The New Brazilian Cinema

Edited by
Lúcia Nagib

I.B. TAURIS

LONDON · NEW YORK

Reprinted in 2006 by I.B.Tauris & Co Ltd
6 Salem Road, London W2 4BU
175 Fifth Avenue, New York NY 10010
www.ibtauris.com
in association with The Centre for Brazilian Studies, University of Oxford
www.brazil.ox.ac.uk

In the United States of America and Canada distributed by
Palgrave Macmillan a division of St. Martin's Press
175 Fifth Avenue, New York, NY 10010

First published by I.B.Tauris & Co Ltd in 2003
Copyright © The Centre for Brazilian Studies, University of Oxford, 2003

Copy editing: Neil Hancox and Stephen Shennan
Translation: Tom Burns, Stephanie Dennison, Vladimir Freire, Lúcia Nagib,
Lisa Shaw and Roderick Steel.

ISBN 10: 1 86064 928 9 paperback
ISBN 13: 978 86064 928 8 paperback
ISBN 10: 1 86064 878 9 hardback
ISBN 13: 978 86064 878 6 hardback

A full CIP record for this book is available from the British Library
A full CIP record is available from the Library of Congress

Library of Congress Catalog Card Number: available

Text prepared by the author as CRC
Typeset in New Baskerville by Luciana Cury, São Paulo, Brazil
Printed and bound in India by Replika Press Pvt. Ltd.

The New Brazilian Cinema

Contents

List of illustrations

Notes on contributors

JOSÉ CARLOS **AVELLAR** was the president of Riofilme, the film distribution company of Rio de Janeiro, during the first years of the revival of Brazilian film production (1993-00). He is currently the director of Martim 21, a distribution company of Brazilian and Latin-American films, and the coordinator of the Programa Petrobras Cinema, that funds films and other activities related to cinema. He is a film critic and film historian, and the author, among other books, of *Cinema dilacerado* (Rio de Janeiro, 1986) and *A ponte clandestina* (Rio de Janeiro/São Paulo, 1995).

IVANA **BENTES** is a film and visual arts researcher and critic. She is Associate Professor of Audio-visual Language, History and Theory at the School of Communication of the Federal University of Rio de Janeiro (UFRJ) and an associate researcher at the Advanced Programme of Contemporary Culture (PACC) of UFRJ. She is the author of the book *Joaquim Pedro de Andrade: a revolução intimista* (Rio de Janeiro, 1996) and the editor of *Cartas ao mundo: Glauber Rocha* (São Paulo, 1997). She is the co-editor of the journal *Cinemais: revista de cinema e outras questões audiovisuais*.

STEPHANIE **DENNISON** teaches Brazilian Culture and Cinema at the University of Leeds, UK, where she also directs an MA programme in World Cinema. She has published articles on Brazilian Cinema, and, among other projects, she is currently co-writing a book on commercially successful Brazilian films (forthcoming with Manchester University Press).

VERÔNICA FERREIRA **DIAS** is a filmmaker with a Master's degree in Communication and Semiotics from the Catholic University of São Paulo, with a dissertation on Eduardo Coutinho.

She has taught Theory of Communication and Educational Technology: TV/VT at the Faculdade Associada de Cotia, Brazil.

CARLOS **DIEGUES** is one of the best-known Brazilian filmmakers. He started filming during the *Cinema Novo* in the 1960s, with *Ganga Zumba* (1964), and has so far directed 15 feature films, among them *A grande cidade* (*The Big City*, 1966), *Xica da Silva* (1976), *Bye bye Brasil* (1980), *Quilombo* (1984), *Tieta* (*Tieta of Agreste*, 1996) and *Orfeu* (1999).

AMIR **LABAKI** is the leading film critic of the daily newspaper *Folha de S. Paulo* and a columnist of the newspaper *Valor Econômico*. He is the founder and director of It's All True – The International Documentary Film Festival (São Paulo and Rio de Janeiro). He is the author, among others, of the book *O olho da revolução – o cinema-urgente de Santiago Alvarez* (São Paulo, 1994) and the editor, among others, of *O cinema brasileiro/The Films from Brazil* (São Paulo, 1998) and *Person por Person* (São Paulo, 2002). He is a former director of the Museum of Image and Sound, São Paulo (1993-95).

MARIA ESTHER **MACIEL** is Associate Professor of Literary Theory and Comparative Literature at the Federal University of Minas Gerais, Brazil. Her books include *As vertigens da lucidez: poesia e crítica em Octavio Paz* (São Paulo, 1995), *A palavra Inquieta: homenagem a Octavio Paz* (Belo Horizonte, 1999) and *Vôo transverso: poesia, modernidade e fim do século XX* (Rio de Janeiro, 1999). She is the co-editor of *Borges em dez textos* (Rio de Janeiro, 1998). She is currently working on literature and cinema, carrying out research on Peter Greenaway.

JOSÉ ÁLVARO **MOISÉS** was the National Secretary of Cultural Support (1995-98) and the National Secretary for Audio-visual Affairs (1999-02) at the Ministry of Culture, Brazil. He is Associate Professor of Political Science at the University of São Paulo and was a Visiting Fellow at St Antony's College, Oxford (1991-92). He is the author of several books, including *Os brasileiros e a democracia* (São Paulo, 1995).

LAURA **MULVEY** is Professor of Film and Media Studies at Birkbeck College, University of London. She has been writing about film and film theory since the mid-1970s. Her books include

Visual and Other Pleasures (London, 1989) and *Fetishism and Curiosity* (London, 1996). In the late 1970s and early 80s, she co-directed six films with Peter Wollen including *Riddles of the Sphinx* (BFI, 1978) and *Frida Kahlo and Tina Modotti* (Arts Council, 1980). In 1994 she co-directed the documentary *Disgraced Monuments* with artist/filmmaker Mark Lewis.

LÚCIA **NAGIB** is Associate Professor of Film Studies at the State University of Campinas and the director of the Centre for Cinema Studies at the Catholic University of São Paulo. She is a film and art critic of the daily newspaper *Folha de S. Paulo*. Her books include *Werner Herzog, o cinema como realidade* (São Paulo, 1991), *Em torno da nouvelle vague japonesa* (Campinas, 1994), *Nascido das cinzas – autor e sujeito nos filmes de Oshima* (São Paulo, 1995) and *O cinema da retomada – depoimentos de 90 cineastas dos anos 90* (São Paulo, 2002). She is currently a Leverhulme Trust Visiting Professor at Birkbeck College, University of London.

LUIZ ZANIN **ORICCHIO** is the leading film critic of the daily newspaper *O Estado de S. Paulo*, where he is also the chief editor of the *Cultura* supplement. He is currently working on a book on contemporary Brazilian cinema.

FERNÃO PESSOA **RAMOS** is Associate Professor of Film Studies at the State University of Campinas, Brazil. He is the author of *Cinema marginal – a representação em seu limite* (São Paulo, 1987) and the editor of *História do cinema brasileiro* (São Paulo, 1988) and *Enciclopédia do cinema brasileiro* (São Paulo, 2000). He directs the series 'Campo imagético' for Papirus Press, Campinas. In 2002 he was a Visiting Professor at the University of Paris III/Sorbonne Nouvelle. He is a former president of SOCINE (Brazilian Society for Cinema Studies).

LISA **SHAW** is the author of *The Social History of the Brazilian Samba* (Ashgate, 1999) and numerous articles on Brazilian popular cinema (1930-60) and the evolution of popular music in Brazil in the 1930s and 1940s. She is Senior Lecturer in Portuguese at the University of Leeds, UK. In the autumn term of 1999 she was Visiting Associate Professor in the Department of Spanish and Portuguese at the University of California, Los Angeles.

ROBERT **STAM** is University Professor at the New York University. He is the author of many books, among them: *Tropical Multiculturalism: A Comparative History of Race in Brazilian Cinema & Culture* (Durham/London, 1997) and *Film Theory – An Introduction* (Oxford, 2000). His recent publications include three books on literature and cinema: *Literature and Film: Realism, Magic and the Art of Adaptation* (Oxford, 2003), *Literature and Film: A Reader* (with A. Raengo, Oxford, 2003) and *A Companion to Film and Literature* (with A. Raengo, 2003). He is the editor, with Randal Johnson, of *Brazilian Cinema* (New York, 1995).

JOÃO LUIZ **VIEIRA** is Associate Professor of Film Language and Theory at the Universidade Federal Fluminense, Niterói, Brazil. He contributed to the edited collection *Brazilian Cinema* (Randal Johnson and Robert Stam, eds, New York, 1995) and has authored, among others, *Glauber por Glauber* (Rio de Janeiro, 1985), *A Construção do Futuro: mais um século de cinema* (Rio de Janeiro, 1995), as well as co-authoring *D.W.Griffith and the Biograph Company* (New York, 1985) and *Cinema Novo and Beyond*, an accompanying volume to the major retrospective of Brazilian cinema organized by MoMA, New York, in 1999.

ISMAIL **XAVIER** is Professor at the Department of Film and Television, University of São Paulo. He has been a visiting scholar at the New York University (1995), the University of Iowa (1998) and the University of Paris III/Sorbonne Nouvelle (1999). His books include *Sertão mar – Glauber Rocha e a estética da fome* (Rio de Janeiro/São Paulo, 1983), *O discurso cinematográfico* (Rio de Janeiro/São Paulo, 1984) and *Alegorias do subdesenvolvimento* (São Paulo, 1993), which has been published in English as *Allegories of Underdevelopment: Aesthetics and Politics in Modern Brazilian Cinema* (Minneapolis/London, 1997).

Foreword

The Centre for Brazilian Studies, established in 1997, is a University of Oxford centre of advanced study and research. One of its principal aims is to promote a greater knowledge and understanding of Brazil – its history, society, politics, economy, ecology and, not least, its culture – through a programme of research projects, seminars, workshops, conferences and publications. The Centre publishes research papers and working papers, and recently published its first work of reference: a guide to the manuscript collections relating to Brazil in British and Irish archives, libraries and museums. *The New Brazilian Cinema* is the Centre's first monograph – published in association with I.B.Tauris.

Brazilian film making goes back to the end of the nineteenth century and has had periods of considerable achievement. But after the great days of *Cinema Novo* in the 1960s and the commercially successful productions of Embrafilme (the Brazilian Film Company) in the 70s and early 80s, the Brazilian film industry entered a period of decline and in the early 1990s totally collapsed or, to be more precise, was dismantled. This book brings together an outstanding collection of essays by film scholars, film critics and filmmakers, mostly Brazilian but also from the United States and the UK, to provide the first comprehensive and critical review of the remarkable renaissance of Brazilian Cinema, both feature length fictional films and documentary films, since 1994. It will be of great interest and value to students of cinema and cinema enthusiasts not only in Brazil but also in the UK, the USA and elsewhere.

The volume has its origins in a conference on contemporary Brazilian Cinema organized by the Centre for Brazilian Studies and held at Wadham College, Oxford in June 2000. At the same time the Centre organized a Brazilian Film Festival under the title 'From *Cinema Novo* to the New Cinema' at the Phoenix Cinema and Magdalen College, Oxford. The conference and the festival were coordinated by Dr Lúcia Nagib, Associate Professor in film history and theory at the State University of Campinas, who was a Ministry of Culture Research Fellow at the Centre in 2000. Dr Nagib has now edited this volume.

I am grateful to the Brazilian Ministry of Culture, and especially Minister Francisco Weffort and Dr José Álvaro Moisés, National Audio-visual Secretary (and a contributor to the volume), for generously providing funding for the conference, the festival and the publication of this book. Additional financial support was provided by the Brazilian Embassy in London and the Fundação Armando Álvares Penteado in São Paulo.

Leslie Bethell
Director,
Centre for Brazilian Studies,
University of Oxford

Introduction

This book presents the first comprehensive critical survey of contemporary Brazilian Cinema to both a Brazilian and an international readership. The period in focus begins in the mid 1990s, when a new Audio-visual Law, promulgated in 1993, started to yield its first results, prompting a boom in film production that became known as the *retomada do cinema brasileiro*, or the 'rebirth of Brazilian Cinema'.

This cinematic 'renaissance' occurred at an emblematic moment of democratic consolidation in the country. Before it, Brazil had gone through decades of traumas: twenty years of military dictatorship, the illness and death of appointed President Tancredo Neves on the verge of taking office, President Sarney's inflationary years and, finally, the obscurantist disaster of the first President democratically elected after the dictatorship, Fernando Collor de Mello, who took office in 1990 and was impeached for corruption less than two years later, in 1992.

The first two years of the 1990s were certainly among the worst in Brazilian film history. As soon as he was in power, Collor downgraded the Ministry of Culture to a Secretariat and closed down several cultural institutions, including Embrafilme (the Brazilian Film Company), which was already in difficulties but still remained the main support for Brazilian Cinema. In 1992, only two long feature films were released in Brazil. The cinematic revival began during President Itamar Franco's mandate, which completed Collor's term, and was developed during Fernando Henrique Cardoso's two terms as President (1995-02).

The Franco government's first measure to foster film production was the creation of the Brazilian Cinema Rescue Award (*Prêmio Resgate do Cinema Brasileiro*), which re-allocated the assets of Embrafilme. In three selections carried out between 1993 and

1994, the Rescue Award was given to a total of ninety projects (25 short, nine medium and 56 full length films), which were completed in quick succession. Thus the bottleneck created by the two years of Collor's government resulted in an accumulation of films produced in the following years. The Rescue Award was followed by the passing of Law no 8685, known as the Audio-visual Law, which adapted pre-existing laws of fiscal incentives to audio-visual projects, thus boosting film production rates.

In six years, from 1994 through 2000, Brazil produced nearly 200 feature-length films, a remarkable figure considering that the whole film industry in the country had been dismantled just prior to that. Moreover, despite the serious problems of film distribution and exhibition, several of the films received an immediate and enthusiastic response from critics and audiences. The first clear sign that the Brazilian cinematic landscape was changing was *Carlota Joaquina – princesa do Brasil* (*Carlota Joaquina – Princess of Brazil*, Carla Camurati, 1995), which, even though initially released only in alternative venues, soon attracted over one million viewers.

In 1998, *Central do Brasil* (*Central Station*, Walter Salles) received the Golden Bear in Berlin, and its leading actress, Fernanda Montenegro, received the best actress award in the same festival. *Central do Brasil* achieved enormous success in Brazil, launching the country back on the international scene after an absence that had lasted since the glorious days of *Cinema Novo* in the 1960s. The film received a long list of awards in Brazil and abroad, including the British Academy Film Award for best foreign film and Oscar nominations for best foreign film and best actress. Its commercial career abroad has also been very successful.

Apart from *Central do Brasil*, many other recent Brazilian films – such as *O que é isso, companheiro?* (*Four Days in September*, Bruno Barreto, 1997), *Orfeu* (Carlos Diegues, 1999) and *Eu, tu, eles* (*Me You Them*, Andrucha Waddington, 2000) – were released worldwide, starting a new market trend set in a wider frame of Latin-American film revivals in the 1990s, which includes Argentina and Mexico as well as Brazil. At the beginning of the Brazilian film revival variety seemed to predominate. Directors ranged from veterans to beginners, resuming old projects or searching for new ideas. Styles moved from the openly commercial to the strictly experimental, in fiction, documentary or mixed films. But after nearly a decade, it is now possible to assert that most of the recent films maintain a strong historical link with Brazilian films of the past and that they share a number of features and tendencies. The aim of this book is to shed a critical light on these new tendencies and historical links.

In June 2000, experts from Brazil and the UK gathered at a conference on contemporary Brazilian Cinema, called 'Brazilian Cinema: roots of the present, perspectives for the future', held in Oxford, under my coordination. The conference, accompanied by a Brazilian film retrospective, was sponsored by the Centre for Brazilian Studies, University of Oxford, and the Brazilian Ministry of Culture, in connection with the commemorations of the 500th anniversary of Brazil's discovery by the Portuguese. Several of the chapters of this book originated from papers presented then; the other chapters were commissioned in an effort to cover all the relevant topics.

Contributors include filmmakers, cultural administrators, film scholars and journalists. Some of them, such as filmmaker Carlos Diegues, the former Audio-visual secretary José Álvaro Moisés and the former director of Riofilme José Carlos Avellar, have participated directly in the Brazilian film revival. All the others, including the American and British specialists, possess a long-standing intimacy with Brazilian film history. Authors had total freedom to express their minds, which has resulted in contrasting, often opposing points of view on the same subject. This was not done to generate polemic for its own sake, but to guarantee a space for the variety of readings a film, a movement or a filmmaker can arouse. The engagement apparent in the expression of these different minds also shows how thought-provoking and inspiring new Brazilian Cinema has become.

The consequences of the dismantling process
Part one of this collection deals with film production in Brazil from the mid-1990s onwards. The opening chapter is a detailed account of the so-called 'rebirth of Brazilian Cinema' by José Álvaro Moisés. As a former National Secretary of Cultural Support (1995-98) and National Secretary for Audio-visual Affairs (1999-02) at the Ministry of Culture, Moisés was in a privileged position to describe and analyse the political context behind the cinematic boom, as well as the genesis of the Audio-visual Law, its flaws, advantages and results. Having introduced the film revival, Moisés goes on to present a retrospective account of the dismantling

process during the short-lived Collor government. He then explains how the Audio-visual Law led to investments reaching R$ 450 million in the production of 155 feature films between 1995 and 2000. He does not fail to recognize the limits of the law, which, despite its power to boost production, was unable to stimulate the commercialization of the films produced. He also points out problems, such as the excessively open selection system that put experienced directors on the same level as beginners, and the brokers' outrageous fees for fund-raising, which go against the public interest. According to Moisés, these and other problems have been dealt with through more recent legislation and measures. In his conclusion, he supports the continuation of the Audio-visual Law (originally due to expire in 2003), once it has been subjected to the necessary amendments and updating.

In the next chapter, Carlos Diegues' view of the same subject is less optimistic. According to this experienced film director, who was among the founders of *Cinema Novo*, none of the cycles or periods of cinematic renaissance have managed to establish a definitive film industry in Brazil, and the recent one is also doomed to failure if urgent action is not taken. Diegues believes that the main obstacle to the development of cinema in Brazil lies not in the production but in the distribution of films. If this issue is not properly looked at, he argues, 'at best, the Audio-visual Law can only create the biggest industry in the world of unreleased films.' Other problems affecting cinema in Brazil are, according to him, declining audiences due to economic recession; the lack of ancillary markets; the absence of the State as a mediator and regulator in the film market; and the absence of television from film production and distribution. Diegues concludes by presenting a long list of suggestions aimed at dealing with all these issues.

Part two looks at recent fiction films as an expression of social phenomena. In his chapter, Ismail Xavier, the author of landmark books on the *Cinema Novo* and modern Brazilian Cinema, starts by drawing a comparison between the national project that animated cinema in the 1960s and the return of national concerns in the 1990s, in films such as *Como nascem os anjos* (*How Angels Are Born*, Murilo Salles, 1996), *Baile perfumado* (*Perfumed Ball*, Paulo Caldas and Lírio Ferreira, 1997), *Central do Brasil*, *Orfeu* (Carlos Diegues, 1999) and *Cronicamente inviável* (*Chronically Unfeasible*, Sérgio Bianchi, 1999). In Xavier's view, if the question of national identity remains a vital force in current films, there are also significant differences as the focus shifts from social teleology to individual psychology, from the oppression of the State to that of organized crime, from the social bandit to the cynical criminal, from revolutionary romanticism to pop culture. His analysis leads to the formulation of what he considers the main motifs of Brazilian Cinema in the 1990s: the 'unexpected personal encounter', related to different forms of migration, and the 'resentful character', related to a sense of personal failure. As regards the former, Xavier explains that 'Brazilian films reveal their connection with the contemporary state of sensibility, showing their concern for the human aspects of the compression of space and time inherent in the world of high technology.' Concerning the latter, he points out the 'discomfort shared by a large group of characters who have their minds set in the past and are obsessed by long-lasting plans of revenge.' Xavier goes as far as to see resentment 'as a national diagnosis', a feeling that grows from the lack of political hopes. He concludes by perceiving, in films such as *Central do Brasil*, a 'figure of redemption' represented by the child, described as a 'moral reservoir that can still generate compassion.'

Approaching many of the films sympathetically analysed by Xavier, Fernão Ramos, in his chapter, adopts a much harder critical position. His goal is to detect a 'bad conscience' caused by representations of Brazil's poor, 'who are lending their voice to the middle class filmmaker.' According to Ramos, 'in many films produced during the revival one can feel this bad conscience shifting away from issues of social fracture to accusations directed at the nation as a whole.' He then proceeds to describe foreign (often Anglo-Saxon) characters that appear in these films as a means 'to provide a point of comparison to the configuration of low self-esteem, to measures of national incompetence.' In his view, *Cronicamente inviável*, with its bitter criticism of the 'unviable nation', is the ultimate expression of a mechanism meant to provide a 'comfortable viewing stance', when the spectator, together with the filmmaker, is placed outside the 'ignoble universe' presented in the film.

The final chapter in this part of the book provides a completely different view of *Cronicamente inviável*. João Luiz Vieira's detailed analysis of the film tries to show that it keeps alive the possibility of radical social transformation through self-reflexive techniques that refuse authority even to the voice-over commentator, with whom audiences usually identify. In Vieira's view, *Cronicamente inviável* is a 'political film in a depoliticized world', that breaks boundaries between documentary and fiction genres, defies conformism and 'posits a thematic and stylistic agenda of resistance to the oppressive and exploitative functioning of local and transnational capitalism.'

Part three focuses on the documentary, a growing genre in contemporary Brazilian Cinema. Amir Labaki, the director of the São Paulo and Rio International Documentary Film Festival, gives a broad panorama of recent production, connecting it with the documentary tradition in Brazil since the pioneers. In the recent revival, documentary production increased at the same time as boundaries between documentary and fiction genres became fluid. Thus he includes in his overview films that contain both fictional and documentary material, such as *O cineasta da selva* (*The Filmmaker of the Amazon*, Aurélio Michiles, *1997*), *Perfumed Ball* and *Milagre em Juazeiro* (*Miracle at Juazeiro*, Wolney de Oliveira, 1999). As the author points out, documentaries have been at the root of several fiction films of the revival. For example, *Socorro Nobre* (Walter Salles, 1996) was a kind of prologue to *Central do Brasil*, and *Notícias de uma guerra particular* (*News of a Private War*, João Moreira Salles and Kátia Lund, 1998) is behind *O primeiro dia* (*Midnight*, Walter Salles and Daniela Thomas, 1999).

Among those entirely devoted to non-fiction film is veteran filmmaker Eduardo Coutinho, to whom a chapter is dedicated by Verônica Ferreira Dias. Not only are his documentaries on Rio *favelas* (shanty towns) and popular religion among the best of the revival, but Dias embraces the idea, already suggested by Jean-Claude Bernardet in the 1980s, that Coutinho is the greatest documentary filmmaker alive in Brazil. This is due, according to the author, to his realist method, which reveals the mechanisms of film production and denounces it 'as a discourse, not a copy or mirror of reality'.

Part four explores the most frequently recurring locations in the films of the revival: the *sertão* (the arid backlands) and the *favela*. That these had been favourite locations of Brazilian cinema since the time of *Cinema Novo* makes comparison between these two historical moments unavoidable. This is indeed the core of Ivana Bentes' chapter, which draws a parallel between recent *sertão* and *favela* films and their predecessors. According to Bentes, 'the *sertão* and the *favelas* have always been the "other side" of modern and positivist Brazil.' However, what in the 1960s originated an 'aesthetics of hunger' (the title of Glauber Rocha's famous 1965 manifesto) has now been turned into a 'cosmetics of hunger'. It is the shift from the 'camera-in-hand and idea-in-mind' (as a *Cinema Novo* slogan used to go) to the steadicam, 'a camera that surfs on reality, a narrative that values the beauty and the good quality of the image, and is often dominated by conventional techniques and narratives.' One of the main targets of her critique is the acclaimed *Central do Brasil,* a film that is rescued by an entirely different approach in the next chapter, on the *sertão* in the Brazilian imaginary, by Luiz Zanin Oricchio.

Oricchio's chapter is especially appealing to non-Brazilian readers, for it contains a detailed explanation of how the *sertão* came to be such a privileged location in Brazilian cinema from the beginning. His account starts with the Rebellion of Canudos, at the end of the nineteenth century, in the backlands of Bahia state, and the extraordinary report on the several battles written by Euclides da Cunha in the classic book *Os sertões* (*Rebellion in the Backlands*). After analysing the developmentalism and the revolutionary hopes that animated films in the 1960s drawing from the Canudos saga, he proceeds to a passionate analysis of the *sertão* films of the 1990s, giving special attention to *Sertão das memórias* (*Landscapes of Memory,* José Araujo, 1997), *Baile perfumado, Central do Brasil* and *Eu, tu, eles.* In his conclusion, Oricchio does acknowledge that, in the new films, 'pre-revolutionary fervour has been replaced by the quest for personal happiness' and 'what was once a battlefield has become a stage for cathartic reconciliation or existential redemption.' However, he does not dismiss these films for being depoliticized, arguing that their social standpoint depends on their historical context. In the past, he claims, 'the world was unjust and everyone knew what they were fighting against.' Now, with the hegemony of globalized capital, 'the world is still unjust, but the targets have disappeared into thin air.'

My chapter goes back to the *favela* and complements the previous chapter on the *sertão*. After an historical overview of the *favela* films up to the present, I proceed to an in-depth analysis of the film *O primeiro dia,* trying to show how it revisits and updates utopian images of the past. This historical connection becomes explicit in the re-elaboration of Glauber Rocha's prophecy, present in *Deus e o diabo na terra do sol* (*Black God, White Devil,* 1964), which says that 'the *sertão* will turn into the sea, and the sea into the *sertão*.' In *O primeiro dia,* this refrain echoes in the turn of the millennium, when the nines 'turn to zero', configuring an empty utopia, a nostalgia for the time when the sea could mean a revolution. The film leads to the conclusion that utopia remains forbidden to the poor: at the end, the northeastern/*favela* hero dies on the beach, looking at a sea he will never reach.

Part five focuses on screen adaptations during the revival. Stephanie Dennison, an expert on Brazilian *pornochanchadas* (soft porn comedies) of the 1970s and 80s, analyses two recent adaptations of Brazil's most famous modern dramatist, Nelson Rodrigues. *Traição* (*Betrayal*, various, 1998) and *Gêmeas* (*Twins*, Andrucha Waddington, 1999) are a good springboard for her insightful account of all the Rodrigues adaptations in Brazilian Cinema. Her argument is that *cinema rodrigueano* is a genre in itself that has undergone interesting variations according to the different political moments in Brazil. She claims that the recent adaptations reveal 'the extent to which the cinematic climate has changed' in the country. In contrast to previous Rodrigues films, the new ones contain 'nothing visually nasty, dirty or cheap', and they also avoid 'nudity, sex scenes and scenes of sexual violence', elements that seem to make up the very core of past adaptations. This is because their aim is to produce 'a watchable, well-made, commercially viable cinema' which can convince audiences that Brazilian Cinema is a safe bet.

Maria Esther Maciel analyses *Amor & Cia.* (*Love & Co*, Helvécio Ratton, 1998), a singular film and, in her view, a peculiar work of literary adaptation. She explains how a chain of doubts permeates the film from its roots. The authorship of the original text is uncertain: although ascribed to Portuguese naturalist novelist Eça de Queiroz, it remained unsigned and untitled and was published after his death. She argues too that Ratton incorporates in it several elements derived from Brazilian realist novelist Machado de Assis. Apart from the doubts and betrayals at the film's own source, the plot itself is a case of betrayal by a woman who gets involved with her husband's best friend and partner. *Traduttore-traditore*: betraying the original text, Ratton brings doubt into the character's act of betrayal, and asserts, through stressing ambiguity, the richness of a period drama, at a time when documentary-like fiction seems to be the fashionable trend.

The chapters in Part six show how social history permeates Brazilian film history. Robert Stam, the author of the best known works in English on Brazilian Cinema, focuses on representations of Indians in 100 years of Brazilian film history. Departing from a contemporary example of a TV miniseries *A invenção do Brasil* (*The Invention of Brazil*, Guel Arraes and Jorge Furtado, 2000), set 500 years ago, at the time of Brazil's discovery, his chapter embarks on a retrospective of Brazilian Cinema, from the silent period up to contemporary production. In this fascinating journey, we meet the 'romantic Indian', the 'documented Indian', the 'modernist Indian', the 'patriotic Indian' and the 'tropicalist Indian', finally returning to the 1990s, when all these types seem to find a place on the screen. Stam's view is that Brazilian Cinema and popular culture 'have both prolonged and critiqued the myths and fictions inherited from *Indianismo*.' He hopes, however, that in the twenty first century, 'the native Brazilian will emerge to speak in a more full-throated manner, as an integral part of the cultural polyphony which is Brazil.'

Lisa Shaw, who has been developing important research on the Brazilian musical comedies of the 1940s and 50s called *chanchadas*, analyses the film *For all: o trampolim da vitoria* (*For All*, Luiz Carlos Lacerda and Buza Ferraz, 1998) as a legacy of both the *chanchada* and Hollywood paradigms, with particular reference to the US war-time musical. Shaw interweaves Brazilian and American (film) histories, which were closely linked in the 1930s and 40s, the time of the Good Neighbour Policy that boosted 'latino' movies, several of them starring the Brazilian singer Carmen Miranda. She then reads *For all* as a 'nostalgia film' that quotes the *chanchada* as well as Hollywood musicals, and functions as a pastiche of the musical genre itself.

José Carlos Avellar, a key figure in the Brazilian film revival as the head of Rio's film production and distribution company Riofilme, also embarks on a voyage through Brazilian film history. He uses some of Pasolini's linguistic ideas on cinema to describe 1960s cinema (or *Cinema Novo*) as equivalent to the 'spoken word', because 'it expressed itself by using the direct and only partially articulated elements of spoken language,' whereas current Brazilian Cinema could be compared to the 'written word', 'as a means of writing down the way of speaking of the 1960s.' For him, cinema in Brazil has undergone a process of 'resensitization' – an expression used by Walter Salles to define the experience of *Central do Brasil*'s main character. 'This process', he explains, 'is to an extent the reunion of the father (the old *Cinema Novo*?) and the nation. It is a way of understanding Brazil.'

Part seven is an Epilogue containing a chapter by British film theorist and filmmaker Laura Mulvey, who reflects on some of the relevant issues raised in the previous chapters. Mulvey is particularly interested in the ways in which the volume addresses 'questions of history: the history of Brazil since *Cinema Novo* and the history of Brazilian Cinema itself.' She includes in her reflections a broad parallel between the Brazilian and the British film experience of the 1960s and 70s. At the end of the 60s, military dictatorship interrupted *Cinema Novo*'s revolutionary utopianism, while in the late 70s Thatcherism put an end to the avant-garde film experiments that were taking place in Britain. Mulvey claims that, in the 1980s, 'a gap, a caesura, in aesthetic and political continuity developed that gives a distinct edge to the way that new cinema movements of the 1990s conceived of themselves.' Unlike the British, she continues, 'the cinema of the Brazilian "renaissance" directly raises the relation between a "then" and a "now" and confronts what meanings these cinema histories might have for the present.' She concludes by arguing that new technologies, through which anyone 'with the simple touch of a digital button can stop and think about the complexities of moving images,' can work as 'a telescope into the past' and be a means of negotiating across the 'great divide'.

This closing theoretical piece is not meant to bring discussion of the experience of Brazilian Cinema in the 1990s to an end. True enough, contemporary cinema in Brazil cannot be called a 'renaissance' any longer, for it has established itself on a stable productive basis with regular hits appearing, such as *O invasor* (*The Trespasser*, Beto Brant, 2002) and *Cidade de Deus* (*City of God*, Fernando Meirelles and Kátia Lund, 2002); indeed, the latter has already reached over 3 million viewers in Brazil. But the rich experience of the 1990s, which re-elaborates a century of Brazilian film history, will certainly bear fruit for many years to come.

Lúcia Nagib
January 2003

Acknowledgements

I would like to express my thanks, first of all, to Leslie Bethell and his collaborators (Nádia Goodman, Margaret Hancox and Jocelyn Bradley) at the Centre for Brazilian Studies, University of Oxford, for their enthusiastic support of Brazilian Cinema. Professor Bethell took the pioneering initiative of sponsoring a Brazilian film season and the conference in Oxford which was the origin of this book, thus decisively contributing to the establishment of Brazilian film studies in the UK.

The events in Oxford and the book would not have been possible without the intellectual and financial support of the National Secretariat for Audio-visual Affairs of the Ministry of Culture, Brazil, and the former Secretary for Audio-visual Affairs, José Álvaro Moisés, who assisted us throughout, providing us with data and documents.

Brazilian filmmakers and their production companies also offered invaluable help, giving oral and written interviews and putting their documents and photos at our disposal. My special thanks to Carlos Diegues, Teresa Souza and Rio Vermelho Filmes Ltda.; Tata Amaral; Sérgio Bianchi; and Walter Salles and Videofilmes. Contributions from other filmmakers are acknowledged at the end of individual chapters.

James Dunkerley and Laura Mulvey were extremely supportive in the first stages of this project. Philippa Brewster was a brilliant reader and advisor. Verônica Ferreira Dias helped considerably with researching the images.

Finally, my deepest gratitude to Stephen Shennan for his tireless assistance with the copy editing and his invaluable opinions on the content and structure of the book.

Part one

Producing films in Brazil

1

A new policy for Brazilian Cinema
José Álvaro Moisés

Showing the world is always a moral act.

Wim Wenders

To awaken history is to gain awareness of our singularity.

Octavio Paz

The best way to draw a character is to use one's imagination. ... the essence [of art] is imagination.

Paulo Autran

Brazilian Cinema has undergone a complete turn-around in recent years. First of all, with the help of new sponsorship laws, production rates have accelerated: 155 feature films were made between 1995 and 2000, compared with less than a dozen during the early years of the decade. Secondly, the quality of these films has improved significantly, enriching film language, diversifying styles and revealing a considerable amount of new talent: 55 new filmmakers have surfaced between 1994 and 2000, a number comparable to the *Nouvelle Vague*, in France, during the 1950s.

Many recent Brazilian films have received widespread recognition for their cultural merit, both in Brazil and abroad. Three have been nominated, in the last few years, for an Oscar for best foreign film: *O quatrilho* (Fábio Barreto, 1995, nominated in 1996), *O que é isso, companheiro?* (*Four Days in September*, Bruno Barreto, 1997, nominated in 1998) and *Central do Brasil* (*Central Station*, Walter Salles,

1998, nominated in 1999). Although the Oscar is a marketing tool for North American filmmaking, it also acknowledges cultural achievement. Brazilian films have also been recognized in other festivals and international competitions, and have received, overseas alone, almost 100 prizes between 1998 and 1999.

Furthermore, contrary to what a section of the press in Brazil asserts, the Brazilian public has gone back to watching national films. In 1998, for example, according to data provided by Filme B (a company specializing in the statistics of the Brazilian film market), there were around 3.6 million admissions for films produced in Brazil, more than 50 per cent above the number of the previous year. In 1999, more than 5.2 million people watched Brazilian films in the cinema and, in 2000, the number climbed to 7.2 million, 12 times more than the rest of the film market had grown in the country. Signs are very promising. Viewing numbers for national films, compared with those for 1995, are six times greater, pointing to a potential for growth which should be properly developed.

The government has played an important part in the new reality of Brazilian Cinema. In 1998, President Fernando Henrique Cardoso included cinema in the Brazilian Programme for Productivity and Quality's (*Programa Brasileiro de Produtividade e Qualidade – PBPQ*) 13 goals, with the aim of claiming 20 per cent of the country's film market by 2003. In 1999, he decided that a new credit line should be made available to finance the sector, through the More Cinema Programme (*Programa Mais Cinema*). With resources from the National Bank for Social and Economic Development (*Banco Nacional do Desenvolvimento Econômico e Social* – BNDES) amounting to R$ 80 million in 1999-00, to which the Ministry of Culture will add R$ 2.5 million annually, the programme offers support for film production and for its commercialization, including the modernization and refurbishment of movie theatres throughout the country; in 2000, 11 projects benefited from this programme and another nine were approved and will receive the money they requested. More importantly, the recognition that the sector is on the verge of requiring new strategic initiatives from the State led the government to create, in September 2000, the Executive Group for the Development of the Film Industry (*Grupo Executivo de Desenvolvimento da Indústria Cinematográfica* – GEDIC), which was a task force designed to define government involvement in the sector. Made up of seven Ministers of State and six representatives from the sector, the group's job is to present short, medium and long term measures to stimulate the development of cinema.

The Brazilian parliament has also taken various initiatives that prove its commitment to creating new opportunities for national cinema. In 1999, the Federal Senate created the Special Cinema Commission, within its Commission for Education and Culture, to bring together suggestions from the government and the film community as to the best legislative measures to adopt for the sector's industrial development. As a result of a proposal made by its president, senator José Fogaça, the commission became permanent; but the Legislature wants to take things even further, as demonstrated by projects presented by senator Francelino Pereira and member of the legislative assembly, Miro Teixeira.[1]

Moreover, there is growing concern about cinema within the general public, as well as the Executive and Legislature. It shows that we are now entering a new era after the dissolution of the institutions that offered public support for the sector at the start of the 1990s – an insane predatory act perpetrated by the Collor government. Without dwelling unnecessarily on the reasons for that predatory rage, I am happy to say that, in contrast to that unhappy moment, we are experiencing a new phase, showing that Brazilian society recognizes more clearly the cultural and economic importance of cinema and audio-visual production.

Both government and society are therefore better prepared today to face the task of building a strong national film industry. The country understands, more every day, how important it is for us to look at ourselves in a cinematic 'mirror'. We realize that we need that fundamental function of self-identification which is made possible by the projection of our common experiences on a screen, to understand each other better and to define with more clarity what we want for ourselves in the new millennium.

The country is experiencing a unique moment in which society and the State need to redefine how they want to associate themselves with Brazilian Cinema, its filmmakers and its public. The critical awareness is greater now, both within society and among those responsible for managing the sector, in terms of evaluating the legacy of past experiences such as the National Institute for Cinema (INC), the National Film Company (Embrafilme), the National Council for Cinema (Concine), as well as recent sponsorship laws, or, going back in time, of the days of such studio enterprises as Atlântida and Vera Cruz, when the State barely

played a role in financing film. The dismantling of film production in the early 90s and its 'revival' later in the decade, have given
us more information to draw on, and provided us with clearer
points of departure to define a new model for the relation
between State and cinema. It also pointed to the need for a project capable of giving film making the permanent conditions
required for survival, so that in the future it will not wilt at the first
signs of economic crises or the government's wrong orientation,
as happened in the last decade.

The Ministry of Culture contributed decisively to the construction of this new model. Minister Francisco Weffort dedicated himself to solving cinema's problems with initiatives that clearly
showed a desire to transform government intent into action, as
proved by decisions taken in 1996 that raised the tax discount
offered to companies that invest in film from 1 per cent to 3 per
cent, and decisions taken in 1999 to recreate the Cinema
Commission, a ministerial advisory committee that draws on the
participation of all the sectors involved in audio-visual production
in the country and makes up a significant part of the process of
defining policies for the sector. But it is not just a matter of drawing attention to the government's successful initiatives, or omit-
ting its faults. Democracy presumes that governments recognize
this when necessary and correct the direction taken for the development of cinema and audio-visual production in the country.

The consequences of the dismantling process
It is important to evaluate the dismantling in the early 1990s of the
public institutions that funded cinema, whose main effect was to
make us lose part of our critical capacity. If in the 1950s and 60s
Brazilian Cinema provided a catalysing force in the formation of
Brazil's multiple cultural identities, it never became an established
industrial activity, even when important public incentives were
offered in the 1970s, by Embrafilme, Concine and some of the sector's protective laws. Those mechanisms carried traces of State
paternalism and supported films that sometimes had little or no
cultural value. Nevertheless, in subsidizing production and, more
importantly, the distribution of national films in Brazil and
abroad, at the end of the 70s they helped national cinema fill close
to 35 per cent of the country's cinemas, which at the time exceeded 3500, with over 100 million admissions a year. This means that,
despite its difficulties in becoming an industry, our cinema was

capable of competing with foreign films, pointing to the industry's potential which unfortunately never reached its full development.

At the beginning of the last decade, however, the entire Brazilian film production and distribution support system fell apart. The dissolution drastically affected Brazilian Cinema's ability to operate with economic efficiency in its home market and, as a result, to compete with imported films. Not even the State's capacity to measure film activity statistically was safeguarded. From being an important cultural experiment, on the verge of becoming an industry, cinema was reduced, in the early 90s, to a fringe economic activity. National production, which had exceeded 100 films a year in the mid 1970s, was almost reduced to zero, with only two films released in 1992. As a result, Brazilian films, which had one third of the market share in the 70s, only managed 0.5 per cent of the market in the early 90s, leaving behind a vacuum which was quickly filled by a more competitive alternative product, namely American cinema.

And so Brazilian film practically vanished from the internal exhibition market, not to mention its total disappearance from the external market. It also lost its public, although, as we know, this was partly due to the technological modernization that had been taking place in the last decades, which ushered in colour TV, home video and, later on, cable TV. Film therefore became an economic activity of little or no revenue, frustrating the cultural community and contributing to an increase in the country's trade deficit. The foreign film invasion of the internal market, especially by Hollywood, becomes clearer when we see that while Brazil imports about 350 films a year for cinema, TV and cable exhibition, as well as home video, in the last six years the country has produced an average of 28 films a year. This quantity is not enough to provide pressure on exhibitors to open up more space for national films, even if there is legislation that safeguards a minimum screen quota.

We currently import more than US$ 700 million per year in audio-visual products, while we export less than US$ 40 million. We face both foreign exchange deficit and the industry's difficulty in generating its own funding and therefore becoming efficient enough to compete with what comes from outside. One should also keep in mind that current international rules for free trade do not yet effectively allow for full competitiveness, reducing the chances of trading in equal conditions. This is why, in fact, American films currently fill more than 90 per cent of Brazilian cinemas, as well as a lot of the country's TV. American cinema – with its large quantities of violence, its questionable portrayal of relations between races and classes, and its own multiculturalism – has become, if not the only, then one of the main references for the cultural education of the Brazilian population, especially of its youth. It is true that the importance of this phenomenon does not compare with the local soap operas, which are extremely creative and capable of communicating with the different regions of the country, as well as being among the most profitable branches of the audio-visual economy; nevertheless, 'canned' films tend to be increasingly present in the electronic media, including open and cable TV.

The problems that remain
Despite all this, in the mid-90s there was a revival of Brazilian Cinema. The phenomenon began with an important change in the State's political outlook on the sector, with the introduction of the Brazilian Cinema Rescue Award (*Prêmio Resgate do Cinema Brasileiro*) in 1994, and grew with the reformulation and modernization of cultural sponsorship laws under Fernando Henrique Cardoso's government. This government democratized such laws, encouraged partnerships with private businesses, increased the discount rate they could have, and made a larger proportion of income taxes available for cultural activities, including cinema. The allocation went from R$ 95 million, in 1995, to R$ 160 million, in 1999 and 2000. Until 1994, this tactic was little used, and did not amount to more than 3 or 4 per cent of potentially available resources in a particular year; in 1996, it went up 100 per cent, and again in 1997, prompting the Ministry of Culture to request an increase. Direct investments in culture and especially in cinema, have increased significantly with the government's policy to reformulate laws and maximize their use, even if it is clear that a film industry will not be established solely through these mechanisms

Due to budgetary increases in the field, from 1995 to 2000 investments in culture grew nine-fold. In just six years such government action prompted investments to reach R$ 450 million in the production of 155 feature films, almost all of which have already been released or are just about to be. Many, such as *Carlota Joaquina – princesa do Brasil* (*Carlota Joaquina – Princess of Brazil*, Carla Camurati, 1995), *O quatrilho*, *O que é isso, companheiro?* and, more recently, *Central do Brasil*, *Orfeu* (Carlos Diegues, 1999), *Eu, tu, eles* (*Me You Them*, Andrucha Waddington, 2000) and *O auto da compadecida* (*A Dog's Will*, Guel Arraes, 2000), were all released in Brazil and/or abroad, and competed for important international prizes. They were very successful with the national audience too, which, in many cases, exceeded 1 million admissions, and in one case, *O auto da compadecida*, exceeded 2 million admissions. In fact, between 1995 and 2000 the most successful films, publicized by the electronic media, were watched by over 25 million Brazilians, proving that they can draw large number of viewers, when they are launched in the market place with sufficient publicity.

This situation allowed for a revival of cinematic production. However, these films are not always able to pay their way with their box-office proceeds alone. This means that production companies do not make profits and, as a result, cannot in the short term foresee autonomy from the State, either through its sponsorship laws, or through its direct investments. In the end, what really becomes compromized is Brazilian Cinema's ability to become competitive and regain its own market share. The problem does not lie, as the press often makes us believe, in the relation between the audience and the films. The predominance of American film in the Brazilian market – and, as a consequence, its enormous cultural influence – is a devastating economic factor, as it is in other parts of the world. This influence is expanding with the implantation of multiplex cinemas that are subsidized by the American government. Even if this does not justify any trace of xenophobia towards American culture by Brazilians, it also does not mean automatic acceptance of the domination of the cinematic market which is happening here and in the rest of the world, with the possible exception of India and China, and perhaps Iran. This process makes a single cultural model available to the general public, being incapable on its own of providing cultural enrichment.

This is why the link between culture and democracy becomes so important. Once this link is seen as indissoluble, one can only reject, in defence of democracy and the integrity of culture, destructive American dominance of the cinema market. In practice, it excludes the possibility of expressing cultural diversity, or makes it extremely tenuous in societies like Brazil's, in which oral tradition is still so strong. This does not mean we have to throw the burden of responsibility onto the shoulders of distributors or on the American film industry, whose creativity is unquestionable: in a market economy, it is the nature of efficient businesses to fill the existing gaps.

EVOLUTION OF INVESTMENTS IN AUDIO-VISUAL PRODUCTION 1995-2000

Investments	1995	1996	1997	1998	1999	2000	2001*	Total R$
Fiscal incentives	28,995,481	75,716,723	114,011,079	73,153,527	60,796,467	53,267,008	28,353,847	432,234,132
Audio–visual Law, Article 1**	16,848,507	50,449,952	75,917,001	39,093,362	37,766,848	25,478,153	3,981,196	245,553,823
Audio–visual Law, Article 3**	4,030,992	7,319,787	3,848,491	3,999,707	3,865,016	6,245,111	3,781,394	33,090,499
Sponsorship	8,055,982	17,946,984	34,245,587	30,060,457	19,164,603	21,543,744	20,591,257	151,608,614
Conversion of foreign debt	–	–	–	–	952,653	5,505,668	–	6,458,321
More Cinema Programme	–	–	–	–	–	5,565,568	–	5,565,568
Government's Budget	1,600,000	3,835,840	9,822,212	5,541,491	11,703,668	13,929,500	14,773,210	61,205,921
Total	30,535,481	79,552,563	123,883,291	78,695,018	73,452,788	78,267,744	43,127,057	507,463,943

SOURCE: Ministry of Culture/The Audio-visual Secretariat

(*) Figures up to 02/08/2001

(**) The Audio-visual Law, Article 1, grants investors discounts of 100 per cent of the amount of their income tax invested in long feature films. Article 3 allows foreign distributors to invest 70 per cent of their income tax on profits made in Brazil in Brazilian film productions.

But what we should do is question the national states, society and specific local cultural communities about the responsibility of letting such strategic spaces become vulnerable to this invasion.

We must also not allow the globalization of consumer markets of cultural wares and mass communication, to deprive us of lasting contact with cultural models other than the one already mentioned, whether these come from France, Italy, Sweden, Germany, England, India, Iran or China, not to mention our Mercosul neighbours or the Iberian countries, whose cultural heritage is so familiar to us. The rarity of seeing Portuguese, Spanish, or Argentinean films in Brazil is symbolic of a large cultural loss.

Limits of the Audio-visual Law
Since 1995, the government has been perfecting cultural sponsorship laws, in particular, the Audio-visual Law (*Lei do Audiovisual*) which paved the way for the production of 155 feature films, more than 100 documentaries and close to 100 shorts between 1995 and 2000. As a result of this we have reclaimed a proportion of our internal market, from 3 per cent, in 1995-96, to close to 10 per cent in 2000; this means that the government's goal of reaching close to 20 per cent by 2003 is in sight. Important problems remain, as we will show in a moment. However, there are still important results which must be recognized. Look, for example, at the number and diversity of talents, many of them women, making directorial debuts in the last four or five years, due to a more democratic and widespread use of the Audio-visual Law. As a result, there have been new languages and trends in cinematic expression, adding colour to a scenario which, until recently, was confined to patterns established in the 1950s and 60s.

There is no fundamental reason, therefore, why the country should drop fiscal incentives. But this does not mean that limitations should not be recognized. First of all, despite its advantages, the financing system created by the Audio-visual Law does not stimulate the commercialization of films produced with its help and this prevents the capitalization of production companies. In fact, of the eighty films made and released in the market between 1995 and 1998, only ten roughly broke even or earned more than they cost to make; over sixty films had poor results at the box-office – even if this is not the only measure of their worth. As a result, instead of offering their producers new capital, in many cases they led to debts incurred by un-recouped commercialization costs. Another important factor relates to the fact that efforts to make a previously inoperative law actually work resulted in the distortion of some of its objectives from 1995 to 1998. Instead of promoting the development of film production and, in this way, pressuring the exhibitors to show more Brazilian films, existing film financing laws included fiscal incentive mechanisms that increased production time considerably, frustrating investor expectations, as well as public authorities and the general public. Secondly, the law allowed producers often to omit from the planning stages the necessary articulation between production and commercialization, that is, between production, distribution, exhibition, and sale of a copyright-protected product to the internal and external markets, including television and home video. Thirdly, it led to a hefty inflating of film production costs, especially when it came to feature films, as a result of producers' perceptions that they had access to a bottomless purse. A film community not uninterested in making money on its investments, backed by an Audio-visual Law that stimulated production almost exclusively, often ended up losing perspective on the complete cycle of how the market works, abandoning certain stages and giving the sector little continuity. Specification of the relation between production, commercialization, distribution and exhibition was absent from the planning stage.

In addition, the urge to make the Audio-visual Law actually work, after the damage incurred by the Collor government, also created problems. For example, before 1999, adequate criteria for the selection of projects were often missing, so that they were almost all accepted unconditionally. This produced enormous saturation in the market for the purchase and sale of audio-visual certificates, which led to a kind of 'cannibalization' of the opportunities of the investment market. An extremely large number of approved but insufficiently qualified projects led to a savage battle for resources in a market which makes available an estimated R\$ 70 to 80 million a year. The result was the fragmentation of resources among hundreds of projects, making it impossible for many of them to complete production. In combination with factors already mentioned, this led to a great abundance of resources in 1996-97, but in 1998-99 many projects could not enter into post-production, which reduced the sector's performance and discredited it with the media, public authorities, and many of its investors.

In fact, between 1994 and 1998, the Ministry of Culture

approved 800 audio-visual projects, but less than 15 per cent reached the final leg; the remainder battled it out incessantly for more resources, saturating market supply even though more than half of them had almost no chance of finishing. This proved that urgent measures were necessary. Furthermore, although not widespread, some practices surfaced that ran counter to the public interest, such as re-buying audio-visual certificates before films were completed; similarly, broker's fees for fund-raising, which the Ministry of Culture had limited to 10 per cent, reached 40 per cent. Such practices drained resources, which were no longer available to fund production, distribution and commercialization of the activity, forcing the government to adopt new measures (see below).

Finally, television, although extremely influential in societies in which an oral culture still predominates, is still far from offering Brazilian Cinema important support. In Brazil cinema has developed almost entirely in film theatres; furthermore, Brazilian television has proved its enormous ability to produce its own images, such as soaps. TV is also strongly anchored in the broadcasting of cheap foreign films, which has led to a situation in which cinema and television 'fall out' with each other.

As a result, the Brazilian film industry does not look towards the financial opportunities that TV and cable offer. As other countries have shown, this could be a better way of showing films, with a better financial return and would also give Brazilian films a mass audience of millions of people, in keeping with the current government's policy of democratizing access to culture. Such circumstances point towards Brazilian film's indispensable integration with TV.

What has been done
Some of the issues dealt with so far allude to structural problems of film production, that must be dealt with in the long term. Other issues have short and medium term solutions. It was based on this conviction that in 1999 the Ministry of Culture adopted a series of measures whose results can already be seen. First of all, the Cinema Commission envisaged by Law 8401, from 1992, was reorganized, because it did not act with the regularity and organization required of it. The reorganization took place in January 1999, and incorporated practically all audio-visual sectors in the country, especially cinema, welcoming all legitimate even if disparate interests, in an effort to create an industry dear to all. In a short

period of time, the Commission has acquired an important role in the definition of policies for the sector.

In second place, the State began and continued to implement a series of permanent acts of responsibility aimed at the sector's cultural development. These included: (1) the Virtuoso Grant Programme, through which directors, managers and technicians can improve their professional skills with courses in Brazil and abroad; (2) a selection process for short films, documentaries, feature film scripts and productions requiring investments under R$ 1 million; (3) Brazilian participation in international partnership deals, especially those aimed at aiding co-productions, such as the Ibermédia and the Brazil-Portugal Accord; (4) support for Brazilian artists wishing to compete internationally with their films, offering help with copies; (5) national awards that recognize the cultural merit of national production, with the creation of the Grand Prize for Brazilian Cinema (*Grande Prêmio Cinema Brasil*); (6) and finally, the start of a programme for the restoration of the country's cinematic assets (begun with the work of Joaquim Pedro de Andrade).

Emphasis was also given to the publicizing of Brazilian films abroad, with the publication of the *Catalogue of Brazilian Cinema 1995-1999*, in four languages, with 10,000 copies made available to international distributors. The Ministry of Foreign Relations, of Industry and of Commerce also participated actively in this process, with a view to spreading Brazilian film culture and opening new avenues for Brazilian audio-visual media abroad. This resulted in close to a nine-fold increase in the Audio-visual Secretariat's budget over the last six years: resources leapt from around R$ 1,6 million, in 1995, to almost R$ 14 million in 2000.

Most important of all were the measures relating to the functioning of the Audio-visual Law. The new measures reduced the number of audio-visual certificates on offer as early as in 1999. First of all, repurchase of certificates before films were completed was prohibited, with the help of the Commission for Moveable Values (*Comissão de Valores Imobiliários* – CVM). This halted practices that were detrimental to the public treasury, which resulted from the reduction in certificate values, since investors discounted from their income tax the entire value announced in the original operation and recovered part of their investment by buying back part, or all, of their certificates from the issuers. It is clear that, as well as inflating the price of some projects, this also generated tax evasion.

Furthermore, the time limit for the use of money received through fiscal incentives was reduced, so that film production could be completed within a specific period of time. Last, but not least, precise criteria were established for the approval of projects seeking public resources. These were based on the experience of the first four years of Fernando Henrique Cardoso's government, which pointed to a need to take into consideration the performance of applicant companies when approving projects. A decision was made to take into consideration the experience and the background of the director and crew. And, since some of the production companies already had as many as ten projects approved, they were induced to operate with leaner portfolios of up to three projects at a time: while one project is being completed, another is half way through production, and the other is in pre-production.

Another reason these measures were adopted was the clear need to move away from the practice of treating everyone like equals, of presuming that someone beginning in the field should have more or less the same rights as seasoned professionals who are recognized for their work and have been awarded prizes at home and abroad. This demagogic phenomenon sometimes plagues democratic systems. One cannot treat someone starting in the film industry in the same way as someone as experienced as director Nelson Pereira dos Santos. This is why criteria were developed to take into consideration the proponent's experience as well as the production company's capacity and performance in previous projects.

The first results
Thanks to the combination of market reduction measures, certificate repurchase restrictions, new criteria for approving projects, and limits of three projects per company, close to R\$ 352 million worth of certificates were withdrawn from the market in 1999, and 300 projects that had exceeded the time allowed for fund-raising were shelved, leaving around 500 projects to make a claim on R\$ 680 million of money earmarked for tax deduction, half the amount available at the beginning of the year. This remainder was much closer to what the investment market could set aside for film over four or five years. The intention was to recognize the merit of those with the best conditions to realize their projects, without eliminating opportunities available to beginners.

The Ministry of Culture also made an objective attempt to integrate its own international aims with those of Latin-American

and European filmmakers to confront America's domination of
the film market. In 1999, just before the Head of State and
European Union, Latin-American and Caribbean Government
Summit Meeting, the Ministry of Culture organized a meeting, in
partnership with the InterAmerican Development Bank – IDB
(*Banco Interamericano de Desenvolvimento* – BID), to define common
cinematic ground between these countries so as to create better
ways to claim part of the Latin-American and European film market. As well as proposing an increase in co-productions in order to
offer the people of both continents a greater diversity of audio-
visual products, the meeting also defined the need to create a
theme cable channel to broadcast, 24 hours a day, Latin-American
and European films. Justification for this initiative referred to the
American film industry's oligopoly which, even in countries that
have extremely protectionist legislation, such as France, gives the
American industry a share greater than 70 per cent. A further
meeting in Rio de Janeiro was followed by another organized by
Cinecittá in Rome, in 2000, with IDB support, and another during
the 2000 Cannes, Venice and Biarritz Festivals in which Brazil also
took an active part.

It is worth mentioning an observation usually made by directors of American distribution companies, that Latin-American
and European producers would take more of their market share
if they improved the quality of their films. This diagnosis, which
certainly refers to a real problem, does not fully comprehend the
reality of Latin-American cinema. Because it lacks the conditions
for competitive equality in its own market, it is very difficult to
create the circumstances in which its quality can be improved.
Quality is also an attribute of the quantity that is produced.
However this factor is dependent, among other things, on cinematic production acquiring business standards and a professional setting which are indispensable to the development of an
industry that has a competitive edge.

The transition to a new model
The short term measures, elaborated by the Ministry of Culture,
were linked to measures that will take longer to mature, and
whose main objective was to prepare for a transition to a new
State/cinema model in Brazil. Following the President's decision,
the Ministry opened a new line of credit to the sector, in August
1999, through the More Cinema Programme (*Programa Mais*

Cinema), already mentioned above, financed by BNDES in partnership with Sebrae and Banco do Brasil. The programme has a new financial concept, and, in order to qualify for credit, projects must include production, distribution and exhibition proposals. Resources are also earmarked for marketing and for the expansion of screening rooms, as well as other aspects of the infrastructure vital to the development of the film industry.

This is a question not only of creating new conditions so that private investment continues, but of complementing the financing system in place – essentially amounting, at the moment, to incentive laws – with public credit mechanisms, as already happens in countries like Italy, France and Canada. As well as creating new leverage mechanisms for the film industry, there is also a desire to create necessary conditions to multiply and diversify the State's financing capacity, since this new mechanism allows for rotating credits, that in turn increase financing. But the programme provides a further advantage: by offering filmmakers better fund-raising conditions, it is also offering a potential investor greater security and providing the filmmaker with the means to repay debts. It is a new way of stimulating capitalization of production companies which, as a result, are taking on board some of the risk of creating a film industry in the country.

'The Rediscovery of National Cinema – Meeting between Brazil and Citizenship' is another medium term project. The initiative articulates the use of resources already secured by federal government, by means of the Ministry of Education, through work carried out by the Ministry of Culture to promote Brazilian filmmaking in society, especially among the young, and to stimulate the growth of an audience. With support from the Secretary for Distance Education, the Ministry of Education, Public Network Television (the Educational TV stations), Senate TV, TV of the Chamber and Canal Brasil, the programme was begun in 1999 during the celebrations of the five hundredth anniversary of Brazil's discovery, with widespread discussion of the contribution made by Brazilian filmmaking to the country's culture and formation. The films are exhibited weekly in the 62,000 schools that participate in the School TV programme, to primary and high school students. The films are also being exhibited on national TV, to a general audience.

As well as these, other more long-term initiatives have also been started. Their full implementation is dependent upon legislative changes that regulate the State's relationship with film. The main necessary changes refer to Laws 8401, 8685 and Decree 1900, from 1992, which has been constantly republished. This set of laws can and must form the basis for a Consolidation of Legislation that regulates the relationship between the State and cinema.

As a first step towards this consolidation, a reconceptualization of Brazilian audio-visual activity has been proposed through a preliminary law jointly discussed by the Ministry of Culture's Cinema Commission, and sent to the Senate's Special Cinema Commission and the Executive Group for the Development of the Film Industry. The aim is to include all the new influences on the sector ushered in by the third technological revolution which uses computers and other media to generate new images, and by new modes of transmission and precision. This is the case with new modes of image digitalization, which are about to give computer users access, from their homes, to a network of films and other audio-visual products; this is also the case with images generated outside the country and broadcast via satellite to television sets.

Secondly, the Ministry of Culture proposed the retention of the Audio-visual Law, set in place in1993, up to and including 2003. A proposal has been made, meanwhile, for it to be extended for another twenty years. Contrary to the opinion that is so frequently put forward by the media, the Ministry of Culture believes that widespread use of policies that offer fiscal incentives is justified. In fact, as regards cinema and all other cultural sectors, the use of tax breaks through sponsorship laws in 1998, for example, did not divert more than 0.015 per cent of all the resources that the State did not claim in taxes. In 1999, due to measures adopted because of the economic crises in Hong Kong and Russia, this percentage dropped even further, to 0.010 per cent. That is also what was used in 2000. It is a minute fraction of the State's tax exemption which will not compromise the programme for economic stability, but has an enormous ability to generate revenue and jobs. Research carried out by the Ministry of Culture in 1997 and 1998 showed that for every R$ 1 million applied to culture, 160 indirect and direct jobs are created. Therefore, an extension of the Audio-visual Law, at least for another twenty years, is an ideal way for Brazil to express its political will to give wings to the film industry.

The third aspect of the proposed consolidation of cinema laws deals with the need to control audio-visual products imported into the country. As happens in every country where the State controls what passes over its borders, Brazil also needs to control audio-visual imports offered to its population, so that the economic effect of the entry of these products may be properly recorded and, as a consequence, appropriate measures may be taken to protect local industry. The dismantling of protectionist laws for cinema took away instruments used by the State to control imports, as well as making it impossible to enforce laws that required imports to be registered with governmental organizations and hence pay a tax for the registry service. Legislation exists to this effect, but, unlike the days of Concine, there is no longer any way of knowing, for example, how many cinemas there are in the country, how many screenings they have, or the number of foreign films that come in and are shown as a whole. The tax levied on this registration service can and should be used to foster audio-visual activity, since, once sold, such films are shown on television, home video and in cinemas. But current legislation does not include fines for companies that do not pay the tax. As a result, the State's inability to charge for this registration generates the disappearance of potential resources which impede it from carrying out its mission to help national producers, as well as to improve conditions for the circulation of their films.

For this to happen, resources and conditions currently not in existence would have to be implemented. Because the State was left unprepared to carry out its job of registering imported audio-visual products, it failed to earn, in 1999, ca. R\$ 24 million. To have an idea of what this means, just remember that a consistent programme for the commercialization of around 25 Brazilian films made in one year costs in the region of R\$ 3 million a year, which goes towards a well-marketed release in the film's home market. Even if the lack of these resources has not completely impeded the first steps of the Commercialization Programme from being taken, as the Ministry of Culture invested close to R\$ 2,9 million in a programme of this kind in 1999-00, it is not difficult to realize that new sources of finance are necessary in order for a larger number of copies to be made available for exhibition and attract larger audiences. And so, even though there is political will to make film registration legally binding, the government lacks the relevant legal instruments necessary to make the law operative, which is why this topic was included in the consolidation of cinema laws.

Beyond the consolidation of legislation that requires the registration of imported products, which includes the introduction of the Brazilian Product Certificate (*Certificado de Produto Brasileiro* –

CPB), the Ministry also proposed the creation of a Contribution for the Development of Audio-visual Activity, as prescribed by Decree 1900, from 1992, which states that part of the activities carried out by foreign distribution companies in Brazil – as already happens in other countries – will be taxed about 10 per cent on the total amount of profit sent overseas. This contribution is already binding, under Art. 3 of Law 8685, which states that foreign companies distributing their product in Brazil may divert up to 70 per cent of the income tax they owe towards co-productions. Currently, as most of the distribution companies in Brazil are American, and because they can draw on a provision of American income tax law that allows them to discount tax paid in Brazil from what they owe in the States, the mechanism implicit in this article acts as a dead legal letter. Save for the few who invest in co-production as a specific way to take Brazilian market share, most do not use the mechanism. Thus, the Ministry suggested a reformulation of the article in order to create, in the spirit of the contribution required in Decree 1900, a new source of money for the sector, based on its own economic dynamic.

A proposal was also made for the updating of the Screen Quota Law, which guarantees Brazilian films exhibition in the home market. The screen quota is not a way of protecting market share, or rather, of creating legislation to completely bar foreign films from certain areas of the national market. It establishes, in a limited way, a minimum number of days for the exhibition of Brazilian films in the country, so as to guarantee access to a local audience. This is indispensable, as other countries have proved, if the general desire is to create conditions for a competitive equality of national cinema in Brazil. Although currently in force, the screening quota is not met at the moment, because the State is unable to enforce the law that instates it. As a result, the Ministry of Culture sealed a partnership with the Public Prosecution Service, in 2000, to analyse the specific cases in which the law was breached and decide on necessary courses of action to be taken against the perpetrators. Moreover, for the legislation to be effective, the Ministry of Culture included a provision, when the laws applying to cinema were being consolidated, that allowed for better monitoring of adherence to the quota law by distributors. It is not just a matter of punishing those that do not comply with the law, but of creating effective ways to reward companies that overshoot the screening quota of Brazilian Cinema with public recognition.

Another important factor applies to the need for obligatory provision of distribution and exhibition figures, by both foreign and local companies, to allow the State to become familiar with the market's performance and to be able to fiscalize its content. In the past, mechanisms used by the State to regulate the exhibition market fell under the jurisdiction of the National Cinema Council, that checked the country's existing cinemas and what they showed. With the abrogation of the relevant legislation, the Collor government assigned to exhibitors, distributors and producers the task of gathering such information, and making it available to the public. A mechanism was created (*Sistema de Informações e Controle de Comercialização de Obras Audiovisuais* – Sicoa) that has not been capable of producing a permanent means for constant and up-to-date information about the workings of the market, although it has received important investments from distributors and exhibitors. At the end of 1999, for example, no one knew for sure in which cinemas throughout the country Brazilian films had been shown with success. With the new legislation, companies must supply the State with this information. Each company, independently, may do this without the need for a special organism. Many companies are already sufficiently computerized, and the need to comply with a law, in order to avoid fines, would give the State the ability to draw up a plan of action based on the situation of the market, as well as what regulatory measures to take, if necessary, to protect the national industry. These remedies do not exhaust the alternative ways of dealing with the problems facing the film industry, but they do provide the government with more effective means to make filmmaking a permanent activity in the country.

This set of measures and initiatives, although they have not exhausted the problems facing the sector, constitute a point of departure for the introduction of a new model for the relationship between film and State in Brazil. This is what Brazilian government is now trying to do through GEDIC. The recommendations of this group, aiming to create an Inter-ministerial Agency for sponsorship and market regulation, will consolidate the achievements of recent years and will hopefully allow cinema to become an industry in Brazil.

Translation by Roderick Steel

NOTES

1. Senator Francelino Pereira, the referee of the Senate's Cinema
    Commission, is compiling all the existing laws on cinema in order
    to prepare a bill for the sector. Senator Luiz Estevão is the author
    of bill n° 139, of 1999, which determines that 5 per cent of the
    box office revenue of foreign films will be destined to financing
    Brazilian films. Miro Teixeira is the author of constitutional bill
    n° 608/98, which prohibits the levying of federal, State or munici-
    pal taxes over audio–visual and theatrical works of any kind for five
    years from the date of the law's promulgation.

2

The cinema that Brazil deserves [1]

Carlos Diegues

Brazil is currently experiencing a boom in film production thanks to the Audio-visual Law which, since 1994, has prompted the rebirth of feature film production. But Brazilian Cinema has never been a permanent activity and has always gone through cycles such as this. These cycles begin with much euphoria, only to end some time later and almost always suddenly, in the midst of a crisis that is never due to the quality of the films themselves.

In my lifetime alone, I have witnessed or participated in many of these cycles or periods of renaissance. These have included the rise of the Rio de Janeiro-based *chanchada* (musical comedies), the Vera Cruz studios, the *Cinema Novo* movement, *pornochanchada* (porn comedies), Embrafilme (the Brazilian Film Company), the new São Paulo-based cinema of the 1980s and so on. All these cycles have signalled, each in its own way, the definitive establishment of a film industry in Brazil.

The Vera Cruz studios closed their doors just as *O cangaceiro* (*The Cangaceiro*, Lima Barreto, 1953) was receiving its prize at the Cannes Film Festival and winning over audiences throughout the world. *Cinema Novo* was knocked for six by the military dictatorship just as films like *Macunaíma* (Joaquim Pedro de Andrade, 1969) were confirming its aesthetic achievements, which were by then combined with popular appeal. Embrafilme was dismantled in 1990, just when Brazilian films were beating all records in terms of market share, not to mention the international awards won for *Dona Flor e seus dois maridos* (*Dona Flor and Her Two Husbands*, Bruno Barreto, 1976) and *Memórias do cárcere* (*Memories of Prison*, Nelson Pereira dos Santos, 1984).

A complex industry

The difficulty in establishing film production as a permanent activity in Brazil has been constantly attributed to the fact that cinema is a new, therefore unknown industry, characterized by unexpected factors that are beyond our control. But cinema has existed for over 100 years in Brazil, and since the first decade of the twentieth century Brazil has produced films, some of which have even been of international significance.

The truth is that cinema is not a new industry, but rather one of the most sophisticated and complex of recent times, that demands constant flexibility, imagination and diversity, even in countries where it has firmly taken root. The difficulties are more extreme in countries where the industry, in spite of its sophistication and complexity, is still impoverished and precarious. This is the case in Brazil.

With the exception of the United States of America (where only a few very low-budget, independent films are made), no other country in the world has an internal market of cinema theatres capable of maintaining a lucrative film industry and recouping production costs. In theory, given the size of its population, Brazil should be one of the few countries able to rely on its internal market alone in order to cover the costs of the industry.

However, in spite of its population of 160 million, only about 70 million cinema tickets are sold in Brazil each year, to about 10 million consumers. This means that only 6 per cent of the Brazilian population goes to the cinema. There are some 1400 cinema theatres in Brazil, which makes it the country with the second highest ratio of inhabitants to theatres.

To gain a better idea of how paltry these figures are you only need to remember that in France, whose population is only about 50 million, 155 million cinema tickets are sold every year, in some 4000 theatres. As far as the USA is concerned, with its population of near 300 million, on average 1.3 billion tickets are sold each year, in approximately 24,000 theatres.

Declining audiences

It was not, as is often claimed, the advent of television as a hegemonic popular leisure activity that was responsible for the decline in cinema audiences in Brazil. Generally speaking, virtually every country in the world has experienced a rise in the number of people going to the cinema compared with thirty years ago, and the figures have remained very stable for the last ten years. This is even the case in the United States, which is streets ahead in terms of the ratio between the number of inhabitants and the number of television sets, and where, as we all know, the most socially influential television in the world is made.

In Brazil the dramatic fall in the size of cinema audiences began in the mid-1980s, and became progressively more severe from then on until it reached today's levels. The decline is particularly evident among the country's lower classes – the cinema theatres that are closing due to falling ticket sales are those situated in small towns in rural Brazil, and in the poor neighbourhoods and outskirts of big cities. The public is no longer going to the cinema as a consequence of the worsening economic recession and its resulting, growing and perverse concentration of income, which excludes the vast majority of Brazilians from today's consumer society. When you have scarcely any money to live on, the first thing to be cut from the household budget is any kind of leisure activity, especially one that can be replaced by something cheaper.

So the people who have stopped going to the cinema are precisely those who traditionally have always ensured the box-office success of Brazilian films, during all the previous cycles of the country's film production. Popular audiences who want to see themselves represented on screen have always been, historically and statistically, the key consumers of Brazilian films.

Having been transformed into a typical middle-class leisure activity, the cinematic spectacle has been subsumed into 'shopping centre' culture in Brazil. It is targeted precisely at the section of the population who, fuelled by dreams and fantasies of a hypothetical 'first world', refuse to recognize or take part in the realities of the country. They equally have difficulty in accepting their Brazilian cultural identity, a pre-requisite for understanding any audio-visual material produced in Brazil.

Ancillary markets
Throughout the world, as a general rule, only about 25 per cent of the total income from a given film comes from box-office receipts. The other 75 per cent comes from the so-called ancillary markets, the numerous alternative forms of dissemination that we know today, particularly terrestrial and cable television, but also videos, laser discs, DVDs, the increasingly important Internet and the nascent digital age.

However, in Brazil films are restricted to only 25 per cent of their potential income, given that the ancillary markets are all but nullified by the lack of popular consumption, and Brazilian producers do not have access to terrestrial or cable television, both lucrative sectors of the audio-visual and advertizing industries. On the rare occasions that Brazilian producers are given access to these media, they are obliged to accept humiliatingly low prices that are offered on the pretext that this is the amount that American films receive. Furthermore, we should remember that on the even rarer occasions that Brazilian films are shown on national networks, they almost always obtain impressive audience figures, as has been proved by opinion polls made by Ibope (*Instituto Brasileiro de Opinião Pública e Estatística*/Brazilian Institute of Public Opinion and Statistics), that anyone can consult. This is precisely because these networks attract popular audiences.

Consequently, the market for Brazilian films is limited to only 6 per cent of the country's population and, furthermore, films can expect only 25 per cent of their potential revenue. In neither case are filmmakers themselves responsible for the situation.

The Audio-visual Law has permitted the resurgence of the production of full-length feature films in Brazil, but it has not guaranteed their impact on the public since it does not address the issue of dissemination. Today everyone is aware that the crux of the issue at the heart of the film industry is distribution and not production.

In order to understand this maxim, you only have to consider the fact that production does not necessarily lead to distribution, but that distribution always stimulates production. There is no point in producing films unless there is a market intervention strategy in place. At best, the Audio-visual Law can only create the biggest industry in the world of unreleased films.

Market share

Political or economic power is essential in order to intervene in the market in a significant way. Embrafilme, for example, had both, in addition to coercive State backing. It produced a wealth of films, with the result that, for several years, it was the second largest film distributor in Brazil in terms of turnover. It was this distribution policy which meant that Embrafilme became a decisive factor in securing market share. During its existence, Brazilian films obtained on average 35 per cent of the market, with peaks of 40 per cent and 45 per cent in certain years in the 1970s. To gain a better idea of the scale of these figures, you only have to remember that French cinema, which has more success than any other national cinema vis-à-vis Hollywood's hegemony, today enjoys only about 25 per cent of its own domestic market.

Now, let us imagine that you are the owner of a supermarket that has two soap suppliers. The first delivers a box of soap every week, whilst the second delivers a box twice a year. Which of the two brands of soap will your customers find more regularly in your supermarket? Consequently, which of the two brands will you display on the best shelf, in the best possible position?

The same applies to Brazilian cinema. The most determined, competent Brazilian producer, with regular output, is not capable of releasing more than one film every 18 months or every two years. Therefore he will never be an important or main supplier for the exhibitor, who needs around 35 to forty films per year in order to keep each of his screens in operation.

Even if Brazilian films break all records at the box-office, with unprecedented ticket sales, the exhibitor will always give preference, priority and better treatment to the films distributed by companies that can supply the product regularly and in sufficient number to keep the theatres open. These are the companies that distribute American films, the so-called 'majors', each of which can offer cinema theatre owners between 15 and 45 films per year.

Distribution policy
Whilst they continue to be distributed on an individual basis, one project at a time, by producers who do not guarantee a regular supply for exhibitors, Brazilian films will always face an uphill battle in their home territory.

I would like us to consider now an example other than that of the United States, where the 'majors' (Disney, Warner, Universal, Fox, Paramount, MGM and so on) have always practised this policy of concentrated, 'packaged' distribution. The success of French cinema, in its efforts to guarantee its survival, owes much to the existence of four big local companies that operate like national 'majors'. Gaumont, UGC, Pathé and Bac (the latter a branch of the Canal Plus complex) ensure, with their diversified film packages, the distribution of all French productions.

This was also how Embrafilme used to guarantee the supply of productions that ranged from the last film in the 'Trapalhões'[2] comedy series to films by first-time directors, and including box-

office smashes like *Dona Flor, Xica da Silva* (Carlos Diegues, 1976),
A dama do lotação (*Lady on the Bus,* Neville d'Almeida, 1978),
Gaijin, os caminhos da liberdade (*Gaijin,* Tizuka Yamasaki, 1980), *Eu
te amo* (*I Love You,* Arnaldo Jabor, 1981), *Pixote, a lei do mais fraco*
(*Pixote,* Hector Babenco, 1980), *Bete Balanço* (Lael Rodrigues,
1984), *Memórias do cárcere, Eles não usam black-tie* (*They Don't Wear
Black Tie,* Leon Hirszman, 1981) and so on. Such hits paved the
way for the launch of more 'difficult' films onto the market.
Without combining quantity and diversity, without economic
power, it is impossible to make your presence felt in the film distribution market.

The lack of ancillary markets for Brazilian films at home means
that Brazil is rowing against the tide of what is happening today in
the rest of the world. The huge variety of new means of dissemination and the constant increase in their number lead to ever
greater demand for audio-visual products, at an increasingly
breathtaking rate.

This growth is even more striking in relation to feature films,
because they take up more television screen time throughout the
world than any other cinematic form. As a consequence of this
demand, world production of feature films is constantly on the
increase, even though some of these productions never reach cinema theatres, instead providing fodder for television or, in many
cases, going straight to video, laser disc or DVD.

The irony is that the ancillary markets need an ever-greater
quantity of films, which in turn exceeds the demand of cinema
theatres. This means that while there is a shortfall of films for terrestrial and cable television, for video and so on, there is a surplus
of films for screening in cinemas, which do not have the capacity
to deal with so many.

This is the reason why, nowadays, films show for such short
periods of time at the cinema, generating about 40 per cent of
their revenue during their first week.

Since there is a bottleneck of films in each cinema theatre,
each awaiting its opening night, films are not shown for long
enough to attain their expected box-office receipts or to realize
their income potential. But because, with this system, the general
box-office income increases, this commercial distortion is perpet-
uated in a vicious circle.

State participation

As we have seen, Brazilian films cannot depend on ancillary markets (which, outside Brazil, make up for the rapid passage of films through cinema theatres), and thus we can understand how, once again, Brazil has to be content with inadequate commercial exploitation that falls far short of realizing its potential. Cinema theatres all over the world have become shop windows that determine the value of each film in the ancillary markets.

Canal Plus, for example, the largest cable channel in Europe, purchases films in accordance with a pricing chart that takes into consideration the performance of each film in the cinema theatre market, and establishes a price three and a half times lower than the average price for films that have not gone on general release. The Brazilian film market follows this global trend, whereby films spend very little time in theatres, but in Brazil they do not have ancillary markets to fall back on.

In the 1950s, when the Kubitschek government decided that Brazil needed an automobile industry, it not only created incentives for national production and raised taxation on foreign goods, but it also started building roads that the vehicles produced in Brazil could use.

In the 1970s, when the military decreed that a telecommunications system was essential for territorial integration and national security, they not only gave telecom companies fiscal advantages, but more importantly they invested in a state-of-the-art satellite system which meant that Brazilian television was one of the first to broadcast on a national network.

Of course Brazil no longer lives in times of import substitution via State investment, nor are Brazilians any longer ruled by an authoritarian regime that demands social control at any price. However, if cinema is something that should be fostered, the Brazilian State has to commit itself to making that existence viable.

Despite the fact that market forces are respected throughout the civilized world, in any country with at least a reasonable film industry the State always intervenes to some extent to keep it going, despite the complex distortions referred to above. It very rarely assumes the role of entrepreneur or investor but almost always acts as mediator or regulator.

Where market forces are absent, corruption ensues, but a complete lack of involvement on the part of the State, on the other hand, inevitably means a return to the dark ages.

The relationship with television

Even in the United States, the home of the free market economy, the regulatory presence of the State is felt through the application of the antitrust laws, which prohibit national television networks, for example, from producing more than 30-40 per cent of the material that they broadcast, obliging them as a result to acquire the rest from independent producers or studios.

Every country, according to its specific conditions, has legislated for the relationship between television and cinema in its own way, for example fostering co-productions via investment of part of their takings, or by requiring the purchase of films via market reserves, or even by requiring that part of the takings made during commercial breaks be ploughed into film production, and so on.

Brazil is the only country in the world where the government has never considered mediating the relationship between the two industries. In other words, it is the only country in the world where the State has never been involved in establishing what the responsibility of television should be with regard to the cinema.

The paradox of Brazilian television is that it is one of the best in the world and one of the most advanced in terms of technology and production values, but from an institutional point of view, it works along the lines of the old sugar mills of Brazil's North-East, where a handful of feudal overlords decide the destiny of people's minds in private conversations on the veranda of their plantation houses.

While in the rest of the world television networks have to meet different economic, educational and cultural objectives set by the State, in Brazil television chiefs do not have to answer in any way to government or society, as if they really were masters of the airwaves which they rent by concession. And tragically we have seen over the last five decades that Brazil's public representatives have not always had the courage to, or simply have not been interested in confronting this anomaly, this institutional anachronism.

In Brazil, television stations do not have any kind of responsibility or duty to the local film industry. Moreover, Brazilians have to sit back and accept that national television is a dumping ground for cheap foreign films, which in turn affects the price of Brazilian films. Filmmakers have to accept 'bargain basement' prices in order to sell their wares in what is for them a primary and often the only market.

The foreign films that are sold to Brazilian television stations have already covered their production costs in full: the Brazilian market for them is of no real financial significance. In the television market of their country of origin they are worth 50, 60 or even 70 per cent of their original cost, while in Brazil these films are sold for a value of around 3 per cent of the average cost of producing a Brazilian film. The same rules are applied to the purchase of Brazilian films by these stations.

As a simple example of how absurd this all is, take the Liza Minnelli Show, with a large orchestra, dance troupe, and so on, which can be bought by a Brazilian cable television channel for around US$ 1000. If a Brazilian producer wants to film an original show by Gal Costa, for example, for US$ 1000 he cannot even hire the most modest of lighting sets.

A flawed project

In my opinion, Brazil's main newspapers dealt with the issue of cinema's relationship with television in their recent proposal for a reform to the Audio-visual Law in an erroneous manner. According to the proposed reform, with the pretext of 'improving the management' of the film industry, the law would enable television stations to raise funds for cinema production. This proposal, which, if approved, would result in the immediate end to independent production in the country, is based on a number of serious miscalculations. The first is to consider production to be the core of the current crisis in Brazilian cinema. We have already seen that this is not the case. The second is to believe that the country's television companies are better prepared than film production companies to make what the latter have been making for decades, namely films. The nature of television production, which is to churn out material like a kind of Audio-visual fast-food store, is completely different from that of the cinema, which more than ever demands personalized products, capable of being transformed into unique and exclusive events.

The third misconception of the proposal is that television companies in Brazil would be more competent than the film industry. Despite all the difficulties and adverse circumstances, the likes of Barreto, Massaini, Pereira dos Santos and Khouri,[3] to mention but a few of Brazil's longer-serving film-people, are still there, more than forty years later, producing films which always make an impact. Whatever happened to the Tupi, Rio, Excelsior, Continental and Manchete television companies? Most of them closed down amid scandal and outcry.

Every day the newspapers say that SBT TV network is desperately looking for a foreign partner to survive and that its chief Sílvio Santos is publicly declaring that without his Tele-Sena lottery game he would have to close down this station. These same papers write that Rede TV is being taken to court and threatened with closure for failing to meet the obligations that it inherited from Manchete. Some stations survive on the back of the religious naiveté of the Brazilian people; others thanks to sports broadcasting, and so on. Finally, perhaps the only truly solid, competent and successful station in the country is TV Globo, despite its current ratings crisis, of which the press constantly reminds its readers. But why hand over to Globo and its characteristic production style the hegemony or even the monopoly on film and audio-visual production, which is what would happen if this law were approved? If this project becomes law, it will be the first time in audio-visual history that cinema finances television and not the other way round, as happens throughout the rest of the world.

Brazilian Cinema has no future if a way of forging an alliance with television cannot be found, if these two industries cannot interrelate in some way. But this alliance must originate from new resources, created by an agreement that is mediated by the State, and not by taking over the meagre resources that already exist, which scarcely support fragile and indispensable independent production in Brazil.

Television companies have to yield some ground: as they say in Brazil, it is not up to the patient to donate blood.

National cinema
Given all the factors outlined above, the disheartening statistics, the challenging circumstances and the history of the industry, it would be easy to conclude that it is not possible to make films in Brazil. But I do not believe that that is the question that should be asked here. The essential question is not whether we can but whether we *should* make films in Brazil. Or rather, is Brazilian Cinema something that should be fostered?

500 years ago in Europe a civilization flourished which represented the best that Western man had achieved to date. The Renaissance placed the individual at the centre of ideas, whereby worldly knowledge replaced superstition and a humanist religion was victorious over darkness. Never before had so many accomplished artists shared the same space and time, producing art with-

out equal. And it was in the name of all this artistic achievement that the conquistadors of the Americas massacred people, destroyed civilizations and carried out the largest genocide in the history of humanity. The devastation was so great that today civilizations such as those of the Aztecs, the Mayas and the Incas are archaeological mysteries to us. We know more about the Egyptians and Phoenicians, who lived more than 5000 years ago, than we do about these peoples who disappeared only 500 years ago.

It is no exaggeration to say that the role of American film in today's global culture is the same as that of the conquistadors of the Renaissance. Everyone likes to watch American films; in certain aspects they mirror another apogee in the history of humanity, a great civilization that we all recognize. Hollywood is a magical word for everyone and some time from now, when today's human and political passions have disappeared, I am sure that that word will be to the twentieth century what Greek theatre was to Antiquity, Italian painters were to the Renaissance and French novelists were to the nineteenth century. However, the fact that Hollywood films occupy 90-95 per cent of the world's screens is not good for humanity, just as it is not good for Brazil. If Brazil cannot produce its own image and occupy a few screens with that image, Brazilians will become living archaeological mysteries, unknown both to others and to themselves.

Structural measures
In order to avoid this tragedy Brazilian Cinema must above all become a permanent activity, a result of the inspiration and competence of its creators, acclaimed by society, inspired by market trends and wholeheartedly supported by the State. To this end I suggest a few opportune structural measures, which should be adapted to future needs at each stage of development.

1) Since cineastes cannot interfere in the country's income distribution, it is essential to encourage the setting up of **popular film circuits** and the opening of film theatres in rural areas, in poor neighbourhoods, in the *favelas* (shanty towns) and in deprived suburbs of big cities, in order to reach a greater public and increase the income potential of national films. The Federation of Brazilian Exhibitors (FENEEC) already has an excellent project that operates along these lines, based on financial mechanisms already in place.

2) In order to create capitalized businesses with the economic strength to intervene in the market and to carry out a concentrated and diversified **distribution policy**, the State must foster, via investment funds generated by the market's financial agents, the establishment of large distributors or national 'majors', by means of mergers, consortia, associations and so on, with financing for these companies and their regular programmes. This initiative does not exclude the encouragement of associations with already existing large distributors, above all those that have already shown an interest in Brazilian cinema (for example, Columbia, Warner, Lumière, Buena Vista and so on), or even with Riofilme and similar companies.

3) Still on the subject of the marketing of films, I suggest that the proportional system of **additional income rewards** be adopted once again, just as it was in Brazil in the 1960s and 70s and as it is in present-day Argentina, France and in other countries. These rewards consist of giving back to the producer part of the taxes levied on cinema tickets, in direct proportion to the box-office success of a film.

4) We must maintain and extend the resources available from **Article 1** of the Audio-visual Law, to guarantee the existence of independent and *auteur* productions, which in the past have been the basis for Brazilian Cinema's critical acclaim and which to this day have been responsible for its most outstanding achievements.

5) The State has to assume its responsibility towards film art and culture, thus creating a permanent system of **direct finance** for documentaries, experimental films and shorts and feature films by first-time directors. These are films that must be produced, even though they may not be absorbed by the conventional market, nor have the means to compete for a place in that market.

6) One of the roles of the State should be the **conservation of the country's cinematic history**.

7) It is essential, as has already been seen, to **integrate the film and television industries**, through new resources, in order to stimulate the growth of both and their international expansion. Price policies that discourage the dumping of cheap films on the Brazilian

market must also be established, along with screen quotas and co-productions. Television stations should not have a given system imposed on them, as that would never work. The State should mediate an agreement capable of benefiting both parties, according to their specific interests.

Translation by Stephanie Dennison and Lisa Shaw

NOTES

1. Summary of the address given to the Cinema Sub-committee of the Brazilian Senate, 8 June 2000.
2. Group of comedians led by Renato Aragão, who are extremely popular in Brazilian TV and Cinema.
3. Cinematographer and producer Luiz Carlos Barreto and his sons, Bruno and Fábio Barreto; producer and director Aníbal Massaini Neto; director Nelson Pereira dos Santos; director Walter Hugo Khouri.

Part two
Fiction film and social change

3

Brazilian Cinema in the 1990s: the unexpected encounter and the resentful character

Ismail Xavier

After the crisis that took place around 1990, Brazilian Cinema experienced a climate of rebirth since 1994-95. The presence of feature films in the market increased from 1994 to 1999. And the new cinema presents such a variety of styles that it makes the description of dominant aesthetic trends uphill work. Diversity – taken not only as a fact but also as a value – is what matters today.

The cultural climate does not favour debate on questions of principle involving film aesthetics and their tense relationship with market values. Pragmatism reigns, under the umbrella created by the legal device known as the Audio-visual Law. The choice between qualifying for the 'art film' circuit and attempting to communicate with larger audiences depends fundamentally on personal convictions shared by those engaged in each project, since there is no immediate pressure for return on capital. Filmmakers are taking the opportunities created by the legislation, aware that they may be living in a production bubble, which is bound to collapse if the cultural policies (currently under discussion) do not change.

Contradictory though it may seem, the proclaimed diversity does not obstruct the identification of significant tendencies in the ways the new cinema has been trying to account for the complexities of contemporary events; or, in other words, the most interesting works face problems of representation that are not exclusive to Brazilian Cinema today. How can cinema effectively speak about people's experiences in a world saturated by manipulated images? One solution has been to insert 'safeguards' in the

film: that is, to make the spectator aware of the process of production, to teach him/her how to read images, creating a structure of interactions in which the film itself, as an event among others, makes explicit its form of intervention within a certain context. I am referring to a tradition set by modern cinema that finds
its continuity in works like Kiarostami's, for instance, where we
find an original combination of realism and self-reference worked
out within a particular national context marked by the contradiction between tradition and modernity.

In Brazil, we have been living with this peculiar tension
between the critique of the image and the acknowledgement of its
central role within the ongoing and necessary inventory of national experience since the 1960s. At that time, some *Cinema Novo*
films presented a solution based on condensation, discontinuity
and all-encompassing allegories. The idea was to articulate an
ambitious political speech dedicated to a 'general diagnosis of the
country'. Conceptual issues, related to the notions of class and
national identity, were connected to formal innovations that
linked young filmmakers with the modernist tradition. Aesthetic
rupture and social criticism went along together, alienating people who expected naturalism and a didactic cinema. The best of
Cinema Novo introduced textual references (not only related to
parody), and a degree of opacity in those very images that con-
veyed its political engagement. Even a canonical realistic film like
Vidas secas (*Barren Lives*, Nelson Pereira dos Santos, 1963) represented, indeed, a rupture that is typical of modern cinema,
engaged as it is in a frontal attack on naturalistic conventions and
studio productions.

Cinephilia, very strong then, meant utopian impulses, a belief
in a better future for art and society. And the filmmaker saw
him/herself as someone who had received a popular mandate that,
in the Brazilian case, was conceived as coming from the very core
of the nation. In *Cinema Novo*'s vision, the nation was seen as a
much more cohesive and 'matter-of-fact' reality than history came
to reveal. We all know the ways of culture and politics in the past
decades, a period in which the filmmaker no longer has had that
conviction and has plunged him/herself into that defensive stance
typical of current art cinema in its relationship to the social and the
political. Looking back, one realizes how the sense of loss – related
to the legitimization of political cinema through the idea of a popular mandate – had come to the foreground already in the late

1960s, when Brazilian filmmakers moved away from a utopian impulse, especially after 1967, the year of Glauber Rocha's *Terra em transe* (*Land in Anguish*). Since this example of exasperated drama of disenchantment, it has become impossible to insist on a pedagogical art akin to populism, and the years 1968-69 brought blatant opposition to that sense of popular mandate, whether from *Cinema Novo* or the so-called *Cinema Marginal* (Underground Cinema), as Brazilians saw the rise of a cultural dissidence that refused any social teleology of redemption. The model of the enlightened intellectual willing to raise a new popular consciousness prepared for national liberation faded. In the early 1970s, film practice was contaminated by a sense of impotence that the film critic and writer Paulo Emilio Salles Gomes, in 1973, turned into a formula: in terms of film, underdevelopment is not a stage with a progressive direction, it is a state of being. The best of Brazilian Cinema in the 1970s turned around this bitter conviction, exploring family dramas, experiences of decadence, acute crises lived by frustrated characters who failed in their endeavours, or catastrophic peregrinations, of poor and rich alike, that ended in misfortune.

This kind of feeling towards the country still has its appeal in current films, at least in those most engaged in discussing social issues. Although different from the films made in the past, recent productions do not proclaim any rupture, revealing a certain continuity of concerns, including the recurrent thematization of emblematic *Cinema Novo* subjects and spaces: the *sertão* (arid backlands) in the North-East and the *favelas* (slums) in Rio. Since the beginning of the decade (in opposition to the late 1980s) a return of national concerns has reunited politics and allegory in a variety of films of quite different styles, reworking and displacing old concerns with identity politics that persisted throughout the 1990s, although today's filmmakers are less convinced than *Cinema Novo* leaders about their posture vis-à-vis the national-popular issue. This is arguably due to their being displaced by the high-profile discourse on national identity incorporated, since the 1970s, by the rhetoric of the winner of the audio-visual battle in Brazil: the Globo Network. This TV channel now displays its hegemonic industrialized version of the national-popular issue in its *telenovelas* (soap-operas). Also many films, especially those engaged in portraying history as a spectacle, tend to reproduce the ideas and the style of tele-fiction for marketing purposes. Since 1995, historical subjects have been at the centre of some very successful films that dealt with questions of identity and Brazilian history and that became closely associated with the idea of a rebirth of Brazilian Cinema which came to the foreground in that year. Such is the case of *O quatrilho* (Fábio Barreto, 1995), *Carlota Joaquina, princesa do Brasil* (*Carlota Joaquina, Princess of Brazil*, Carla Camurati, 1995), and *Guerra de Canudos* (*The Battle of Canudos*, Sérgio Rezende, 1997).

Light comedy, historical satire and epic melodrama were the traditional genres, common to film and television, that those three filmmakers explored, following the established conventions, in order to communicate with large audiences. Such forms of spectacle suppose the transparency of the past and are not engaged in raising questions of representation. These are made visible only in low budget films concerned with self-expression and authorship, establishing forms of dialogue with the national experience different from the parameters created by classical cinema and television. Here the filmmakers strive for an original approach either to the contemporary scene or to well known episodes of the past, facing both the crisis of a more canonical realism and the necessary changes to be undertaken when the impulse is to rework the national allegorism initiated by *Cinema Novo*. In narrative-dramatic films, authors like Tata Amaral, Sérgio Bianchi, Paulo Caldas, Lírio Ferreira, Beto Brant and Murilo Salles resist the pressures of a more conventional cinema and try to develop a new critical interaction with film genres, defining their own strategies of allusion (sometimes sheer allegories) in order to discuss the present conjuncture. Canonical realism is rare. Its only major example, not by accident, focuses on a story taken from the nineteenth century Portuguese writer Eça de Queiroz, *Amor & Cia.* (*Love & Co*, Helvécio Ratton, 1998), an ironic playing on the bourgeois codes dealing with adultery. In contrast to Ratton's comic-realistic tone, what is dominant in most films is the performance of passion dramas, the anatomy of crime and other forms of rage in works that deal with excesses but are concerned with the idea of the well-made scenario. Violence is their major theme, character psychology their privileged field of discussion.

In fiction films, the introduction of a degree of reflexivity can nevertheless generate a realistic effect, even when the proclaimed intention is of another kind, like in *Os matadores* (*Belly up*, Beto Brant, 1997), *Um céu de estrelas* (*A Starry Sky*, Tata Amaral, 1997) and *Como nascem os anjos* (*How Angels Are Born*, Murilo Salles,

1. Dalva (Alleyona Cavalli) and Vítor (Paulo Vespúcio Garcia) in *Um céu de estrelas*.

1996). In all, the critique of media comes to the foreground to deal with the opposition between the rules of media discourse and the rules of effective violence in society.

Os matadores demystifies the professional killer after giving us the impression that we are looking at a genre film willing to seduce us through the exhibition of glaring violence and the celebration of friendship among peculiar characters devoted to a certain expertise. The major encounter involving the young and the older professional killer ends up having a surprising dénouement. The trajectory of the ambitious young protagonist, a car thief who leaves the big city and reaches a kind of frontier zone aspiring to become a famous killer, turns into a fiasco. Instead of an action-film we face the study of a psychological type, the exposure of the flaws of his precarious project paralleled by the fantasies lived by a Paraguayan who also follows the stereotype of the killer. Both characters fail and their story reveals a situation in which law and order have become a private affair. The State is absent, and law is administered by a local boss who counts on professional killers with no charm; they are just regular employees.

Tata Amaral's *Um céu de estrelas* deals critically with melodrama as embodied by specific characters in its story. The setting is a working class section of São Paulo's labour zone. The central conflict involves a young woman, Dalva, about to move to Miami, her disapproving mother and her ex-fiancé (Vítor). The entire action takes place in her house on the eve of her departure, when she is forced to face Vítor's aggressive opposition in a confrontation that ends with the death of her two obstacles – the mother and the ex-fiancé. The dramatic episode sets Dalva free from both but in undesirable circumstances. At the end of the story, taken by the police, to whom she has to explain what happened in the house, she is devastated. The young man's behaviour is a disaster from beginning to end. First, he forces his way into the house and looks at Dalva's luggage all set to go. He takes a gun from a bag and points it at his own head: blackmail. Later on he kills Dalva's mother, when she arrives home to blame him for all of her daughter's miseries. Called by the neighbours, the police and a television crew surround the house; they talk about kidnapping. The tension grows, and when the police are about to break into the house, Vítor gives his gun to Dalva. Interpreting his wish, she kills him just before all the apparatus set up outside reaches them to banalize their experience of a shared crisis which is more complex than the public opinion voiced by the TV reporter can grasp. The scenes of their confrontation inside the house show quite well their inner anguish and shared feelings of love, desire and fear. Contrasting with this, the two melodramatic gazes, the mother's and the modern and powerful gaze of the TV, exude inadequacy, even stupidity. This critique of melodrama gives room to a realistic questioning based on an economy of psychological motivations tempered by occasional references to a socio-cultural background. Dalva and Vítor are seen as similarly vulnerable protagonists of a working-class drama commodified in the press as *fait-divers*.

In Murilo Salles' *Como nascem os anjos*, the critique of film genre and television coverage involves the systematic exploration of unexpected encounters and implausibilities. The first sequence shows an awkward confrontation in which a slum dweller, called Maguila, surprisingly kills a dangerous armed man linked to the drug dealers who control the *favela*. This is the first of a series of surprises. Branquinha, a sub-adolescent who is proud of her affair with Maguila, together with her friend Japa, flee from the *favela*, following the condemned Maguila. A succession of random turns leads them to a rich house exactly at the moment the owner is about to leave. The garage door is open and the proprietor (who happens to be an American businessman) looks at these unknown poor people with fear. Branquinha tries to explain ('we are not

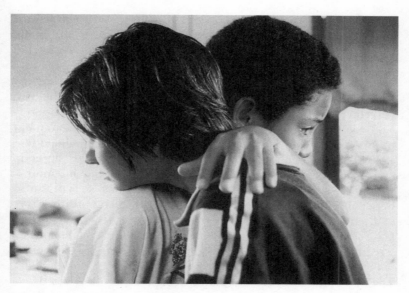

2. Branquinha (Priscila Assum) and Japa (Sílvio Guindane) in *Como nascem os anjos.*

outlaws') but misunderstanding prevails, and another awkward and implausible violent scene creates an unintentional kidnapping: the house chauffeur is killed, the *favelado* Maguila is wounded, and the two children grab the guns forcing everybody to enter the house. Again an unplanned kidnapping creates the basic framework for the action. A complicated series of events involving the police, and again television, leads the two children to their deaths. Inexperienced and always nervous, they end up killing each other in the house under the gaze of the bourgeois man and his daughter.

In Murilo Salles' film the idea of the 'unexpected encounter' presents itself in its most systematic version: a garage door opens and sets people of opposite classes, who have never seen each other before, face to face. From beginning to end the plot line follows a path created by sudden decisions, accidental gestures, unmotivated turns. Other films of the 1990s are not so radical when exploring this motif of the accidental, but they also construct their plots around unexpected or singular encounters. In the city space, a man can bump into an extraordinary occurrence at any moment, as we see in the first scene of *A causa secreta* (*The Secret Cause*, Sérgio Bianchi, 1995). An old woman can meet an unknown child who ends up changing her life, as we see in *Central do Brasil* (*Central Station*, Walter Salles, 1998). In rural spaces the singular event can be produced by migration, when two people with no past history in common and representing figures of otherness for each other meet in a scene treated with special care by the film: such is the case of Brant's *Os matadores* and Caldas' and Ferreira's *Baile perfumado* (*Perfumed Ball*, 1997).

We know that unexpected encounters are not new in fiction. But in this context they seem to create a paradigm that, observed film after film, creates a new sense of what is plausible in the representation of classical themes. Brazilian Cinema's dominant tone is symptomatic in its suggestion of a general malaise in society, featuring a collection of failed attempts at developing relationships of love or friendship. And the films permeated by this renewed sense of failure display another recurrent feature of the new cinema: a screen full of disastrous gestures performed by resentful characters.

The new social environment and the singular (or unexpected) encounter

Beto Brant's and Murilo Salles' films show us territories administered by organized crime and private security forces, social spaces where the State has lost control of violence. Examples of authoritarian intimidation have been enacted in many Brazilian films since the 1960s, and there is a recurrent scene that condenses a set of ideas about discretionary power: a character displays a gun to show off his own power and exhibits his knowledge in a speech about how to use a gun. We were introduced to this kind of emblematic scene in Ruy Guerra's *Os fuzis* (*The Guns*, 1963), which presents a well-known version of it: in a small town in the North-East a soldier shows off his expertise to humiliate the peasants. In Caldas' and Ferreira's *Baile perfumado*, we again see a soldier teaching people, this time his companions, how to use a new gun. Both 'teachers' belong to the official armed forces, manifesting the presence of the State in the backlands. *Como nascem os anjos* takes us to the city, where we see that same kind of attitude displayed by an exhibitionist gangster who addresses his companions and other curious people from the *favela*. Turning the tables, this last film produces an unexpected resolution of the scene. At a certain point, the audience leads Camarão, the gangster-professor, to a confrontation with a poor devil from the *favela* who dares to comment on his performance. Surprisingly, this time it is the bandit who is killed by the supposedly stupid listener, who ends up show-ing his knowledge of the gun and firing at his oppressor.

Apart from this ironic inversion of competence, the scene marks a clear change in the source of intimidation, no longer the State but organized crime, a central motif in the new cinema. Nowadays in Brazil, arms and drug dealers control territories, and make them a kind of frontier space where 'anything goes', where erratic events happen in which normal people are kept in between two violent forces, submitted to all kinds of accidents, including being killed by so-called 'stray bullets'. These are little allegorical capsules that mark their presence in the newspapers almost every-day, featuring the most 'unexpected encounters' we can imagine. The fiction film *Orfeu* (Carlos Diegues, 1999) and the documen-tary *Notícias de uma guerra particular* (*News of a Private War*, João Moreira Salles, 1998), the latter in a more systematic way, show the nature of the three-fold conflict between police, gangsters and the people. Given the three opposing sides, the recent films usually concentrate on the experience lived in loco by the poor, far from the central and invisible power game that involves international connections which are kept off the record as a kind of structuring absence (here the exception comes again from João Moreira Salles' documentary). This idea of a central and structuring absence pervades other kinds of political film – an outstanding sign of our epoch – like *Doces poderes* (*Sweet Powers*, Lúcia Murat, 1996) all organized around off-stage conspiracies, media plots, political marketing, blackmail and murder.[1]

Focused on the experience of violence, in the city and in the countryside, Brazilian Cinema now tends to emphasize ethics and psychology, even when the issues at stake are social and political, as in films that bring the point of view of the major victims – the encircled population of the *favelas* – to the centre. This is what *Como nascem os anjos* does, exploring Branquinha's disastrous behaviour derived from the adolescent nature of her desire, a plunge into vanity that leads her and her friend to the final accidental shooting in which they die. Here the accidental reveals itself to be the rule, the typical and recurrent event that affects a community under a stage of siege and living the syndrome of the 'stray bullet'.

In Beto Brant's *Os matadores*, the gangsters are all professionals. In Murilo Salles' film, the gangster-professor in the *favela* scene, Camarão – whom I take as a model for this kind of character – is arrogant, authoritarian. Lucinho, from Diegues' *Orfeu*, although surrounded by people that remind us of Camarão, is more humanized (he is the protagonist's great childhood friend). Nevertheless, the film constructs a 'bad image' of him, not bothering to explain why he is so different from *Orfeu*, the musician, or why he is engaged in drug dealing and crime. The three films – *Como nascem os anjos*, *Os matadores* and *Orfeu* – make an effort not to romanticize the gangster. They deprive him of the aura of a representative of the people, moving away from the conception of the outlaw found in films from the 1960s and 1970s. Those were bandits whose violence, although seen as mistaken, had some legitimacy as an answer to social injustice. The outlaw could be a hero, and we followed his drama closely, suffering his defeat in a final cathartic moment. Now things have changed, and the most spectacular move in the representation of the bandit occurred exactly in the *cangaceiro* film already mentioned – *Baile perfumado*. Before, as the centre of the drama, the *cangaceiro* (an outlaw of the *sertão*) was understood as a social bandit, an avenger eager to enforce justice, right wrongs. Although limited in his consciousness of the more complex mechanisms of class domination, he was seen as someone not far from revolutionary action. This is what we see in Glauber Rocha's *Deus e o diabo na terra do sol* (*Black God, White Devil*, 1964). This film composed a teleology that turned the *cangaceiro*'s words and gestures into prophecies, as a kind of proto-revolutionary stance. The figure of the bandit in *Baile perfumado* is very different, and the most famous *cangaceiro* leader, Lampião, displays a more cynical position.

In Caldas' and Ferreira's film, there is a mingling of the *sertão* and the city, and bourgeois values play a part in *cangaceiro* land. There is no teleology linking him with the future revolution. Glauber Rocha isolated the *sertão* as an autonomous world; that was a condition for turning it into an allegorical space capable of representing the nation and its history. In *Baile perfumado* there is no encapsulated world. Everything circulates, and exchange values connect *sertão* and sea. Perfume, bottles of whisky, all appear in the *cangaceiro* land. Lampião and Maria Bonita go to the movies, and the filmmaker Benjamin Abrahão films the *cangaceiros* in the *sertão*. In fact, the axis of the film is this singular encounter between the bandits and the filmmaker. The man with the movie camera is the protagonist, and the images he actually produced were the inspiration for the work done in *Baile perfumado* on the *cangaceiro*'s vanity. In Rocha's film, there was vanity, but there was sacrifice and that longing for justice typical of the social bandit. Now this type has disappeared and the Lampião who emerges in *Baile perfumado* is merely ambitious and displays a farcical aspect. Music and editing style celebrate him as a mass culture icon, a peculiar item in a gallery of masks that displaces politics in its myth-making process. From romanticism we pass to pop.

In contemporary cinema, violence does not come out of the search for justice; it comes out of professional routines or, alternatively, from outbursts of rage on the part of frustrated characters not taken as spokesmen for values, but explored in their uncertainties as people mixed up in schemes that are beyond their control. There emerges a form of drama that responds to a world of tactical confrontations that do not seem to fit into strategies larger than the struggle for survival. Violence is acknowledged as a general rule, and it is something that might come when least expected; a fact that reinforces the motif of the singular encounter, a motif that, when linked to migration, reminds us of a new configuration of social networks that goes beyond Brazilian Cinema.

Large displacements in space, and the interactions between local and alien elements, have had a significant effect on the dramatic structures of cinema in several countries. Wanderers, travelling characters, unexpected cross-cultural encounters are frequent in today's cinema, a kind of epochal symptom that Brazilian film comes to share even when it recounts events that took place in the past. Fragments of world history come to light, whether in an apartment with corroded walls in a rundown building in downtown São Paulo – the hidden Nazi in *Sábado* (*Saturday*, Ugo Georgetti, 1996) – or in the American businessman's house 'invaded' by children in Rio, in *Como nascem os anjos*. In *Um céu de estrelas*, Dalva's project connects Mooca, a lower middle class section of São Paulo, to Miami. And *Baile perfumado* signals changes in our perception of a multicultural experience when it accentuates, for the first time, the fact that Benjamin Abrahão was a Lebanese immigrant (including some parts in which his voice-over monologue comes in Arabic). Eurídice, in Diegues' film *Orfeu*, is of indigenous descent, and she has flown from Acre (a state in the North of Brazil) to land in Rio, finding Orfeu in the *favela* (this ethnic multiplicity is not to be found in Vinicius de Moraes' play that was adapted in *Orfeu*). All these details seen together say something about the new configurations of identity politics, and

the motif of the encounter ends up having an allegorical dimension. In different ways, Brazilian films reveal their connection with
the contemporary state of sensibility, showing their concern for
the human aspects of the compression of space and time inherent
in the world of high technology.[3]

As in other national cinemas, Brazilian films present a new
vision of displacement, including that which took place in colonial
times. Djalma Batista's *Bocage, o triunfo do amor* (*Bocage, The Triumph
of Love*, 1997) presents a revision of cultural values associated with
Portuguese colonization. The crossing of the Atlantic and the
Portuguese expansion are taken in their identity-forming dimension, without repeating the stereotype of the bad-mannered and
ridiculous colonizer, stressing the affirmative aspect of the cultural
complex created by people's displacements and interactions. The
fresco of overseas expansion comprises the framework for the homage to the poet Bocage and, through him, the Portuguese language. Expressing the new sensibility of compressed time, the
'compilation film' *Nós que aqui estamos por vós esperamos* (*Here We Are
Waiting for You*, Marcelo Masagão, 1999) condenses the history of
the twentieth century without dealing with Brazil, except for
Garrincha, the football player, and an allusion found in a
Mayakovsky poem, a detail that confirms the country's eccentricity
already suggested by the rest of the film. In Walter Salles' and
Daniela Thomas' *Terra estrangeira* (*Foreign Land*, 1995), the
encounter of two young protagonists results from their flight from
Brazil. They are adrift in Portugal, and their experience follows the
pattern much explored in the US cinema: two lovers try to escape
from a criminal organization. Here the characters' involvement
with criminals is taken as an undesired contingency – in the beginning, they have no other choice. Their sense of impotence finds its
counterpoint in romantic, almost suicidal, gestures that seal the
pact uniting the young couple in their escape. Disenchantment
and libertarian impulses dominate a film that does not fail to mention the inaugural Portuguese adventure across the ocean, alluding
to Brazil as a peripheral country that went wrong.

These ironic remarks on Brazil related to the question of centre and periphery allow for a significant comparison involving *O
que é isso, companheiro?* (*Four Days in September*, Bruno Barreto, 1997)
and Murilo Salles' *Como nascem os anjos*. In Bruno Barreto's film, the
kidnapping of the American ambassador belongs to a well-defined
political context, and the film represents the ambassador as the

3. Alex (Fernanda Torres) and Paco (Fernando Alves Pinto) in *Terra estrangeira*.

more lucid figure in the entire episode, a voice of reason, a man of larger views in comparison with the young political activists who kidnap him. In Murilo Salles' film, we have a more unexpected, singular confrontation. Once in the house of the rich man, the children are taken to be invaders, and the fact that their supposed victim is an American does not change the central conflict in substantial terms. It is a detail that alludes to a certain conjuncture that frames the drama, but does not belong to the axis of the conflict between the children, the police and the television network. What matters here is that the role played by the American in *Como nascem os anjos* is equivalent to that of the Ambassador in Bruno Barreto's film. Both exhibit the same virtues: good sense, serenity and comprehension. A game of mirrors binds the two episodes, the kidnapping decided by politics and the pseudo-kidnapping carefully designed as an accident. Both films treat the American as an exemplar of civility who uses his enforced predicament to observe with understanding nervous Brazilians who threaten or kill each other. There is an ironical lack of symmetry in these encounters, a sense of otherness that undermines effective contact.[4]

The sense of estrangement and fragile solidarity acquires, in other films of the decade, a class dimension. Walter Salles and Daniela Thomas, in *O primeiro dia* (*Midnight*, 1999), take the par-

ticular topography of Rio de Janeiro to define the terms of the singular encounter, and separation, of two people located on opposite sides of the class line. The time is New Year's Eve; the place,
the top of a building in middle class district Leme, next to a *favela*.
A young woman sees her marriage broken and plunges into an
acute personal crisis. She goes to the top of the building to commit suicide. A fugitive, after killing a friend to fulfil his duty to the
jailers who helped him escape, enters the same building and goes
to the top to hide and survive. On this suspended stage the unexpected encounter takes place, alluding to an overall network of
social relationships that is typical of Rio. The moment they get in
touch is great but ephemeral, since the feast and the promised
rebirth are effective only at the moment at which the bandit saves
the little bourgeoise. Their lives have very few things to be shared,
and he will be killed the next morning on the beach.

Another dimension of the singular encounter involves the
position of the filmmaker as citizen before the people he takes as
his subject. I have already commented on the fact that filmmakers
have lost their convictions regarding the legitimacy of their intervention in people's lives and their popular mandate. At the same
time, in society, discussions about the abuses perpetrated by television in its search for sensational topics have become a cliché.
What is implicated here is that the filmmaker has to be cautious;
his/her interaction with people (someone could say 'the Other')
can be questioned, introducing a specific discomfort. This is clear
when we think of documentary films but it also comes as a problem in some fiction films that deal with the poor. An example of
how the new cinema is concerned with the complicated relationship that filmmakers establish with social agents of a different sort
would be José Joffily's *Quem matou Pixote?* (*Who Killed Pixote?*,
1996). This question was in fact generated by the actual assassination, many years after Hector Babenco's film *Pixote, a lei do mais
fraco* (*Pixote*, 1980), of the young man who had played Pixote in
1980. In his film, Joffily gives his answer – the police. But not
before giving all the evidence about the problems brought by the
boy's encounter with cinema, a source of envious reactions on the
part of his brother and friends, which he was not emotionally prepared for and ended up ruining his life.

A psychological syndrome produced by interaction with the
media is also at the centre of Branquinha's drama in *Como nascem
os anjos*. In films from the 1970s and early 80s, like Babenco's *Lúcio*

Flávio – o passageiro da agonia (*Lúcio Flávio – Passenger of Agony*, 1977) and *Pixote*, a realistic approach highlighted television as a source of lies that favoured the established order, contrasting television mystifications with the truth rescued by cinema, a rhetoric that filmmakers have used for a long time. Now there is a new understanding of the role of cinema and television in the formation of the subject, filmmakers becoming less self-assured about their redemptive role in society. Modesty seems to be the rule, and documentary films, when dealing with popular religious cults, prefer a politically timid ethnographic description. This is clear in *Santo forte* (*Strong Saint*, Eduardo Coutinho, 1999) and *Fé* (*Faith*, Ricardo Dias, 1999), films that, despite their differences, have that concern for a cautious approach in common. And João Moreira Salles, who made the best documentary of the 1990s, *Notícias de uma guerra particular*, insists on the necessary respect for the people interviewed so that the encounter cannot turn into manipulation.

This problematic side of shooting and contact with people can be overcome in different ways, and there are instances in which the filmmaker finds a rare experience of joy in a singular encounter lived as a happy discovery. I am referring to Bia Lessa's and Dany Roland's *Crede-mi* (*Believe Me*, 1997), a work that was first intended as a documentary film related to a theatrical experiment they performed in small towns in north-eastern Brazil. The film gained a new dimension when Lessa and Roland realized that their real task was to compose a particular image of popular festivals in order to render visible the persistence of a medieval ethos in that area. This enabled them to find significant traces linking the local culture to Thomas Mann's novel, *The Holy Sinner*, which they had taken with them to use in the experiment with the local actors. Based on this unexpected encounter, they wove a narrative taken from Mann, as enunciated by different local voices and images, composing a singular allegorical journey that gives you the sense of following a collective voice. Lessa's and Roland's experience is of an aesthetic kind, and contrasts with other documentary films in which the encounter is motivated by political engagement. Tetê Moraes' *O sonho de Rose* (*Rose's Dream*, 1996) presents interviews with peasants, some of them militants from the MST (the Landless Movement). The filmmaker's aim is to give us an account of people's lives during the ten years that separate the time of the shooting of the film from the time of a previously organized struggle that the same people had to conduct in order to take possession of their lands. Ten years before, Moraes had documented that struggle, and now (in 1996) she performs a back-and-forth movement to compare people as they appeared and acted in the past with their present condition and thoughts. The film's structure is simpler but reminds us of Eduardo Coutinho's extraordinary editing work in *Cabra marcado para morrer* (*Twenty Years After*, 1984), which gave an account of people's experience during the twenty years of dictatorship. The reencounter, the threads of memory that were bound together, made the film an event that changed the life of those who had been involved in Coutinho's project since the 1960s. At that time, the figure of the encounter could find its expression in the field of social history, linked to an ongoing political struggle that included the filmmaker as an active participant in a collective action.

In a significant turn, *Baile perfumado* is revealing in its exposure of the new self-image of the filmmaker. The singular encounter between Benjamin Abrahão and Lampião, even though fuelled by good will towards the *cangaceiro*, has catastrophic results. Ferreira and Caldas, expressing this new vision, emphasize the image of the filmmaker as a smart fellow, capable of making feasible the apparently impossible. However, the director's identification with Abrahão does not imply any mandate, any utopia. Besides, the film underlines the connection between Abrahão's film making and the modernization that resulted in Lampião's death, when economic changes put an end to the *cangaço* as social phenomenon. The image of Lampião on the screen was offensive to the modernizing projects of the New State (*Estado Novo*) in Brazil, established by Getúlio Vargas in 1937, and Abrahão's work ended up having negative consequences in the *cangaceiro*'s life, although it assured him a place in history. We see in those images a precious document but also the signs of death, a fatality not only for the *cangaceiros* but also for the filmmaker, who was eventually killed because of that encounter. Death is a shared destiny, but there is no ideological framework uniting the bandit and the filmmaker. Both lose their revolutionary appeal.

The new cinema moves us far away from the 1960s metaphors that turned the camera into a gun and the filmmaker into a proto-guerrilla fighting against the power of the industrialized media. The idea that cinema is an ambivalent medium with contradictory effects comes to the fore – cinema can destroy human relationships, it can even kill. Or, as a form of art, cinema can fail in its mission of reconciling the artist with him/herself or with the world. This sense of failure has something to do with the enigmatic experience enacted in Babenco's *Coração iluminado* (*Foolish Heart*, 1998). The protagonist is an Argentinean filmmaker obsessed by an adventure of his youth, a passionate love affair with a slightly deranged young woman. They make a death pact whose romantic exaltation is finally frustrated. They end up rescued by other people. Decades later, he is back in Argentina to experience different kinds of tension related to his past, including a failed attempt to see the former lover, now married to a bourgeois man. Resentful, he ends up expressing his frustration in an ambiguous scene in which he kills a half-real, half-imaginary woman who had been continuously appearing to him in a series of unexpected encounters in the city. In the last and fatal encounter, the enigmatic figure is subjected to all the aggression he had been accumulating since his youth. Here, the filmmaker is himself the (imaginary) murderer. And he acts out of resentment, a paradigmatic motif in the Brazilian Cinema of the 1990s.

The resentful character

The discomfort shared by a large group of characters who have their minds set in the past and are obsessed by long-lasting plans of revenge and aggressive ruminations, is a significant feature of current Brazilian Cinema. Through these films, resentment could even be taken as a national diagnosis. The protagonist of Beto Brant's *Ação entre amigos* (*Friendly Fire*, 1998) is perhaps the most typical example. His revenge is carefully planned and carried out in a film that privileges the 'well made scenario', the calculated effect, rhythm, *grand finale*. A former political activist, the protagonist is obsessed by the idea of killing his former torturer, a character he cannot forget. A group of friends, his old comrades, are invited to participate in the action. The idea is to fix the murder for a weekend, one of those usually dedicated by the group to fishing. The plan puts in motion a machine that reproduces the past: the same group, again a mission. This time, however, their action has no political meaning. The friends hesitate, timidly contest the idea but finally join in. Their present personal weakness projects a shadow of inconsistency over their political action in the past. Not surprisingly, things go wrong again, and the effect of the narrative is to link the details of past and present in order to show the irony of destiny acting on both occasions. The personal revenge succeeds, but the group has to pay the price of a new revelation. Before dying the torturer reveals how they were caught in the past – one of them had betrayed his comrades. The protagonist's outburst cannot be arrested and, his main enemy dead, he rushes to the station to catch the hypothetical traitor (not the real one), the only friend who has not followed him to the end in his stupid revenge. He kills the old friend under everyone's gaze, sealing his mistake. From beginning to end psychology prevails over political reason, in the character's mind and also in the film. The film's dramatic structure and conception of characters, whilst denouncing past repressions and the torture practised by a terrorist State, offers a reductive view of their experiences.

A curious symmetry links the rejected fiancé from *Um céu de estrelas* and the betrayed husband from the third episode of *Traição* (*Betrayal*, 1998), 'Cachorro' ('Dog'), directed by José Henrique Fonseca. What strikes me about these films (quite different from each other in terms of quality) is the fact that both portray men who have lost their self-esteem and invade the privacy of their women in an attitude of retaliation resulting in their own death. They want to attack but their internal division makes them hesitate, directing their violence against displaced targets and in the end against themselves. In *Um céu de estrelas*, Dalva's fiancé is romantic; in 'Cachorro', the betrayed husband is grotesque, as grotesque as the taxi driver of another film, *Perfume de gardênia* (A *Scent of Gardenia*, Guilherme de Almeida Prado, 1995). Here a wife leaves her husband to become an actress. He is obsessed by her image but delays his revenge for ten years. He then works out a plot for a perfect murder; however, when he finally kills her, something goes wrong: to his despair, his own son is accused of the crime and arrested in his place.

Um copo de cólera (*A Fit of Rage*, Aluizio Abranches, 1999) presents no crime, no extreme act of revenge, but resentment dominates a young man's crisis in his interaction with an intelligent and independent woman. Based on Raduan Nassar's book, the film translates to the screen the protagonist's self-exposure, typical of a first person narrative, not without some difficulties. The result is not always ideal but, in any event, the use of the actor's voice and gestures succeeds in expressing an internalized anger that this time is turned into a long discourse. Virility for him means domination and aggression, childish fantasies, rancour and regressive behaviour, showing his attachment to old patriarchal rules hidden

4. Júlia Lemmertz and Alexandre Borges in *Um copo de cólera*.

behind a modern façade. In Walter Lima Junior's *A ostra e o vento* (*The Oyster and the Wind*, 1997), the patriarchal figure turns a conflict of generations into a disastrous experience. He lives alone with his daughter in a lighthouse isolated in the ocean, and he resents his predicament as a man abandoned by his wife in the past and rejected by his adolescent daughter in the present. Poisonous feelings, repression and eventually death are his response to his daughter's liveliness, charm and erotic appeal.

In different social contexts, the new cinema signals the absence of love and friendship through which private life turns into a nightmare and social life into aggression, not only as an answer to poverty but as a response to personal failure. These obsessions, revenge plots and humiliations are reminiscent of Nelson Rodrigues' family dramas. People are envious and bad in *Quem matou Pixote?*, in which the young man who played Pixote in Babenco's film is a victim of jealousy in familial disputes. In the films shot in the *favelas*, we often see young characters getting involved in random aggression which derives from feelings generated by personal rivalries that add to the poverty in the creation of a violent environment. The machinery of mimetic desire and resentment is clearly at work in Branquinha's case (in *Como nascem os anjos*) and when, in *Orfeu*, Lucinho harasses Eurídice and ends up killing her by accident.

A different machinery of death is presented in a film like Walter Salles' and Daniela Thomas' *O primeiro dia*, already mentioned above. The fugitive kills his friend following the rules of an organization that reigns above him; his crime is an act of enforced discipline. However, before shooting him he gives his victim enough time for a chat among 'friends' and for a kind of ritual in which the man about to die starts praying. He creates his own liturgy of resentment, a conversation with God that has a basic premise: life is a universal cheat. This ritualistic scene epitomizes the motif of the 'poor (or the oppressed) killing the poor', which is expanded in its implications in Sérgio Bianchi's *Cronicamente inviável* (*Chronically Unfeasible*, 1999). Here we find the most uncomfortable representation of that violence among the poor which is provoked both by social inequality and a disseminated sense of failure that haunts society. In Bianchi's view, frustration permeates all kinds of social interactions involving Brazilians, rich and poor alike. It is a kind of 'national condition' that finds its typical expression in the variety of outbursts of rage that permeate the entire film. Irony, including self-irony, sets the tone of a representation that, from the very beginning of the film, makes explicit its basic concern: how to render visible the Brazilian malaise? How to deal with the sense of a general degradation that affects all classes in society? The filmmaker's choice is to turn his film into sheer provocation. He creates a mosaic of shocking sketches attacking Brazilians' idyllic self-image, thus rendered pathetic, and revealing a general hatred disguised in the cliché of the national penchant for conciliation. The film displays a gallery of resentful Brazilians, either ashamed of what they are or of the place they live in. What is left for them is the experience of sharing prejudices of all kinds. The final result of *Cronicamente inviável* is a non-conformist discourse that sometimes falls back into resentment, but in the end launches a productive challenge making us see, in a microcosm, a society in which charity rhymes with cruelty, pedagogy with frivolity, everything inviting mutual aggression and the 'dictatorship of happiness'. Bianchi's sad picture of Brazil is a moment of synthesis for the scenario of resentment presented so far.

The figure of redemption

Comedy – a genre involving reconciliation plots – is a good anti-dote to this gloomy picture created by the serious dramatic films featuring frustrations and grudges. Following the pattern of reconciliation, *Amores* (*Loves*, 1998), by Domingos Oliveira, brings the best counter-image to the psychological landscape presented so far. Its informal conversation about sex and current family life involves a group of characters who overcome their griefs and perform a more harmonious assimilation of the vicissitudes of modernity. *Amores* is a kind of anti-*A ostra e o vento*, featuring a father who faces similar predicaments but always acts quite differently when compared with the man from the lighthouse.

Apart from comedy, another instance of the struggle against resentment is a kind of return to the past that, in opposition to what we have observed so far, brings to our attention protagonists that are seen as embodying positive values, people whose trajectory is narrated as a tribute to their exemplary lives. This happens in a historical drama focusing on a well- known revolutionary figure treated as a national hero: *Lamarca* (Sérgio Rezende, 1994). However, as a political film, Carlos Reichenbach's *Dois Córregos* (*Two Streams*, 1999) is a more interesting example of such a return to the past. It also focuses on a political activist from the 1960s, now a more low-life character, if one considers his role as an exemplary guerrilla, but nonetheless depicted as a reservoir of noble feelings displayed in private episodes involving his children and especially his niece, who narrates her past experience and certainly idealizes his figure in her recollection. Despite this, her mediation in the composition of the portrait allows for a significant contrast: that between the grotesque male figures that surround her in the present (the 1990s) and the dignity of her dead uncle. In other words, the locus of noble feelings and ideas remains tied to the past.

In *Dois Córregos*, the antidote for present disenchantment and bitter loneliness is the recollection of the past. In *Central do Brasil*, the antidote is the overcoming of the past. The experience of liberation is produced by another unexpected encounter (our central motif here), now involving a resentful middle-aged lady (Dora) when she faces an emblematic figure of innocence. Given its melodramatic tone, the film builds radical polarizations, including the worn-out cliché created by the opposition between the 'demoniac' city and the sacred countryside. Without this cliché, the end of the film would lose its strong emotional effect. At the beginning, Dora is a condensation of what we have seen so far of rancour and egotism, with the addition of a mean disposition to cheat poor people. Later in the film, the bad side of things must reach a paroxysm before Dora learns to feel compassion and perform a good action to save an unprotected boy (Josué) from his extreme vulnerability in a dangerous environment. In Josué's long voyage home – to the countryside where his family dwells – he and Dora follow quite closely Wim Wenders' scenario concerning the relationship between adult and child (*Alice in den Städten/Alice in the Cities*, 1973), which begins with feelings of mutual hostility and evolves towards solidarity and love. In a story well adapted to the Brazilian social environment, we see the process of a gradual identification involving the two characters, and follow Dora's interaction with popular religion in 'deep Brazil', the very axis of her personal conversion. She has to live a rite of a symbolic death and rebirth in her journey towards the plain identification and solidarity with the Other, paralleled by self-reconciliation, that closes the film.

There is a happy ending in *Central do Brasil* that asserts Dora's encounter with Josué as the only redeeming experience among all those described here. For this reason, Walter Salles' allegory of hope can be taken as a rigorous counterpoint to the collection of bitter experiences enacted in many Brazilian films of the 1990s, and also in the 1980s. We should note how Josué appears as a new Pixote, who this time succeeds in finding his substitute mother figure, contrasting his own story with the disgraceful experience of the original Pixote, who searched for the nursing mother in the figure of the prostitute, but found a character who followed the codes of realism, not the codes of the moral parable. Josué is the contemporary boy who shares with the little Italian of Benigni's *La vita è bella* (*Life is beautiful*, 1997) and Wenders' Alice, in *Alice in the Cities*, the grace of a return to a protected life, at home or elsewhere, despite everything. This was impossible for many other children who have filled the screen through the 1990s, a decade in which children became emblematic characters in cinema. They come to the foreground even in a film like Bianchi's *Cronicamente inviável*, where they feature as a kind of ecological reservoir not yet polluted but about to be, if society continues to be what it is. Bianchi's option is for a bitter parody, a theatre of cruelty, a strategy that places him in opposition to works like *Central do Brasil* in

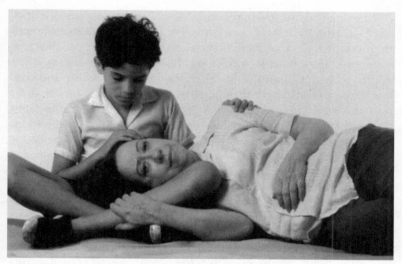

5. Dora (Fernanda Montenegro) and Josué (Vinícius de Oliveira)
  in *Central do Brasil.*

which children come to legitimate edifying sentimental dramas,
when these can be taken seriously, making acceptable a morally
schematic plot of biblical inspiration. Walter Salles, with his talent,
offered us the best of all those parables. Its tearful ending is indeed
a piece of melodrama, but it looks for an aesthetic sanction in that
collection of dense and revealing images that its documentary
aspect is able to produce (like the faces displayed in the beginning
of the film). Its central journey becomes the *locus* of a reverse
migration that establishes a dialogue with *Cinema Novo* films.

Serious dramas concerned with moral parables and redemption are rare today, at least in the more interesting sectors of film
production, and Walter Salles' work constitutes a kind of counterpoint to the dominant tone of recent Brazilian Cinema, more concentrated on experiences of failure, frustration and death.
Dealing with the complexities of current social life, the films
emphasize individual encounters, singularities, tending to leave
aside narrative forms more directly concerned with the exposure
of the social-historical forces that condition human action. There
is, in any case, a suggestive social diagnosis made by those structures related to the motif of the unexpected encounter which I
take as a significant feature of current cinema in general, not only
in Brazil. Moreover, the recurrent figure of the resentful character

can be seen as the most revealing social symptom, since it produces a strong effect when we observe the films' interaction with their context. Each of these films tends to adopt, in a peculiar and sometimes problematic way, a psychological or strictly moralist approach to social and political experiences. But when one considers the overall effect produced by film after film, one realizes how this new cinema expresses genuine anxieties coming from the very texture of our everyday life in the contemporary situation. One realizes how this cinema refers, in different ways, to personal feelings permeated by a sense of impotence before complex machineries of power that seem to be out of reach. One should say 'out of sight', sometimes far away in the off-screen space. Perhaps this is so because they are alien, not available to visual representation, at least within the dramatic structures chosen by current films. Although apparently abstract, these machineries play a significant role in our lives, conditioning different forms of violence, including those developed within the private sphere, familial conflicts marked by closed circuits of mimetic desire and resentment.

We live in a society in which the proclaimed set of values is centred on the idea of equality; the institutional framework promises democratic representation, and advertising triggers desire and simulates equal opportunities of consumption. However, the practical world frustrates expectations because, in it, equality and opportunity are virtual, abstract, and not real possibilities. Competition, as a general rule, segregates the losers from the winners, or the betrayed from the betrayers, as a moralist loser might say. Innocence? It is recognized in the figure of the child only, this kind of moral reservoir that can still generate compassion, embody ideal values and promises, becoming for this very reason an emblematic figure of a contemporary cinema that seems to say again and again: the child is the only universal left.

NOTES

I would like to thank Maria Elisa Cevasco for helping me with the translation of this chapter.

1.   The emphasis given to 'conspiratorial hypotheses' in contemporary political films is discussed by Fredric Jameson in the first chapter, 'Totality as Conspiracy', of *The Geopolitical Aesthetic: Cinema and*

Space in the World System (Bloomington and London, University of Indiana Press and BFI Publishing, 1992).

2. In all those cases, we could refer the *cangaceiro* image to the model presented in Eric Hobsbawm's book, *The Bandits* (New York, Laurel Editions, 1969).

3. This compression of space and time in our contemporary experience is focused on in different essays on the postmodern condition; see specially David Harvey, *The Condition of Postmodernity: An Inquiry into the Origins of Cultural Change* (Oxford, Blackwell Pub, 1989).

4. *Amélia* (Ana Carolina, 2000) deals directly with this opposition between centre and periphery, ironically enacted in the unexpected encounter involving the French diva Sarah Bernhardt and three Brazilian women who come from the countryside to Rio de Janeiro to meet her. The filmmaker created this imaginary encounter inspired by a real accident that took place in Rio de Janeiro's Opera House in the beginning of the twentieth century: in the final scene of the performance of Puccini's *Tosca,* the famous actress fell down and broke one of her legs.

4

Humility, guilt and narcissism turned inside out in Brazil's film revival

Fernão Pessoa Ramos

Our modesty begins with cows... And so we may ask – why do even Brazilian cows react like this? The mystery seems obvious to me. Every one of us carries a potential for umpteen hereditary humiliations. Each generation passes onto the next its frustrations and anxieties. After some time, the Brazilian has turned his narcissism inside out, and spat at his own image. And here's the truth of it – we don't find personal or historical pretexts for high self-esteem. If you're not with me, then so be it. And everything haunts us. So much so that a mere 'hello' is gratifying to us.

Nelson Rodrigues, 'A vaca premiada',
from the collection *A cabra vadia*

The fracture dividing different classes of Brazilian society is a recurrent theme in our cinema. It is expressed thematically in what we could call the 'representation of the popular'. After the interregnum of the 1980s (when the most creative form of national production was aimed at a close dialogue with classical cinematic genres), the theme of social class has made a comeback, bringing with it associated existential dilemmas. The classic motifs around which the theme has gathered historically (carnival, African-Brazilian religions such as *Candomblé*, soccer, north-eastern folklore) have recently acquired new density.

In end-of-the-millennium Brazilian Cinema, representation of the popular is accompanied by elements that, historically, single it out. The central axis that guides perceived notions of what represents the popular starts in the 1960s and encompasses the feeling of guilt, or a bad conscience, caused by the representation of the 'other' by filmmakers using a voice that is not their own. This bad conscience, causing a crack in the enunciation of the popular, was acutely detected by film critic Jean-Claude Bernardet in *Brasil em tempo de cinema*.[1] As a rule, it is made up of low self-esteem born of a feeling of responsibility for the terrible living conditions endured by the country's poor (identified as the 'popular' section of society), who are lending their voice to the middle class filmmaker. For this reason there is not, and never has been (the few exceptions prove the rule), a cinema which can be classified as being 'popular' in Brazil, which is made by members of this social class who actually do have a culture and language of their own, despite their minimal conditions for survival.[2] The goal of this chapter is to detect the representation of this popular culture in the cinema of the 1990s and to learn its specific history.

In many films produced during the revival, one can feel this bad conscience shifting away from issues of social fracture to accusations directed at the nation as a whole. These accusations constitute what we can call the 'statute of incompetence'. The establishment of this statute brings with it, as its defining trait, a certain joy whenever it is exclaimed. Individuals who suffer a dilemma when dealing with the fracture of society (such as the epic dilemmas that Glauber Rocha's characters Paulo Martins and Antônio das Mortes wrestle with) are no longer at issue.[3] The true villain has now become the nation as a whole, without further distinctions being made. More specifically, the country's institutional side is being accused. The police, in particular, are invariably presented as incompetent, corrupt and sordid, as is the health service, public sanitation, administration services, etc. The constant demonstration of incompetence exacerbates the feeling of chaos.

In contrast to this situation there usually surfaces the figure of a foreigner, generally Anglo-Saxon, who, in so many of the films made during the revival, icily observes situations from a distance, pondering everything presented before him. The Anglo-Saxon is there to provide a point of comparison to the configuration of low self-esteem, to measures of national incompetence. This wallowing in incompetence, and the delight taken in exhibiting it to the foreign authority, is what I shall designate by the expression 'narcissism turned inside out'. This expression now describes what has perhaps become a contemporary form of nationalism. The term is imported from Nelson Rodrigues' rhetoric, which he used to describe the Brazilian soul in his chronicles about soccer. The easy and perverse pleasure that Brazilians take in booing their own national team (a true symbol of ego realization) is, to the dramatist, a type of self-flagellation. The writer's sensibility was quick to spot this trait of nationality, maybe even connecting it with the iconoclastic cascades that fill so many of his own texts. Rodrigues, boasting the sharp and bitter vein that is his own, also added the expression 'mongrel complex' to describe the relationship Brazilians have with their foreign alter-ego. National 'humility' is based on this complex.

After destroying all sorts of myths, after repeatedly undermining all attempts at affirmative action, the only thing left to iconoclastic pleasure is to attack its own ego, which defends itself by exhibiting the incompetence of the collective as something outside of itself. To reaffirm this outward trend, it becomes ever more necessary to emphasize a general and obsessive criticism in such a way that exclusion from the criticism itself becomes total, making it impossible for the critic to be included in it. In an attempt to dissociate himself from the negative picture, the critic seems to be saying, 'I insistently criticize the nation, hence proof that I must lie outside the nucleus criticized' (the expression 'only in Brazil...', reflects this well). Narcissism turned inside out, in truth, appears as an aggressive answer to a dissatisfied nationalistic need. It is this movement that I will shortly try to describe with examples in film.

The unviable nation

Central do Brasil (*Central Station*, Walter Salles, 1998) seems to be a good film with which to embark on this course, even though the redemptory figure of the Anglo-Saxon is missing. The protagonist Dora's bad conscience towards the poor is evident and her oscillation constitutes the film's main motivational force. To betray or not to betray the people is a dilemma that appeared constantly in Brazilian films of the 1960s, though these films dealt with greater existential questions in less melodramatic ways. The 1990s, however, provide no fuel for the existential-political tragedy. Political action with the power to transform no longer appears on the horizon, giving way instead to the sordid and the incompetent.

In *Central do Brasil* the narrative movement is clear. Its starting point is a vision of a country accentuated by negativity, which then leads to a movement towards redemption by means of the catharsis of pity. The cruellest of crimes (the murder of children for the extraction of organs) is portrayed as an everyday occurrence in Central do Brasil, the train station at the heart of Brazil. Added to the list of Dora's petty crimes is this other crime, a little larger in scale, which seems only 'a little wrong', as far as everyday actions go. Shooting dead children for petty theft also seems to be an everyday occurrence in Central do Brasil station. The driving force behind Dora's guilt is conceived in such a way as to carry a lot of weight, reflecting a need to present a very sordid scenario in which the country is passively immersed.[4] We should also point to a complete absence of any institutional organization that comes into conflict with this scenario. The lack of opposition leads to a dark scenario, from where a cathartic redemption emerges, gently massaging the audience's ego. From her petty crimes to the unmentionable crime (sending children to their deaths and to have their organs extracted) Dora is propelled by her guilty conscience, which encompasses the feelings the film making class has (as do a good deal of the film's audience) towards the popular universe that permeates Central do Brasil.

The representation of the guilty conscience, meanwhile, is too excessively awkward to be left in such a way, without a development through which it can be rescued. And so it is that the second part of the film is dedicated to this rescue. Dora is purged of her hesitations about the sacrifice of the boy during the procession sequence, when she physically immerses herself in the crowd and finds herself absorbed into popular faith, sharing with the people their most authentic cultural manifestation. One of the film's key moments, the procession unleashes a kind of personal conflict which is experienced internally, resulting in the protagonist's definitive conversion to the boy. The turn-around is well marked and the conflictive element that impeded reconciliation with the popular cause disappears from the horizon. Even the actress in Fernanda Montenegro seems more at ease in her role. By means of pity-induced catharsis, the distance between the contemplated crime and the size of the conversion is fully explored. The ecstasy takes place during the procession, but the figuration of pity spreads throughout the film. Catharsis induced by pity allows the narrative structure to retain elements of forced passivity within the sordid dimension of a nation that kills its own children or sends them abroad. The sordid and unviable nation is burdened with sustaining the configuration of opposite poles, indispensable to a catharsis induced by pity. It is worth noting that what I have called 'inside out narcissism' gives room for a range of emotional exaltations normally related to more traditional nationalistic material.

In *O primeiro dia* (*Midnight*, Walter Salles and Daniela Thomas, 1999), a similar movement takes place, in which the institutional dimension of the State absorbs negative personalities. The personality of the benign thief – who extorts money from corrupt cops and tries to blackmail them – is built on the systematic corruption of the penitentiary system. The protagonist, another gentle criminal, embodies the 'outsider', who is driven to crime by these same corrupt cops. The evil prison warden embodies the negative pole, planning the release of the protagonist and his death, as well as demanding that he kill the gentle thief, who is a close friend. Once again the 'outsiders' embody the story's positive elements. The penitentiary system's systematic corruption serves as a backdrop for the exploration of catharsis, which is once again driven by pity. The New Year sequence on the roof of a building serves the same structural purpose in this narrative as the procession in *Central do Brasil*. The representation of the moment of ecstasy brings together both central characters (the gentle criminal and the abandoned girl) and, from up high in the communion, prepares the viewer for the descent into bereavement and the redeeming finale where pity will take its shape. After the assassination of the gentle criminal on the beach (again the unviable nation stands to blame in the background), catharsis can be unleashed with no holds barred, providing the viewer with all the egotistical gains of pity.

In *Orfeu* (1999), directed by Carlos Diegues, we are faced with a representation of popular culture that constitutes the film's dramatic core, and opposes the nation's sordid institutional side. It is worth noting Diegues' return to a film (*Orfeu negro/Black Orpheus*, Marcel Camus, 1959) that served as a negative point of reference for the *Cinema Novo* generation. The representation of popular culture put forward in the original *Orpheus* was defined at the time by such adjectives as 'spectacular' and 'alienating'. Camus' film created a consensus among the *Cinema Novo* of how not to depict popular culture, with its humble posture, folkloric slant, and mythical perspective typical of foreigners. Diegues' reinterpretation of the myth of Orpheus, based on Vinicius de Moraes' play, is indicative of the resurgence of the theme of popular culture in Brazilian Cinema at the end of the century. *Orfeu* seems to be the author's way of settling a score with the debt of his earlier years.

In this film, the representation of the popular reappears at odds with the contradictions of the 1990s. The idyllic setting of

Orfeu negro is completely cast aside and replaced with a scenario featuring an unviable nation framed in black. In contrast to the violent gangs and youths immersed in drug dealing is the idyllic world in which Orpheus is still finding enough room to realize himself. Singing to a rising sun, within a frame that depicts an unviable nation, may seem contradictory, but the delicate dream-like tone that permeates most of Diegues' films makes it work. Myth, fantasy and the rawness of reality come together. The unviable nation again appears represented by the corrupt and hardened police. The prejudices repeated by the sergeant in charge of the police raids are muttered in order to highlight the institutional interference in the shanty town (Orfeu explicitly states that the police are 'the only thing the State sends up the hill'). The sergeant is prejudiced, violent, and advocates, among other things, the sterilization of the poor and their extermination. Popular culture is seen as an idyllic manifestation to rescue one's identity, that leads to the assertion of the myth of Orpheus and the fantastic tone that permeates the positive fictional universe.

Orfeu presents a significant portrait of the dimensions of popular culture in the revival of Brazilian cinema. The purist vision of this culture, as source material for the construction of a national narrative, in opposition to a typical Hollywood approach, is missing. The presence of rap music, and the questioning of traditional values inherent in Rio's samba schools, is seen positively. The creation of a dialogue with foreign elements is praised.[5] At the same time, one must emphasize popular culture as the most legitimate form of expression of the people. Through it the people living in the shanty town can build a positive identity, in opposition to collective institutional incompetence and the arbitrary will of the group of armed drug dealers. The idyllic shanty town from *Orfeu negro* disappears to make way for the unviable nation, but the idyllic side of popular culture remains intact, even though immersed in a sordid reality. This is the central dislocation carried out in the myth in *Orfeu*, to which is added a rift in the popular universe, also now represented by its darker side (the violence of the drug dealers). Meanwhile, even within this negative dimension, the populace possesses a system of values that is denied to the State's institutional agents. Popular culture (especially samba and carnival) continues to be idealized in its purity, no longer though with necessarily national roots, but serving as an ethnic reference point within a sordid social scene.

The feeling of an unviable nation based on a splintered society rises fully to the surface in *16060* (*Sixteen-oh-Sixty*, 1997), by Vinicius Mainardi, in which a woman from a shanty town, her children and the family of a rich man are forced to live in the same mansion. A sordid scenario links the groups represented. The rich man accidentally orders the killing of the shanty town dweller, and as a result is forced to endure an ambiguous feeling of guilt (like Dora, the character is the incarnation of a bad conscience). The shanty town dweller, meanwhile, is also opportunistic, and goes as far as sacrificing one of her own children: she refuses the medical treatment offered by the rich man and, in order to come out on top, has another child with the rich man's son. Big and small crimes are layered on a story where a lack of ethics is the rule. The characters are drawn in single dimensions, with artificial and schematic outlines. The configuration of the catharsis by the shanty town dweller's pity, or her son's death, does not appear on the film's scenario. This merely makes apparent the inevitable and widespread character of opportunism.

Class conflict is reduced to pulling a series of tricks. Within the schematic frame of the characters, the tendency is to show the rich people in the worst possible light. Their get-together at a dinner for friends, when they go and visit the poor family in the basement, is reminiscent, in its forced stereotyping of the rich, of some of the episodes of the film *Cinco vezes favela* (*Favela Five Times*, various, 1961), produced by the National Students Union. In the latter case stereotyping is also used as a narrative artifice, although there is a countermove when it comes to the positive aspects of the popular character. What is significant is that polarity no longer exists: everyone is sordid and opportunistic in the unviable nation. The main concern is how to draw up a sordid panorama. In contemporary Brazilian Cinema's representation of the popular, it seems that the figure of the foreigner is the only one capable of fleeing from this situation.

This panorama of opportunism and corruption that runs through the social classes also appears in *Alô?!* (*Hello?!*, 1998), a comedy directed by Mara Mourão. In the film, a wealthy executive and his wife carry out a series of scams throughout the country, while simultaneously being extorted by a wide range of characters. No one has any ethics and the film's objective seems to be to point out how widespread this lack of character is, in all sectors of Brazilian society. The maid organizes an extortion racket against the butcher based on her control of the maids in the other apartments. Her nephew is a small-time swindler who swindles his aunt's boss, who in turn swindles her clients in her boutique. The man of the house has an illegal account in Switzerland, where he deposits the money he steals from his partner, while also swindling the real estate market. The chain of corruption is inevitable and omnipresent in every direction you look. There is, however, some joy in this set-up. Laughing at our own incapacity is something that we did to an even greater extent in other phases of Brazilian Cinema, and was a recurring theme in the early musical comedies called *chanchadas*. But in those films the laughter was less tense and related to specific elements. In the current scenario, the naughty laugh seems to have been replaced by the nervous laugh, which hides the necessity for accusation.

Cronicamente inviável (*Chronically Unfeasible*, Sérgio Bianchi, 1999) is the film that has managed to accurately delineate this climate, summarized in its title. The representation of incompetence reaches absolute generality in this case. Everyone is accused and there is not one exception the viewer can hold onto in order to rescue the slightest inkling of identification. We never find the gateway to ego recuperation offered by catharsis through pity, as outlined so far. Nor is the redemptive figure of the Anglo-Saxon present as a point of reference for the establishment of a constructive critical posture.[6] The nation as a whole is unviable and the film goes through its social agents, one by one, in order to prove this thesis. Starting with land reform protestors, and moving onto Indian leaders, the black movement, homosexuals, the rich, teachers, NGOs, charities, projects to help abandoned minors, and so on, everyone is reduced to another example of incompetence, of opportunism and sordid intentions. Motives may vary but the agenda remains the same: to confirm the unviability of the nation by showing up its incompetence. Any timely attempt to deal constructively with social chaos is destroyed with a gleeful exclamation mark.

Narcissism is turned inside out in its clearest form in this case. Within the horror that the sordid exhibition represents, all that is left is the negation of belonging to the collective whole as a strategy for the recuperation of self-esteem. The film offers identification with a stance (the critical attitude professed by the narrative tone as a whole) which, in turn, allows the spectator to be excluded from the universe being criticized. Once I identify myself with the film (as regards the posture it maintains through its bitter critique) I may excuse myself from belonging to the universe being depicted.

Cronicamente inviável, in reality, provides a comfortable viewing stance, in which identification with the narrative, although it offers a critical point of view, signals a distancing from the ignoble universe that is presented.[7] The narrative focus generates this critical stance with a dual strategy. It initially offers the spectator the possibility of identification, grotesquely hammering away at bourgeois values that can be easily eschewed (such as the speech made by the character played by Maria Alice Vergueiro, about the responsibility for her act, the second time a child is run over; or the various diatribes shared by the bourgeois group with the restaurant owner), to later dislocate this identity to a less evident place, where complicity with criticism is established. It is interesting to note that the film and its makers are excluded from the iconoclastic machine-gun fire that sprays Brazilian society. A reflexive dimension that deals with the theme of the enunciation is totally absent from the film. The truth is, it is the critical stance itself, and not the content, that the viewer is identifying with. We are once again leaning towards the mechanism described above: bitter criticism, in its universality, creates a position to which identification is directed. Once in this position, we can comfortably move towards collective unviability, because it has been proven that we are not a part of it. Our relationship with chaos consists of a general and absolute criticism, and need not leave behind any trace or measure of our belonging. In this way, the critical posture must not embrace the enunciator of this same critique, in this case, of the film itself. Should this occur the circle would open and the exercise of redemption, made possible by impeding the development of a sense of belonging, would be constricted.

The representation of a shredded nation in *Cronicamente inviável* (though not as grandiloquent as in *Central do Brasil*), also causes a delight in the type of collective identification that is so particular to nationalistic representation, only now it is defining identity in terms of collectivity, the other way around. Belonging, collectively, is defined in terms of identification with the critical stance the film so forcefully puts forward. The sheer delight taken in incompetence becomes the driving force for turning narcissism inside out, and becomes an exotic brand of nationalistic sentiment

The watchful foreigner

The formulation of an incompetent nation also creates an opening for another type of ego recuperation when dealing with the sordid nation. In some of the films of the revival, sinister pleasure is taken in using the foreigner's (in particular an Anglo-Saxon) gaze upon the country as a reference point when developing the unviable nation. In *Como nascem os anjos* (*How Angels Are Born*, Murilo Salles, 1996), an American citizen is trapped in an impasse created by national incompetence. On the one hand, the film presents a picture of social fracture among shanty town dwellers. They are shown as clearly incompetent and incapable of coherent actions with a rational goal. Two irresponsible children and a character bordering on mental deficiency confirm a diegetic pole to which the Anglo-Saxon's mediatory character comes into opposition. Outside the confines of the home, the nation's institutionalized incompetence consists of police activity, which deals in an authoritarian fashion with the children who invaded the American's home. The national microcosm – abandoned shanty town kids who prostitute themselves, irrational and violent criminal behaviour – provides a backdrop for this scenario. It takes the Anglo-Saxon mediator to deal in a rational and progressive manner with this scene, requesting the presence of NGOs and human rights organizations to accompany the minors. The film also incarnates the thought that, left to itself (without a competent nation's interference), the conflict would certainly come to a different end. Incompetence and opportunism spread beyond the police to the press, which is always seen exclusively as sensationalist. The absurdity of the situation is presented in an even worse light to the nation by television. Once again, the nation takes pleasure in exposing its own misery. There also seems to be no way in *Como nascem os anjos* of shedding some light as to possible courses of action that might rescue the collective whole from chaos. The narrative flow is aimed at echoing and exposing this chaos, making the ridiculous gleam. At the end of the episode, it is the American who turns to the (television) cameras and gives the film its ponderous, explanatory closing statement.[8]

In *Jenipapo* (*The Interview*, 1996), by Monique Gardenberg, we are again confronted with the Anglo-Saxon character (an American reporter) in the centre of the action in the fictional universe, in contrast to the national culture of institutional violence and corruption, within a complex existential conflict. The back-

6. Michael Coleman (Henry Czerny) in *Jenipapo*.

drop is made up of popular political movements in the country-side and the social forces that oppose them. Both sides of this conflict merely serve as supporting acts to the American's actions and his insertion into the priest's universe. Both protagonists are foreigners, embodying in a distinct manner the picture of resistance to barbarity. The reporter overcomes some ethical boundaries to give the priest a voice and give shape to the conflict that will provide the film with its dramatic core. The priest brings together social movements which, without his help, would be dispersed, acting without any effect. Contradictions inherent in Brazilian social movements seem to be reduced to the dilemmas provoked by the fact that the priest's reputation is being affected.

The media paint the same picture. The chief editor and the reporter are portrayed as lacking autonomy, entirely within the same frame of action carried out by the American reporter. It is the foreign perspective that the American reporter has of Brazilian society, which gives the film's well put together drama its peculiar quality. In and of itself the universality of the incompetence and the corruption does not supply enough to drive the film's action. In the exchanges between the two foreigners we feel, quite clearly, precious concerns and liberal tendencies so typical of Anglo-Saxon contemporary thinking. Also, in this case, the foreigners are the only ones capable of drumming up enough personal depth to deal with existential

7. Andréa/Maria (Fernanda Torres) and Charles Elbrick (Alan Arkin) in
O que é isso, companheiro?

issues. This happens again in *O que é isso, companheiro?* (*Four Days in
September*, Bruno Barreto, 1997), as we will see below.

Amélia (2000), a film by Ana Carolina, makes clear this tension
with the foreigner, within a story in which the national character
has a more active voice. The country bumpkin Minas Gerais character interpreted by Miriam Muniz comes into direct conflict with
a fictitious Sarah Bernhardt. The film conjures two separate cultural and ideological planes, and explores the tensions between
them. The dimension of nationality is evident. The exhibitionism
of popular culture for Sarah Bernhardt's enjoyment appears, but
does not becomes a pivotal axis. Few are the occasions in which
the exhibition of plebeian innocence becomes the focus of attention. Tension between the two parts is played out throughout the
film, offering distinct moments of resolution, and moving towards
an end in which revenge is premeditated. On the other hand,
although the foreigner is mocked several times, there is no section
in which the simple women affirm themselves in relation to their
oppression. They are fragile and are taken in by the foreign culture. Their different personalities are constructed on the fringes
of mental retardation, at times almost making it seem as if the
explicit aim of the film is to irritate. The typical set-up of self-

8. Carlota Joaquina (Marieta Severo) in *Carlota Joaquina – princesa do Brasil.*

destructive characters in Brazilian Cinema is repeated: they scream a lot and indulge in all sorts of acts, without the slightest bit of objectivity, until, through exhaustion, they are immobilized by their own incoherence. Perhaps the most important scene takes place when the country bumpkin played by Miriam Muniz stands up to assertively recite the poem *I Juca Pirama*, which is the cry of a warrior. Her voice quickly withers away and the affirmative moment becomes ridiculous. However, her posture is in no way humble and the confrontation is clearly delineated.

The final revenge, that leaves the protagonist crippled, explodes like a tardy affirmation, and provides a response to the minor humiliations that appear throughout the film. Paradoxically, it confines the trio in the universe they come into conflict with. We may say that in *Amélia*, the figure of the foreigner does not fit into the usual picture created by the revival, insofar as it is not marked by an exhibitionist-plebeian stance (whether of popular culture, or of the incompetent nation) for this foreign character.

In *Carlota Joaquina, princesa do Brasil* (*Carlota Joaquina, Princess of Brazil*, Carla Camurati, 1995), we encounter the plainest type of narcissism turned inside out with the foreign reference point. The

Anglo-Saxon character appears projecting his usual explanatory voice, explicitly taking hold of the narrative in flash-back form. In a ponderous tone, a Scot amuses and entertains himself with the incompetent and ridiculous scene that sets the stage for the historical hodgepodge. Within the diegetic universe, the English diplomat is the one to arrogantly dominate the situation. He carefully delineates his interests, demonstrating utmost dexterity in the way he negotiates the chaos and the orgies that the Portuguese rulers revel in. And so it is that we find, in the nation's very inception, the very trait of incompetence and dereliction that so came to characterize the nation over the centuries. During one of the key moments of the founding of the nation (when the European court arrived), the Anglo-Saxon reference serves as a parameter to measure the dimension of our incompetence and cowardice. The exhibitionist pleasure taken in drawing up this inferiority complex is also characteristic. The tone used is one of authentic humility, and all the incompetents have left is the pleasure of entertaining the ponderous foreigner who evaluates them. The exhibitionism of the ridiculous has a comic tone to it, to which is added the need for approval that the humble feel. An unseen voice seems to be repeating: 'At least enjoy our blundering because it is so innocent, infantile, and all it wants is that marginal amount of approval so common to laughter.' The unviable nation seems to have even greater value when it is exposed with humility, in order to amuse the foreigner with his condescending gaze.

The humble affirmation of our incapacity is a historic trait of Brazilian Cinema. In key films of the revival, a more aggressive charge is given to this humility, from which a new picture of an unviable nation is drawn. Paulo Emilio Salles Gomes takes pleasure in mentioning our 'creative incapacity in copying', while also prizing the humble position of that person condemned to not be original, but, even so, to be creative, as if due to some uncontrollable destiny. This vision is backed by a valorization of slapstick comedy's creative spirit and of the relationship, also very present in this genre, between humility and the show of incompetence put on for the foreigner. In this scenario, the Brazilian basically appears as the humble person who, when faced with a foreign presence, exhibits with panache an incompetence at copying. The exhibitionism of humility – so present, for example, in the characters played by Oscarito in the *chanchadas* – acquires a ripe tone when exposed to, or confronted by, the foreigner.

Humility also serves many times as a base for a hefty dose of exhibitionistic national culture, particularly in its popular form. Humility and representations of the popular walk hand in hand, as Glauber Rocha pointed out with precision. The tradition of humility is transformed in recent Brazilian Cinema. Now, the exhibition of humility – muddled or incompetent – loses its comical and slightly ironic tone. Humility now serves as a shell for the representation of the unviable nation, drawn out in a much more aggressive, and less ironical bias. It is in the reappearance of this aggressiveness that the posture of humility finds satisfaction in the figure of the contemplative foreigner.

The configuration of the humble posture in terms of the Anglo-Saxon character is also found in *O que é isso, companheiro?*. The character of the American diplomat is the only one with a sensible voice, amidst crack-brained adolescents, authoritarian torturers and members of the military. The most densely drawn character in the film, the ambassador, negotiates existential conflicts that lead to a complex evolution of his personality. Even though he represents an imperialist nation, he develops a humanistic sympathy for the kidnappers, taking an interest in the left-wing bibliography they present, and sharing a sensitive poetic vision of his predicament (by describing, for example, the hands and skin of his kidnappers). These, on the other hand, are much plainer. They encompass specific types (the tough guy, the pretty girl, the intellectual, the dazzled boy, etc.), that provide parameters for the establishment of pivotal points that allow the ambassador's personality to grow. The only kidnapper who could compete in terms of maturity and complexity with the ambassador, the old communist leader who commands the operation, remains in the background and does not evolve in any way.

The fascination with the liberal Anglo-Saxon's ideological universe and his existential stance is the point of view chosen by the film to illustrate this particular moment in Brazil's history. The Brazilian group's incompetence in planning and carrying out the kidnapping is made explicit. The kidnapping is decided arbitrarily, based on an adolescent's sudden enthusiasm. The kidnappers eye with suspicion magazines on Woodstock and manifest infantile points of view about a North American Black Rights movement (Black Panthers), demonstrating a repressed passion for the cultural universe they feel they can combat. The group's actions are littered with basic mistakes that end up jeopardizing the operation: buying large quantities of food, showing off wads of money, being recognized near the hideout, leaving newspaper cuttings around with the address of the place they have moved into, etc. These mistakes are highlighted in order to emphasize the group's lack of preparation and their inevitable incompetence. The film does not take up more important issues that arise from the armed kidnapping of an ambassador. It focuses entirely on the exhibitionism of the picturesque element that is national incompetence. In this case, the 'humility' which is shown to the foreigner is not the 'popular', but is instead distraught youth. On the axis of the exhibitionist stance of popular culture is the exotic, the curious, innocent intensity, traits that the film confers upon the incompetent youths.

The exhibitionist stance of the popular also appears in *Bella Donna* (*White Dunes*, Fábio Barreto, 1998), that uses the creation of a popular culture which is all spectacle as the pivotal point of its fascination with the well-structured foreigner. *Bella Donna* is a film saturated with this exhibitionist trend, which paves the way for the Anglo-Saxon woman's infatuation. The desire of the national-popular figure of the fisherman to exhibit himself and to win the attention of this woman becomes the motivating force of the film's narrative action. Folkloric routines make a comeback. As in various other films in which popular exhibitions take place without a bad conscience, the incompetent nation does not appear in the background in this film.

Carmen Miranda – Bananas Is My Business (1995), a documentary by Helena Solberg that shows Carmen Miranda's rise to fame, is slightly more bitter in its presentation of the exhibitionist nature of exotic national culture and its reception in the Anglo-Saxon universe. The proximity of a humble posture and humiliation, as two sides of the same coin, is rarely taken up in Brazilian audiovisual production. The conflict surfaces and it is no longer enough just to be humble and have an exotic culture in order to make a mark on the entertainment business. The contradictory and conflictive dimension of the representation of a third-world culture, and the way in which it is appropriated by Hollywood, is depicted with rawness and lack of glamorization in the film.

Conclusion

The relationship between the spectacular, the posture of humility and the representation of popular culture occupies, historically, a central role in Brazilian Cinema. In his manifesto 'An Aesthetics of Hunger', Glauber Rocha rises up against the proximity of the spectacular exhibitionism of popular culture to the digestion of such representations by the elite. The director sees the way out as being the narrative incorporation of violence that characterizes an affirmative stance by the popular classes, impeding, in a Brechtian way, the fruition of the popular by the viewer, based on a reading of humble exhibitionism. The solution pointed to, in order to destroy this bond of fruition, is violence, the opposite to humility. The exhibition of the popular as a spectacle runs through various Vera Cruz productions (in particular, its greatest success, *O cangaceiro/The Cangaceiro*, Lima Barreto,1953), in films that, not always rightly so, are considered to be close to the *Cinema Novo* (such as *O pagador de promessas/The Given Word*, Anselmo Duarte, 1962). Maybe its most characteristic expression was in the early Orpheus film (*Orfeu negro*), by Marcel Camus, which has already been analysed.

I have sought to delineate, in this chapter, the representation of the popular in the cinematic revival, relating it to the posture of humility and the image of an unviable nation. Humility, very often, accompanies the portrayal of a nation marred by a narcissism turned inside out. The figure of the foreigner is used as a reference point with which to draw away from a sharp critique, allowing for the creation of space required for the exercise of modesty. Popular culture can take shape as an idyllic element, and distance itself from collective incompetence, serving as a base from which the viewer can rescue him/herself. In Walter Salles' and Carlos Diegues' films we can see this rescue taking place through cathartic mechanisms that explore the inverse polarity established between the sordid nation and the presentation of the popular element. In some other cases – and in this chapter we recall such films as *Cronicamente inviável, Alô?!* and *16060* – the picture of the unviable nation goes beyond the institutional framework, and also targets the realm of the popular. The recurring Anglo-Saxon character has been analysed as the specular staple when representing the unviable nation and defining the space for the exercise of humility. The nation is represented 'for someone', in what we have described as an exhibitionist-humble manner. This happens in such films as *Carlota Joaquina, O que é isso, companheiro?*, *Como nascem os anjos* and *Jenipapo*, among others. The driving force behind this, at the heart of these considerations, is a type of 'bad class conscience' which still determines a significant amount of Brazil's cinematic output.

Translation by Roderick Steel

NOTES

1.   Jean-Claude Bernardet, *Brasil em tempo de cinema* (Rio de Janeiro, Civilização Brasileira, 1967).
2.   The closest thing to popular production (as petty bourgeois as this style of production was) could be seen in *Boca do Lixo* ('Trash Mouth') films of the 1970s and 80s – so named after the area in São Paulo where they were made. These featured enough of an organic aesthetics to be considered a genre in and of themselves. These semi-pornographic romps were structurally linked to the lower class, as well as drawing their audience from this class. The people who made them were also lower middle to lower class. Their ideological universe tended to reflect their desires for social climbing, made clear by sexual metaphors in which male prowess was asserted over female desire.
3.   Paulo Martins is a character in *Terra em transe* (*Land in Anguish*, 1967). Antônio das Mortes is a character in *Deus e o diabo na terra do sol* (*Black God, White Devil*, 1964) and *O dragão da maldade contra o santo guerreiro* (*Antonio das Mortes*, 1969).
4.   In his interview in João Moreira Salles' *Notícias de uma guerra particular* (*News of a Private War*, 1998), the ex-Secretary of Security for the city of Rio de Janeiro rejoices in the chaos that surrounds him. His speech flows like a waterfall as he talks about the nation's unviability and the inevitability of civil conflict. We come to feel that his raison d'être is tied to his ability to show us the impossibility of taking a positive course of action. The moment we join him in his gleeful celebration of so many failed attempts to take action, we cease to include ourselves in the group being criticized. The constant tense music in the background reaffirms this exclusion, drawing this part of the film to a close without offering any way out for the unviable nation.
5.   Religion, another element dear to representations of popular culture, is also vigorously thematized in the film. Orpheus' father is converted to Protestant fundamentalism while his mother remains a follower of the African-based religions, such as *Candomblé*. Since *Cinema Novo*'s early days, *Candomblé* has been central to representations of popular culture (in *Barravento/The Turning Wind*, 1961, we can feel Glauber's protestant origins coming face to face in quite an ambiguous way with the mythology of the African-Brazilian religions). In *Orfeu*, Protestant fundamentalism is shown negating po-

pular culture, itself mirrored positively in *Candomblé*. In the middle of the parade, Orpheus' father is seen praying in isolation. He does not drink, and does not take part in impromptu samba dances. In the final scenes each parent is seen summoning a different divine power to help Orpheus.

6. There seems to be a significant absence of any foreigners among the list of incompetent entities. A few years ago there was always a tourist or American businessman being made fun of in Brazilian films. Internal score-settling seems to take over in *Cronicamente inviável*. The other person left off this list, as discussed later, is the filmmaker and his film.

7. In a good part of the film, there is a voice that centralizes this opposition, oscillating between a professorial monologue and an independent voice-over that comes from a narrative enunciation (in the form of a free indirect conversation).

8. Many of the films of the revival feature television as a mediator, often placed within the film as a central narrative element. One gets the feeling that dramatic content, when expressed exclusively by the film, is judged to be insufficient to get a rise out of the audience. It's as if a further boost is needed, and only the media can provide it. In *Como nascem os anjos* television is used as the parameter to exhibit the boy and to determine his future actions when it flashes on its screen his partner's frustrations with the repercussions of their criminal actions. In *Orfeu* the protagonist's murder is stopped by the chief drug-dealer when he sees himself on television. All the film's characters are shown on television at some moment or other. In *Jenipapo* (*The Interview*, Monique Gardenberg, 1996), television is used as the mediator with which to configure the concrete dimension of the journalist's voice and the space conceded by the priest. In *Um céu de estrelas* (*A Starry Sky*, Tata Amaral, 1997), a radical choice is made in which the film's action becomes mediated by television, and the film's enunciation is eclipsed by the medum's interference. *Doces poderes* (*Sweet Powers*, Lúcia Murat, 1996) thematizes the idea through interviews given directly to the camera, in a non-narrative style closer to that used in televized journalism. In *O que é isso, companheiro?* (*Four Days in September*, Bruno Barreto, 1997), appearances of Repórter Esso TV programme are key to the film's dramatic moments. Indeed the kidnappers' main goal is to have their message and their faces shown on television, which eventually happens and leads to massive celebration on their part. In *O lado certo da vida errada* (*The Dark Side of the Wrong Life*, Octavio Bezerra, 1996), the boundaries between television and life itself become inextricably connected. In *Zoando na TV* (*Playing on the TV*, José Alvarenga, 1999), in a completely different universe, there also seems to be some difficulty in defining boundaries. Television mediation is central to the creation of an identity shattered by idealized notions of the common people and notions of an unviable nation. The echo-box that TV media offers to the drama appears as a necessary element to the full exhibition of the

unviable nation. The film's narrative seems to depend on the cathartic position of the spectator, fostered by the impact of the TV news report, in order to narrate properly. Without television there is no drama, there is no movement within the fictional action – or at least this seems to be the idea around which so many of these films are based.

5

Chronically Unfeasible:
the political film in a depoliticized world

João Luiz Vieira

Since its general release, at the beginning of June 2000, Sérgio Bianchi's latest feature, *Cronicamente inviável* (*Chronically Unfeasible*) has been causing something of a stir, not only among critics but also the general public. Most Brazilian-made films have had very limited runs in recent years. However, despite the fact that the film opened only in Rio de Janeiro and São Paulo, and only in two theatres in each of these cities, box-office figures indicated from the start a surprisingly successful career for a film that makes no concessions to seducing the public. Instead, it harshly deploys situations of violence, outrage and despair.[1]

Coincidentally or not, as soon as the film was released, a number of events took place on the political scene that seemed to echo the film's content. At that moment, Brazilians were being exposed to a series of socio-political scandals that had become mobilizing and disturbing media events; one of them was the failed attempt by the city council to impeach Celso Pitta, mayor of São Paulo, charged with corruption. This was just the tip of a gigantic iceberg.[2]

However, nothing seemed to compare, in terms of media events, with the remarkably negative repercussions of the official celebrations of the '500 Years of Brazil', which climaxed in April 2000 with cases of extreme violence from repressive forces against Native and Afro-Brazilians. The latter were questioning the meaning of the celebrations while Native Brazilians were demanding, once again, the demarcation of their lands in southern Bahia, near the sites where the Portuguese actually arrived 500 years ago.

Thus, the year 2000 was a privileged moment in which, more than ever in recent history, questions of national identity were foregrounded. Bianchi's film is an in-depth survey of some endemic problems as well as more recent tragedies of Brazil.

Sérgio Bianchi is one of the very few independent filmmakers in Brazil who have succeeded in producing feature films on a regular basis, despite the political upheavals and economic crises that have marked the post-dictatorial 1980s. Born in Ponta Grossa, a town in the southern state of Paraná, in 1945, and based in São Paulo since the 1970s, Bianchi belongs to the generation of filmmakers that followed the *Cinema Novo* movement of the late 1950s through the early 70s, when film financing systems in Brazil were undergoing great changes. However, his early ability to balance State co-sponsorship with a range of financing and production strategies enabled him to develop a distinctive authorial style in film, breaking boundaries between documentary and fictional narrative modes, while focusing on environmental issues and the wide panoply of social distortions that accompanied the Brazilian 'economic miracle' during the 70s and its tragic aftermath with globalization.

Cronicamente inviável evokes the sense of anger mixed with disgust that has deeply affected contemporary life in Brazil, at social, political, cultural and intellectual levels, while defying conventions of social or magical realism that have customarily been used to represent Latin-American social dilemmas for both domestic and foreign consumption.

A question immediately came into my mind as I watched the film for the first time: How does one film 'anger', 'disgust' and 'hatred'? Bianchi seems to know the answer. *Cronicamente inviável* is a cry – 'vomit' is perhaps a better word – against a state of general conformism that seems to be affecting social life in Brazil. The film interweaves violence, social prejudice, corruption and several other themes through parallel narratives of fragments of the lives of six characters, thereby discussing the difficulties involved in surviving, both mentally and physically, in the often chaotic society of Brazil, under the assumption that everyone is troubled by them regardless of their political option or social status.

The story evolves around an upper middle class restaurant in São Paulo, owned by Luís (Cecil Thiré), a refined, well-mannered man in his fifties who manages to be simultaneously ironic and poignant. Alfredo Buch (Umberto Magnani) is an intellectual, a writer – he could also be a university professor – who departs on a strange journey into the country, attempting to understand, through a bitter view of reality, the problems of social oppression and domination. Adam (Dan Stulbach) has just arrived from

9. Maria Alice (Bety Gofman) in *Cronicamente inviável.*

Paraná and is looking for a job as a waiter in Luís' restaurant. He stands out among the other employees due to his European descent, which is apparent in his physical features and education, as well as in his rebellious tendencies. Maria Alice (Bety Gofman) comes from Rio's upper-middle class and is constantly trying to keep a bit of humanity when dealing with people from the lower classes. She is married to Carlos (Daniel Dantas), who has a pragmatic view of life and believes in rationality as a way of taking personal advantage from the country's social instability. The couple has a maid, Josilene (Zezé Barbosa), with a long-standing record of underpaid housework. Finally Amanda (Dira Paes), the restaurant's manager, is a captivating woman with an obscure past, hidden behind the many tales she tells about herself to her friends and sophisticated customers.

This schematic summary of the film's possible plots is however er subverted by the filmmaker. Through a careful and sharp editing style, Bianchi questions the very foundations of the film language – its 'inner workings' or 'logic', its unspoken tenets and ideology – of nearly all of Brazil's recent production which, by and large, flirts with audiences through seductive strategies of all sorts. Viewers who are unfamiliar with Bianchi's aggressive style are taken by surprise by the film's opening images:·a man with a torch sets fire to a hornet's nest. Thus, the explosive tone of the film's style and themes becomes explicit from the beginning, with this prelude acting like a warning: those who play with fire may end up burned.

Brazilians' fascination with mainstream models, be they international (such as Hollywood), or national (mainly TV Globo), has a long history. Bianchi has little patience with such light-hearted romanticism in the face of the urgent crisis derived from the increasingly ominous situation of present-day Brazil. His film contests commonsensical interpretations through a radical framework that decentres its parallel narratives in order to explicate their historical contingencies. This conflicting interweaving of narratives produces a saturation of meaning through the evocation of conflicts within the Brazilian social arena. The film purposefully defines Brazil as a social and geographic totality by means of editing leaps that link together different regions of the country for no apparent reason. It cuts from the more developed South-East – the upper-middle class posh restaurant in the South Zone of São Paulo – to Carnival in Salvador, in the north-eastern state of Bahia, then back to Santa Catarina in the South, then back again to Salvador and then on to Mato Grosso, in the Midwest, followed by Rio de Janeiro, the poor South-East areas of São Paulo again and up to the Amazon borders. This technique is nothing other than a discursive device which translates the mechanics of capitalist social relations in order to reveal the reified cultural fabric of the country, mingling the social with the geographical. It is an eloquent representation of the internal diaspora.[3]

The film questions the idea of evolution connected with 'change'. Instead, it depicts the capitalist economy as a politics of exploitation, *inclusion* and *exclusion*. Bianchi's camera acts like a knife – a new metaphor aptly directed at the editing process – , pointing to everything and everyone at the same time: manipulated landless people, indigenous Brazilians, intellectuals, community-based activists, right and left wingers, viewers and the filmmaker himself. Echoing his 1982 short-film *Mato eles?* (*Should I Kill Them?*), *Cronicamente inviável* functions as an assault on the assumptions and sensibility of contemporary Brazilian moviegoers, who in the last decade have by and large been concentrated in the middle classes, which are accustomed to documentaries that flatter our humanist sense of compassion, whether they are progressive films or more conventional television docudramas, such as TV Globo's weekly *Globo Repórter*.

At first, one is led to identify with the character of the intellectual, Alfredo, whose voice-over comments sound like the traditional progressive consciousness, detached from the masses, that sees and analyses everything, requesting the spectator's complicity. Alfredo's presence and voice-over – most of the times synchronized with his actual point-of-view shots – interweave themes and landscapes through the narrative while, simultaneously, the book he has written, *Brasil ilegal* (*Illegal Brazil*), cross-cuts different scenes, such as a TV chat show, in which fake and actual activists discuss some of his contradictory and provocative issues. He exposes his arguments as if he were rehearsing a documentary or writing another book, and he sutures the narrative as a cynical *flâneur* contemplating similar modes of violence – whether sitting on a chair on a polluted beach in Salvador, or walking through Rio de Janeiro streets replete with the now banal and standard police raids against street kids. Throughout the film there is no suggestion that this strategy is meant as a mockery of our illusion of omnipotence, our self-aggrandizing fantasy that our own heightened consciousness and sensitivity might actually change the situation. By the end of the film, however, we are informed that Alfredo, the travelling writer and intellectual, is involved with the illegal traffic of human organs. All illusions are thus broken, and we are left alone and helpless.

It has become a commonplace – especially in post-modern critical discourse – to acknowledge the fact that 'every film is political' in a pluralist sense, in which all cultural phenomena are necessarily inflected with the 'biases' of specific, antagonistic points-of-view. Going in a different direction, *Cronicamente inviável*, like all of Bianchi's works, does not fall into this 'ethics' because it purposefully exposes the conditions in which the non-sovereign status of characters and spectators of conventional texts is legitimized. In the film, both have a decentred position.

Cronicamente inviável replaces ethics and aesthetics with politics, showing the struggle for control over the means of production in all social spheres, whether of State power, of material resources or of cultural representations. The film cuts across these areas more than any other recent Brazilian film. This politics, we are constantly reminded, is none other than that of class struggle, intertwined in a single fabric with questions of gender, race and sex. The most eloquent sequence, where all these issues seem to be inextricably linked, juxtaposes different people, times and landscapes in a continuous flow of exploitation. At a certain point, the pervasive voice-over intervenes to compose a fictional past for the character of Amanda. From the restaurant in São Paulo, the film jumps to the Brazilian Midwest where little Amanda is one more child among the hundreds of underpaid charcoal workers. She looks sad, dirty and lost in the heavy, polluting smoke of the burnt forest charcoal. But, soon after, another more optimistic past is constructed for her, whereby she becomes the daughter of a stereotyped peasant family in a colourful, sunny, utopian country-side, like in a story book. The soundtrack plays 'typical' guarania music while Amanda's mother nicely combs her daughter's clean hair. She is dressed as a sort of tropical Little Red Riding Hood, then picks a cashew fruit directly from a tree and runs to a fairy tale waterfall to meet her friends.

This is one of the many recollections with which Amanda enter-tains her customers at the restaurant, all of them eager for some sort of Brazilian exoticism. What Amanda tells her guests is one of the dozens of mythical tales about the creation of the Earth, some of which explain the popular phrase 'God is Brazilian'. The phrase becomes a pretext to engage the audience in a long discussion on God's agenda for Brazil. None of the interventions are in the least complimentary. Maria Alice raises the argument that 'if God is Brazilian, he only comes to the country to sleep. And he will very naturally relieve himself as he wakes up. That explains a lot. God a Brazilian? No. He only sleeps and shits here.'

The mention of God links the space of the São Paulo restaurant where this conversation takes place with a quintessential icon of 'Brazilianness' – a close-up of Rio de Janeiro's celebrated postcard image of Christ the Redeemer, synchronized with standard *Bossa Nova* rhythms. Overlooking Rio's spectacular bay, Alfredo hands over a strange suitcase to a man, while his voice-over distils anoth-er iconoclastic diatribe, a sort of perverse semiotic reading of the world famous statue. Re-interpreting the traditional welcome to all visitors to the country, Alfredo reads Christ's open arms as a total reversal of God's commandments: 'Come from all over the Earth, all races, creeds and cultures. Exploit without pity. Set fire to every-thing. Respect not the land or those who live on it. Respect neither young nor old. Come and fuck everything up!' This is reminiscent of the most radical Buñuel.

Another sequence that interweaves different characters, loca-tions, times, races and genders projects a past onto Josilene, the maid. Much in the way that little Amanda's picturesque peasant past was constructed, Josilene is, at first, a little girl, seen with her family, all dressed up coming out of an idealized poor house in a *favela* (shanty town) in Rio. Josilene's Afro-Brazilian family are on their way to Maria Alice's birthday party in her rich mansion. Through a series of juxtaposed images, some of them resembling party snapshots in photo albums, parallel connections are unveiled like archaeological layers that point to a historical tradition of relations between masters and slaves that have hardly changed over time. Josilene's mother worked for little pay as a maid in Maria Alice's family. Her father's job also depended on Maria Alice's dad, according to the voice-over narration on the images of the present party.

Twenty years later and Josilene's brother, Valdir, also works for little pay as a cook at the fancy restaurant in São Paulo in which the film is centred. In order to follow the voice-over narration, the images are edited in jump cuts worthy of an experimental tradition that includes, among others, Glauber Rocha, Orson Welles and Jean-Luc Godard. At the end of the birthday party sequence, the young Josilene is happily jumping and playing, when rhythms of a Carnival samba school slowly rise. This sound bridge and a straight cut link the narrative to the present time, and we see Josilene, now an adult, parading with a samba school in Rio's Sambadrome during Carnival. As she is consciously searching for her bosses who watch the parade, the usually fast paced rhythm of the samba slows down almost to the point of freezing the narrative flow as the omniscient voice-over starts again questioning the film, the characters and the audience watching the film: 'Why will an adult dressed in gold and silver march along a street almost like in a corral, closed in by boxes still occupied by her masters?' For this question, an interpretation is provided to justify domination at all levels, with the same voice-over narration. Josilene feels a certain complicity – as the voice-over explains – in the pleasure of domination, in the hope that someday she, too, may become a master.

Cronicamente inviável can be placed within a post-modernist tradition in Brazilian Cinema if we look at it through the motif of 'garbage'. This is a tradition that goes back to the Brazilian Underground Cinema, the *Udigrudi* in its parodic Portuguese version, referring to a group of young Brazilian filmmakers in the late 1960s who questioned and offered an alternative to *Cinema Novo*. For the Underground, *Cinema Novo* had become *embourgeoisé*, respectable and cautious both in its thematic and cinematic languages. As *Cinema Novo* moved towards relatively high-budget films, characterized by technical polish and 'production values', the *Novo Cinema Novo*, as it started to be called, demanded a radicalization of Glauber Rocha's 1965 manifesto 'An Aesthetics of Hunger'. Parallels with the present situation apply: almost 100 per cent of Brazilian films nowadays follow the recipe dictated by 'high quality' films, with budgets increasing enormously. But going back to the late 60s, the then young filmmakers rejected well made cinema, in favour of a 'dirty screen' and 'an aesthetics of garbage' – a provocative proposition which makes today's overrated Dogma movement somehow outdated. A garbage style, they argued, seemed appropriate to a post-colonial country picking through the remnants of a world dominated by First World monopoly capitalism.

Bianchi's film, besides being 'ugly' and 'dirty', abounds with images of garbage, literal and metaphorical human detritus. Following the opening scene of the man setting fire to the hornet's nest, there is a black screen with the credits and the sound of dishes being cleared of leftovers before washing (as it turns out later, the location is the restaurant kitchen). The images that follow show the garbage being separated and recycled into different containers outside the restaurant by two employees – one of them, as it turns out later, is Valdir, Josilene's brother – a key scene that will be presented twice and which immediately calls attention to the film's reflexive mode of representation. At the first presentation of this scene, two beggars approach and start picking whatever they can eat out of the cans. For the first time here, the disembodied voice-over questions the *mise-en-scène* for being too explicit and suggests another way of organizing it which is 'more in tune with reality'. The same action is then repeated, with the beggars approaching the trash cans, but this time one of the employees aggressively pushes them away, warning that they are not allowed to eat from there, then proceeds to feed a dog with the leftovers.[4]

Human detritus is presented several times over the narrative, twice at least in connection with body parts. One of these moments is in Salvador, also during Carnival, when two men urinate on the street. A woman scoldingly asks them whether they could not do that at home. In a sequence of comic effect, it turns out that they are pissing at the door of their own house.

As pointed out by Robert Stam, garbage is hybrid, it is the site of the promiscuous mingling of rich and poor, centre and periphery, the industrial and the handicraft, the domestic and the public, the durable and the transient, the organic and the inorganic, the national and the international. The ideal post-modern and post-colonial metaphor, garbage is mixed, syncretic, a radically decentred social text.

I would like to bring these impressions on a remarkable contemporary Brazilian film to a close by quoting Fredric Jameson's pertinent words, when he argues that all Third World texts are 'necessarily allegorical' in that even those texts invested with an apparently private or libidinal dynamics 'project a political dimension in the form of a national allegory: the story of the private individual destiny is always an allegory of the embattled situation of the public Third World culture and society.'[5] In a world characterized by conformism, it is quite rewarding to witness the permanence of a cinema that defies conformism and posits a thematic and stylistic agenda of resistance to the oppressive and exploitative functioning of local and transnational capitalism. Bianchi's *Cronicamente inviável* therefore, by avoiding the traditional kinds of love affair and seductive relation between text and audience, brings to the fore the social mechanisms in all their exploitative force and, in so doing, keeps alive the possibility of radical transformation.

NOTES

1. As of the end of 2000, *Cronicamente inviável* was being distributed with only six prints. However, it had reached a total of 67,031 spectators in Rio and São Paulo alone. Thus, it had become more successful in terms of admissions per screen than, for example, the two Brazilian 'blockbusters' of the year, Guel Arraes' *O auto da compadecida* (2,113,613 admissions for 199 prints) and Tizuka Yamasaki's *Xuxa Popstar* (1,208,192 admissions for 304 prints). Not to mention that these two films, contrary to *Cronicamente inviável*, benefited from massive publicity campaigns. Source: Database Sicoa (*Sindicato das Empresas Distribuidoras Cinematográficas do Município do Rio de Janeiro*).

2. The list is too long to itemize in the space and scope of this chapter, but just as a reminder I would like to point out, besides Celso Pitta's failed impeachment process, (1) the continuing charges against multinational laboratories producing counterfeit drugs – most of them using only 10 per cent of the active ingredient required; (2) the arrest of a man who threw an egg at the Minister of Health dur-

ing a peaceful demonstration, on the basis of the National Security
Law (*Lei de Segurança Nacional*) – a convenient remnant of the arbitrary laws of the military dictatorship, still in effect according to the
needs of the moment; in the last few years, it has been used, for
example, against leaders and militants of the Landless People
Movement (*Movimento dos Sem-Terra* – MST); (3) the escalating
police violence against teachers from State and federal universities
and public servants who were entering their sixth year without a single raise, despite considerable inflation; (4) the news that the
Brazilian Congress Commission had voted to roll back forest protection requirements of the Forestry Code, so that mega-landown-
ers could legally cut and burn the Amazon forest even more vora-
ciously; if successful, this act would represent the victory of cattle
farmers and the international trade of rare Brazilian wood; the
amendment to the existing law, if approved by the Congress, would
entail a 25 per cent increase in Amazon forest destruction, which
means 4500 km² a year at 1998 rates. The supporters of these proposed changes are the *bancada ruralista* (the ranchers' caucus),
which include members of the Congress representing approximately 1 per cent of Brazil's landowners who occupy half of Brazil's
agricultural land, while half of the landowners have some 30 per-
cent of the land. Landowners in pristine Amazon rainforest areas
are currently required to keep 80 per cent of their holdings forest-
ed, while owners in the highly endangered tropical savannah
regions must keep half. According to this new disastrous law,
ranchers could cut up to half of their forests and 80 per cent of the
savannah areas.

3.   A similar device can be found, for example, in the brilliant documentary *Boca do Lixo* (*The Scavengers*, Eduardo Coutinho, 1992), or
even in classics of modern Brazilian cinema such as *Iracema, uma
transa amazônica* (*Iracema*, Jorge Bodanzky and Orlando Senna,
1974) or *Bye Bye Brazil* (Carlos Diegues, 1979), among other titles
belonging to what could be considered the Brazilian road movie
genre.

4.   The whole scene and its presentational mode echoes in some ways
the famous Brazilian short film *Ilha das Flores* (*Island of Flowers*,
Jorge Furtado, 1989), in which animals take precedence over
humans on the distribution of organic garbage. In the Furtado
short film, pigs are more important than people.

5.   Fredric Jameson, 'Third World Literature in the Era of
Multinational Capitalism', Social Text 15, Fall 1986, p 76.

Part three

Documenting a country

6

It's all Brazil

Amir Labaki

It should come as no surprise that the revival of Brazilian film production, that restarted in the early 1990s, is marked by a new trend towards non-fiction. Brazil already boasts a rigorous tradition of documentary filmmaking, proof of which can be seen in the excursions made into this medium by every great Brazilian filmmaker, from pioneer Humberto Mauro to award-winning Walter Salles, and from the still underestimated Alberto Cavalcanti to 'prophet' Glauber Rocha.

The vitality of the Brazilian documentary can be seen in the striking dialogue maintained throughout the country's history between this type of production and fiction film making, especially in the post-war period. Humberto Mauro's educational shorts (from the mid 1930s through the 1970s) sought to register nationalistic cultural traditions, while at the same time the experiments carried out by studios such as Atlântida (in the 1940s and 50s) and Vera Cruz (1949-1954) established solid industrial bases for Brazilian fictional cinema. The Brazilian New Wave, known as *Cinema Novo* (from the early 1960s through the early 70s), was equally interested in fiction and documentary, allowing the genres to affect each other mutually. Almost all of its leading exponents – Glauber Rocha, Leon Hirszmann, Joaquim Pedro de Andrade, David Neves and others – worked extensively in non-fictional production. It was not by chance that two of their contemporaries, Eduardo Coutinho and Eduardo Escorel, inverted the equation, giving pride of place to documentary film making, although they also made fiction films.

It is interesting that this dialogue also fertilized Brazilian film production in the period marked by a production 'revival', which started in 1995. Similar themes catalyzed congruent, complementary and even hybrid approaches. Boundaries between genres became even more permeable. In some cases, documentary and fiction are found in the same film, even, albeit rarely, in the same scene.

In one exemplary case, two pioneers of Brazilian documentary film making gave origin to biographical surveys with a hybrid format. In *O cineasta da selva* (*The Filmmaker of the Amazon*, 1997), Aurélio Michiles rebuilds the trail blazed by Silvino Santos, a Portuguese immigrant who, in the 1920s, devoted himself, like no one before or after him, to filming the Amazon. And Lírio Ferreira and Paulo Caldas dedicated their debut film, *Baile perfumado* (*Perfumed Ball*, 1997), to Lebanese immigrant Benjamin Abrahão, an amateur filmmaker who, in the 1930s, made the only moving images of Brazil's foremost *cangaceiro* (outlaw of the backlands), Virgulino Ferreira, called Lampião.

Drawing on unique archival material, still in need of proper restoration, Michiles created a predominantly non-fiction film, even though he chose an actor (José de Abreu) to personify Silvino Santos as narrator. Ferreira and Caldas, on the other hand, knew exactly how to incorporate the short excerpts filmed by Abrahão, slotting them into a somewhat expressionistic dramatization of the meeting between a filmmaker and a *cangaceiro*. *O cineasta da selva* and *Baile perfumado* are reflexive, impure, hybrid works, made more complex and yet understandable due to a studied mix of cinematic genres.

Wolney de Oliveira goes a step further in *Milagre em Juazeiro* (*Miracle at Juazeiro*, 1999). He not only combines fictional and non-fictional elements, but also mixes temporalities. Current still photographs of public religious manifestations alternate with dramatized scenes of the extremely popular Father Cícero in the state of Ceará at the end of the nineteenth century.

Milagre em Juazeiro was made at the same time as two other powerful documentaries on the subject of religion, albeit executed more formally. *Fé* (*Faith*, 1999), by Ricardo Dias, and *Santo forte* (*Strong Saint*, 1999), by Eduardo Coutinho, have different forms but similar postures. *Fé* brings together for the first time Brazil's largest mystical celebrations, as a kind of apotheosis of beliefs. *Santo forte*, on the other hand, zooms in on the syncretic religious experiences of people who live in a single shanty town in Rio de Janeiro. As critic and filmmaker Jean-Claude Bernardet observed at the 1999 Havana Film Festival, two apparently disparate films develop from the same neutral and impartial starting point of the religious manifestations they cover.

Four productions by brothers Walter and João Moreira Salles represent two exemplary and exceptional diptychs on the direct and perceived influence of documentaries on fictional works. The non-fictional short *Socorro Nobre* (1996) mobilizes personalities and themes which are later developed by the director, Walter, in the feature film that won him the Golden Bear in Berlin in 1998, *Central do Brasil* (*Central Station*). Letters are at the heart of both films. In the documentary, a prison inmate writes to a famous artist, sharing with him her feelings about beauty and loneliness. In the work of fiction, a letter brings together the two protagonists, an old wheeler dealer (Fernanda Montenegro) and an orphan boy (Vinícius de Oliveira), who embark on a trip from Rio de Janeiro to the North-East in search of his father. Both films are about paths crossing and not crossing, about violence and sensitivity, blood ties and familial affinities.

Similar connections can be seen between the documentary *Notícias de uma guerra particular* (*News of a Private War*, 1998), by João Moreira Salles and Kátia Lund, and *O primeiro dia* (*Midnight*, 1999), by Walter Salles and Daniela Thomas. In the former, the bitter strife of daily life in a Rio de Janeiro shanty town is laid out in a raw manner never seen before. Interviews with community members, young dealers and policemen make up a mosaic of a chronically violent situation without an imminent visible solution. *O primeiro dia* opens on a scene of turn-of-the-millennium Rio from exactly the same universe, whence it borrows one of its main protagonists, a small-time criminal (Luís Carlos Vasconcelos) whose destiny is linked to that of a middle class teacher on the verge of a nervous breakdown (Fernanda Torres).

However, this interaction in an area of contemporary Brazilian film production is not the rule. Current Brazilian documentary filmmaking is made up mostly of traditional genres such as biography, news report or archive film. Exceptional cases break away from tradition and turn these same genres inside out, bringing fiction to the documentary, and prompting film-diaries. Thematic diversity is greater than stylistic diversity. During this period of renewal, the Brazilian documentary has rebuilt itself as a practical medium; it now confronts the challenge of reinvigorating itself as an aesthetic principle.

One of the fundamental breaks from the previous cycle, which took place during the lead up to democracy at the end of the 1970s and early 80s, has been the virtual abandonment of the political saga as chosen theme. The new heir to the tradition established by Sílvio Tendler with films like *Os anos JK* (*The JK Years*, 1978) and *Jango* (1983) is *O velho – a história de Luiz Carlos Prestes* (*The Old Man*, 1997), in which Toni Venturi reconstructed the life of Brazil's most important communist leader, who died in 1990. The tragic lives of victims of the military regime also provided the theme for the short film *Vala comum* (*Common Grave*, 1994) by João Godoy, about the discovery of a mass grave, in the outskirts of São Paulo, which was filled with the bones of 'disappeared' militants.

The short-lived Fifth Centenary celebrations of the discovery of Brazil by the Portuguese gave pride of place to projects aimed at casting light on the diverse interpretations of the Brazilian national experience. *O povo brasileiro* (*The Brazilian People*), a kind of testament left behind by anthropologist Darcy Ribeiro, became, in 2000, a TV series directed by Isa Ferraz. Observations made by Gilberto Freyre, a sociologist from the north-eastern state of Pernambuco, a pioneer in the study of miscegenation, resurface in *Gilbertianas* (2000) by Ricardo Miranda, also inspired by a television series by Nelson Pereira dos Santos.

And in a post-resurrection ode, Brazilian Cinema itself becomes a privileged theme. Helena Solberg researches the psychological impact of a myth in *Carmen Miranda: Bananas Is My Business* (1995). A critical evaluation of anthropological film material appears in the archive film *Yndio do Brasil* (*Our Indians*, 1995), by Sylvio Back. Among the portraits of filmmakers one finds films on Roberto Santos by Amilton Claro (*Roberto*, 1996), on José Mojica Marins (*Maldito/The Damned*, 2000), by André Barcinski and Ivan Finotti, and on a north-eastern film artisan, *Simião Martiniano* (1998), by Clara Angélica and Hilton Lacerda. And Laís Bodanzky and Luís Bolognesi record in the filmed diary *Cine Mambembe* (1999) their marvellous project for exhibiting film in town squares throughout the interior of Brazil, baptizing various generations in cinema.

In a parallel move, Brazil's music history also begins to be told by documentaries which are for the most part biographical. Among these are films on the life of a São Paulo based samba composer, Geraldo Filme (*Geraldo Filme*, Carlos Cortez, 1998), and Rio de Janeiro based Nelson Sargento (*Nelson Sargento*, Estevão Pantoja, 1997), as well as on the renowned *Bossa Nova* musician Laurindo de

10. Luiz Carlos Prestes in *O velho*.

Almeida (*Laurindo de Almeida – muito prazer/Laurindo de Almeida – Pleased to Meet You*, Leonardo Dourado, 1999) and Bahia composer Dorival Caymmi (*Um certo Dorival Caymmi/A Certain Dorival Caymmi*, Aloísio Didier, 1999). And never before had the rise of Brazilian rock been presented in such a compelling manner as in *Paralamas close-up* (1998), by Andrucha Waddington, Breno Silveira and Cláudio Torres. Experimental filmmaker Carlos Adriano also explores the biographical genre, but with an original approach that deconstructs the life of a fleeting idol of São Paulo samba in *A voz e o vazio – a vez de Vassourinha* (*The Voice and the Void – The Turn of Vassourinha*, 1998).

It is as if a new geography is being revealed. Way beyond picture postcards, a reinvigorated generation of documentary filmmakers is presenting the nation with snapshots of refined freshness. With biologist and composer Paulo Vanzolini for a guide, *No rio das amazonas* (*In the Amazon River*, Ricardo Dias, 1996) brings us closer to real people and places in the North of the country. The same effect is achieved for the North-East with digital video by David França Mendes and Vicente Amorim in *2000 Nordestes* (*2000 North-Easts*, 2000). *Ao sul da paisagem* (*South of the Landscape*, 2000), a part of a series by Paschoal Samora, has uncovered for cinema corners of Brazil that are totally unknown, capturing not only spaces but their particular times. In the same vein it is also worth noting *Terra do mar*

(*Sea Land*, Eduardo Caron and Mirella Martinelli, 1998), which focuses on life on a small island in the South of the country. New angles are being tried even for portraits of large cities. The cinematic imaginary of São Paulo is presented in two short features, *São Paulo – sinfonia e cacofonia* (*São Paulo – Symphony and Cacophony*, Jean-Claude Bernardet, 1995) and *São Paulo – cinemacidade* (*São Paulo – Cinemacity*, Aloysio Raulino, 1995). Fiction and documentary come together to tell the story of four centuries of one of Brazil's main port cities in *Brevíssima história das gentes de Santos* (*An Extremely Short History of the Peoples of Santos*, André Klotzel, 1996). João Cabral de Mello Neto's poetry guides one's eyes over a new vision of the city of Recife in *Recife de dentro para fora* (*Recife from the Inside Out*, Kátia Mesel, 1997). The world's most mythical beach appears on New Year's Eve in *Copacabana* (Flávio Frederico, 1998).

Great themes and famous personalities fortunately do not exhaust the possibilities of recent Brazilian documentaries. A wide gamut of narrative strategies has been used to portray ordinary people. A whole series with this focus, based on the founding principles of 1960s *Cinéma Verité*, has been developed by the Rio based production company Videofilmes (run by the Salles brothers), resulting in *Seis retratos brasileiros* (*Six Brazilian Stories*, 2000). Working in pairs, renowned journalists and filmmakers have sought out some of the country's typical stories beyond the news headlines. They accompany the day-to-day life of a family on the outskirts of São Paulo, five workers in Rio, a group of immigrants who return to their home in the North-East, the annual preparations of a Rio samba school, the decadence of a rural aristocracy and the rise of a local evangelical church.

Previous experiences in short filmmaking bet on a similar search for intimacy with the anonymous. In *Três despertares* (*Three Awakenings*, 1998), André Francioli, a film student at the University of São Paulo's Film School, ECA, pointed his video camera at his own family. *Pombagira* (Maja Vargas and Patrícia Guimarães, 1998) documented the relationship between a group of women and *pombagira*, a sensual spirit received by a medium in the Afro-Brazilian religion called *Umbanda*. And in *Burro-sem-rabo* (Sérgio Bloch, 1996), the camera observes the routines of people collecting paper.

Two documentaries boast rare levels of sympathy with unusual anonymous characters, who are shown in their routine life. In *A pessoa é para o que nasce* (*People Are What They Are Born for*, 1999), Roberto Berliner penetrates the lives of three blind sisters who sing

11. *Terra do mar.*

in the Brazilian North-East. Chico Teixeira confronts the commonplace with dwarfs in *Criaturas que nasciam em segredo* (*Creatures Who
Were Born in Secret,* 1995).

Lives of normal people have also prompted attempts at new
interpretations of enormously complex phenomena. In examin-
ing the plague of urban violence, *O rap do Pequeno Príncipe contra
as Almas Sebosas* (*The Little Prince's Rap against the Wicked Souls,*
Paulo Caldas and Marcelo Luna, 2000) questions what leads
young people sharing similar backgrounds to choose such different paths as music and crime. In the first of three episodes in the
exceptional series *Futebol* (*Football,* João Moreira Salles, Arthur
Fontes and Rudi Langemann, 1998), two potential football stars
are followed over a two and a half year period in what becomes a
true Brazilian version of *Hoop Dreams* (Steve James, 1994). And
finally, moving beyond national boundaries, Marcelo Masagão
brings together real and fictional characters, famous and
unknown, in his ambitious film about the twentieth century, *Nós
que aqui estamos por vós esperamos* (*Here We Are Waiting for You,* 1999),
edited on a computer using archive footage.

*

At the beginning of the twenty first century, the documentary genre has acquired a new status in the Brazilian audiovisual panorama. The traditional masters are still active, while a new generation has arisen. Feature documentaries are no longer exceptions or eccentricities. Didacticism is being abandoned in favour of more complex approaches. Broader subjects have also been inviting broader audiences to understand the Brazilian puzzle. There are fewer certainties, fixed models and definitive explanations. The challenge is no longer to give right answers but to present new questions. Nothing is taken for granted – but it's all Brazil.

Translation by Roderick Steel

7

A cinema of conversation – Eduardo Coutinho's *Santo forte* and *Babilônia 2000*

Verônica Ferreira Dias

Eduardo Coutinho started his career in the cinema in 1962. He was part of the first *Cinema Novo* generation, who proposed social and political changes in the country through the experience, by both filmmakers and audiences, of so-called 'Brazilian reality', an expression very much in vogue then. They aspired to a political, critical and realistic cinema through the presentation of themes, locations and characters marked by Brazilian miseries. Even if the actual result sometimes showed 'populist inclinations' (in the words of Ismail Xavier)[1] and preconceived discourses, the attempt made by that generation to replace Hollywoodian comedies, dramas and love stories with 'genuinely Brazilian' subjects and approaches ended up changing the course of Brazilian film history.

The Centre for Popular Culture (*Centro Popular de Cultura* – CPC) was the headquarters where artists developed their project of social change through art. In the early 1960s, the CPC sent troupes all over the country to perform but also learn from local cultures. Coutinho was one of the filmmakers travelling to the North-East of Brazil in 1962, with a CPC film project that remained unfinished. During that period, he started working on another film, *Cabra marcado para morrer* (*Twenty Years After*), which he would continue making until 1964, when it was interrupted by the military dictatorship. The film had to wait 20 years to be completed. On its release, in 1984, *Cabra marcado para morrer* was considered by Jean-Claude Bernardet to be a 'watershed' in the development of documentary film making in Brazil.[2]

Between his work at the CPC and the release of *Cabra marcado para morrer*, Coutinho had experience with fiction film (he wrote the script of *Dona Flor e seus dois maridos/Dona Flor and Her Two Husbands*, Bruno Barreto, 1976) and with TV documentaries, working on the programme *Globo Repórter*, of the Globo TV network. In his TV documentaries, Coutinho developed the method he has been using since, namely the use of interviews as a structuring element; the legitimization of the utterances of the characters, usually common people, through the refusal of interpreting voices, such as those of experts or voice-over commentators; and the explicit presence in the picture of the filmmaker, his team and the technical apparatus, thus revealing the mechanisms of production and disclosing them as a discourse, not a copy or mirror of reality.

Since 1979, Coutinho has devoted himself exclusively to the documentary genre and has come to be considered Brazil's greatest documentary filmmaker. His recent productions, *Santo forte* (*Strong Saint*, 1999), *Babilônia 2000* (2000) and *Edifício Master* (*Master Building*, 2002), were shot in digital video – then transferred to 35 mm film for screening in cinemas – a technique which has enabled him to refine his method, allowing for longer takes (thus reducing the interruptions in the interviews) and increasing the crew's mobility.

The *favelas* (slums) on the Rio de Janeiro hills were the location of *Santo forte* and *Babilônia 2000*, which approached them through a new perspective. The Rio hills have already been portrayed in a wide variety of cinematic images, being shown as a place sometimes 'close to heaven' (as an old samba goes), sometimes 'close to hell'. They are the cradle of music as well as violence. They have represented exoticism *par excellence* in *Orfeu negro* (*Black Orpheus*, Marcel Camus, 1959), and the crude Brazilian reality that *Cinema Novo* wanted to change, as in *Cinco vezes favela* (*Favela Five Times*, various, 1962). More often than not, however, the *favela* was 'the otherness', observed by a foreign camera-eye that went up the hills to verify a thesis.

Lúcia Nagib observes in this book that recent Brazilian films often return to old themes, such as the *favela*, to reinterpret and update them. She notes that

> the privileged locations of the *favelas* in the Rio hills offer the
> most overwhelmingly pictorial views of the city, which is the
> reason why Nelson Pereira dos Santos used the city, with its

12. Eduardo Coutinho in *Babilônia 2000*.

tense proximity between rich and poor districts, as the 'main character' in *Rio 40 graus* (*Rio 40 Degrees*, 1955); Santos' images, incidentally, would be quoted and re-elaborated in several later films, from Marcel Camus' *Black Orpheus* (1959) to Carlos Diegues' *Orfeu* (1999) and *O primeiro dia* (*Midnight*, Walter Salles and Daniela Thomas,1999).

In the film *Babilônia 2000*, this privileged situation is commented on by the *favela* inhabitants themselves and shown as such. From high up on the hill, the camera focuses on Copacabana, the most famous beach in Rio de Janeiro, on the last day of the year, with thousands of people on the sand awaiting the fireworks that will soon burst over their heads and before the very eyes of those on the hill. However, in Coutinho's picture of this *favela* hill, the characters are well aware not only of the beauty of the place, but of the problems they have to endure there, such as violence from the police, racial prejudice, etc.

In *Babilônia 2000*, around 100 people became film characters in front of the camera of an outsider coming from a different social class. However, here as much as in *Santa Marta – duas semanas no morro* (*Santa Marta – Two Weeks on the Hill*, Eduardo Coutinho, 1987), the resulting picture is not only the vision of this outsider who went up the hill, but the image of the *favela* inhabitants as they would like to be seen by the 'asphalt' people; this is made clear in the film itself in the conversations between the interviewer and the interviewees. Luiz Zanin Oricchio explains this process thus:

> It is a subtle manner of making political movies. We are far from CPC's didacticism, which was important at the time, but would have no meaning today. It is not a case anymore of making pamphleteering movies, no matter how well-intentioned they are. Nor should one put oneself 'in the place of' the oppressed people or give them voice from a middle class point of view... Such attitudes always carry some artificiality... Truth is what Eduardo Coutinho cares about in his films. Any pretended sympathy for the oppressed is avoided, so that a real sympathy can emerge, which is indeed political, because it captures a divided and unjust society.[3]

The population of Babilônia hill are used to appearing in films and television programmes, when the subject is violence, drug dealing and poverty.[4] Therefore, they partly react to being filmed as real actors. A child, when asked if it was good to live in that *favela*, replies: 'No, it's bad, because there are daily water cuts, just try this tap. But it's good to live up here'. It is a paradoxical utterance: despite the problems, one needs to tell the 'Other' that it is good to live in the *favela* as a way of self-defence, but also to fulfil the 'Other's' supposed expectations.

Because they are constantly being asked to appear before a camera, the *favela* people go as far as constructing a script to suit the filmmaker's probable wish. Take, for example, the following dialogue from *Babilônia 2000*:

Roseli (a character): *I'm here peeling potatoes for a mayonnaise salad. Oh, I'm not going to appear on TV, no way.*

José Rafael (the cameraman): *This is not television, this is cinema. We are making a movie.*

Roseli: *Oh, really? So one can be an actor, an actress?*

José Rafael: *Sure, you already are.*

Roseli: *Please come on in, if you'd like to have a beer. No... where is it going to show? Wait a minute! This will be shown in the United States, there will be a contest... I have to change clothes, improve my looks. Or is it poverty that you want?*

Daniel (executive director): *But this is no poverty at all.*

Roseli: *What you want is the community, right?*

...

Daniel: *May we go in and have a bite?*

Roseli: *Sure, just step in. There is no lack of food. Our poverty is all here, if you want to come and see. We were all born here.*

Rosana (a character): *It's great.*

Daniel: *Why is it great?*

Roseli: *Why, because we were brought up here, we were born here. We are not any more a product of our environment, but we were brought up in this environment and we won't forget it. We don't live here any more, me and her, we don't live here. She lives in Vitória* [the capital of Espírito Santo state], *I live somewhere else. But my parents will never leave here. They live by themselves in this house. I live by myself in an apartment where there would be room for them as well, but they don't want to move. They want to stay here. This you're doing is for what purpose? Tell me what it is for.*

José Rafael: *This is a documentary we're doing about the turning of the millennium. And we'd like to hear your opinion about what's going to change and what's not going to change.*

The conversation goes on, the team enters the character's house to meet the saints the house owner worships, and there another character emerges, Roseli's father.

Roseli: *... this is my dad.*

The father: *I'm the head of the household.*

Roseli: *But your film, explain to me about your film.*

The father: *It's a film they are going to make... I know... isn't it?*

José Rafael: *It's a documentary about the turning of the millennium, we want to hear about what will change, what won't change. What do you think, mister?*

With this additional interlocutor, the conversation is prolonged. This is probably what makes Roseli so curious about what is being recorded, for this does not look like the kind of films she usually appears in.

The constant use of the *favela* hills as a film location has also made their inhabitants aware that they have the opportunity to use the film as a way of publicizing their community. Why not make a film *about* the hill, so that it will change from a film location to the subject of a film? Another character in *Babilônia 2000* says:

> Every month, if I'm not wrong, there are, let's say... three to four foreign teams shooting films here. There was the recording of a 'Você decide' ['You Decide', a Globo TV opinion poll

programme] at Neném's house. He plays in the beach soccer team. The programme will be broadcast next Wednesday. I think a film would be even better to show this community, which I think is the best in Rio de Janeiro, I'm sure of that.

The film was made. One of its characters, Duacir da Silva, nicknamed 'People', declared to the newspaper *Folha de S. Paulo*, after watching *Babilônia 2000* in a preview on the hill, a year after the shooting: 'The film came out very well. I'm proud to see so many people I know appear in it. The film shows what a *favela* really is. It shows how we really are.' This could happen because the hill had ceased to be just scenery and had become the film's subject.

Reinterpreting religion

Santo forte revolves around religion, another old motif, like the *favela*, that has been reinterpreted in recent Brazilian film production. Several other documentary films on the subject were made in 1999-2000, such as *Fé* (*Faith*, Ricardo Dias), *Milagre em Juazeiro* (*Miracle in Juazeiro*, Wolney de Oliveira) and *O chamado de Deus* (*God's Call*, José Joffily). In all those films, and in particular in *Santo forte*, religion, which used to be considered alienating or the 'opium of people' in the early *Cinema Novo* time, is seen as an honourable cultural expression that deserves to be respected and reflected on. It even ceases to be associated exclusively with poor people – a housemaid in *Santo forte* says that she used to visit the same *mesa branca* ('white table', or spiritualist session) as her employer.

Santo forte begins with character André's account of his wife's mystic experience. She 'received' in her body a *pombagira* (an evil deity of the pantheon of the syncretic African-spiritualist religion *Umbanda*) whose intention was to kill her husband. The wife was 'cleared' of this evil spirit by *vovó* ('granny', another figure of the *Umbanda* pantheon). During his account, brief shots of the deities' images were inserted.

The next sequence is opened by the title: 'Rio de Janeiro, 5 October 1997', and followed by aerial shots of the mass celebrated by Pope John Paul, II, in Aterro do Flamengo, on the Rio sea-coast. The aerial camera travels over the crowds, then over Rio's upper class districts, with their fancy buildings and green areas, soon reaching the impressive agglomeration of hundreds of houses covering the entire surface of a hill: the *favela*. The sound of the mass and the prayers lingers on over the images of the hill, announcing

13. Teresa in *Santo Forte*.

the leitmotif of the film: the Catholic discourse is overpowering and penetrating the hill, as if asserting that Catholicism is the 'official' religion of Brazil.

In the next sequence, the camera is back on the ground, hand-held by the cameraman who accompanies the film crew through the crooked, steep paths of the *favela* hill, called Vila Parque da Cidade, in the Gávea district of Rio. It is now December 1997, as a title informs us, indicating that two months have passed between the Pope's mass and the present scene, a self-reflexive device aimed at exposing the artifice of the editing.

The interviews that follow will fulfil the editing intention, which is to describe how popular religion has survived despite the 'official' religion superimposed from above. Take, for example, the following dialogue:

Coutinho: *If somebody in the street asks you what your religion is, Spiritualism, Umbanda, whatever else, what would you say?*

Taninha: *I'd say I'm a Roman Catholic.*

Coutinho: *But you're an* Umbandist *as well?*

Taninha: *Sure, I'm a Roman Catholic and* Umbandist *as well. I like to follow* Umbanda.

Practically all of the film interviewees were 'Catholic from birth', but in the course of their lives 'tried' other beliefs, thus experiencing religious syncretism.

The invasive but distant narrator
Just like the overwhelming sound of the Pope's mass, the film crew
also invades the hill, coming as they do from another social stratum.
They are however allowed in by a local inhabitant, called Vera, the
intermediary between the film crew and the *favela* people. Their
role is explained in the following dialogue:
Vera: *Gávea is a rich district. It has wonderful houses and buildings.
It is quite a contrasting view, the little* favela *in the middle of all this. We
are here facing the statue of Christ the Redeemer, we can see the sea and the
top of the Sugarloaf.*
Coutinho: *Where are we, Vera?*
Vera: *In Vila Parque da Cidade, a small community in Gávea, Rio
South Zone. We are around 1500 inhabitants... it's hard to tell precisely
how many we are, because the population grows every year.*
Coutinho: *How come you are so well acquainted with it up here?*
Vera: *Because I've been living here for nearly 35 years. I work in this
community, I've been a health agent here. I was the one who opened the
door for this documentary to be made in this community. I was the one who
brought you, the film crew, to the inside of the community and showed to
you who they are.*
     This dialogue contains two characteristics of Countinho's films.
Firstly, there is no omniscient voice-over, or *voz do saber* ('knowl-
edgeable voice'), a concept developed by Jean-Claude Bernardet to
mean the voice of experts or voice-over commentators that gives
'technical' or 'official' information, in conflict with the 'voice of
experience' of the ones directly involved in the facts.[5] Indeed, Vera
is the one entitled to introduce and explain the documentary,
since she has been living in the *favela* for 'nearly 35 years' and is
'well-acquainted' with the place. Even the inexact figure she gives
about the *favela* population is presented as more interesting and
informative than official statistics.
     Secondly, since the crew is visible and they talk about their
documentary, the film artifice is revealed, a fact that automatical-
ly prevents any claim for absolute truth or realism. Furthermore,
the negotiation between the different parties is explicit, showing
that there is acting rather than spontaneity on the part of the
favela population.
     True enough, *Babilônia 2000* starts with Eduardo Coutinho's
voice-over, which seems to contradict his usual method. However,
rather than providing any information about the people or their
stories, this voice refers to the film making itself:

Babilônia hill, Copacabana beach, Rio de Janeiro. On the morning of the 31 December 1999, five film teams with digital cameras went up the hill to register the last day of the year. The teams spread over the *favelas* Chapéu Mangueira and Babilônia.

The illusion that cinema, thanks to its capacity of representation, movement and presentification, is capable of reproducing reality is destroyed when the voice-over commentary develops in the past tense. The film crew 'went up the hill', says the voice-over, while the images show them actually going up the hill. Image and sound are shown as disconnected elements, made separately, then put together through human interference and manipulation. This makes it possible for the spectator to understand that the moments of recording, editing and exhibiting are different, and he/she can have a reflexive reaction to what is being shown.

At the end of the film, it is also made clear that the interviews have been manipulated, when, over the final credits, we hear statements that are different from those made during the film. This shows that the interviewees' images and statements have been selected at the editing.

A cinema of immanence

In Coutinho's films, if objective reality is constantly denied by means of a number of narrative techniques, realism seems to be the ultimate goal to be reached through a striving for immanence, that is, an effort to restrain the meaning of an image to what is inherent in it. The relation of Coutinho's work with other realistic cinematic approaches is clear. The new waves (*Cinema Novo*, *Nouvelle Vague* in France and their neo-realist basis), with which he was connected from the beginning, had already explored self-reflexivity, the Brechtian distancing effect, the documentary style, improvisation, all of which aimed to reach reality by destroying the reality-effect. *Cinéma Vérité*, another possible reference for Coutinho's style, also used the interview as a means of capturing reality as it happened.

Coutinho's peculiarity, however, is in his systematic rejection of whatever image or sound could add further meanings to what is being shown and said during the interviews. Coutinho's films can be called 'conversation films', for orality prevails over spectacle. In *Santo forte*, a film about religion – mainly Spiritualism and African-

Brazilian syncretisms – there are no images of ceremonies, services or spiritual phenomena, although they are profusely commented on by the interviewees. The sole visible rituals are the Pope's mass, only briefly shown, and a few other images shown on TV and watched by the characters. In the same way, no extra-diegetic music is added. The only music in the film is that sung by the characters or played on the radio on location.

As to the editing, there is no attempt at connecting the different shots through a planned continuity. The shots are put together through rough and clearly perceptible cuts. Characters are photographed from a fixed angle, in close-up or medium shots, with little variations allowed by a zoom. They are even shown in frontal, frozen positions, in the kinds of test shots usually discarded in the editing, but used by Coutinho both as a way of introducing the characters and as a distancing effect.

The more this search for immanence is stressed, the more disturbing some sudden, silent images become: the frozen shots of wooden images of saints and of empty spaces. The images of saints are inserted in the middle of accounts of spiritual phenomena, and could suggest that human beings are being compared with saints. The images of empty bedrooms, parlours and backyards, where the characters had supernatural experiences, could suggest the invisible presence of spiritual beings. However, because these images are neither visually nor orally explained, such interpretations would not be easily verifiable. The fact remains that, because the religious experiences narrated happened in the past, Coutinho refuses to stage them in the present, as this would turn them into lies. What remain are empty spaces and still life images of saints. It is up to the spectators to create their own images on the basis of the characters' accounts, as when, for example, Teresa (one of the interviewees) mentions a 'squad of spirits' in her now empty backyard.

Negotiating reality
In Coutinho's conception of documentary film making, reality is only attainable through revealing the negotiations that necessarily happen during the shooting. Here are a few examples of these negotiations.

The editing of *Babilônia 2000* tries to be faithful to linear time, starting with morning scenes and ending with night scenes. It also tries to keep the sequences in the same order in which they were recorded. This enables audiences to follow the facts as they happen, as if in a 'counting down' of the time before midnight and the New Year. Illusionistic though it may seem, this is in fact an entirely metalinguistic, self-reflexive technique. The first mention of time in the film is nothing other than self-commentary. At the end of the first interview, Coutinho says: 'Well, it's 11.25am, the 31 December. You were the first person we talked to.' In the next scene, Consuelo Lins, the executive director, says: 'Jéssica, it's 11.25am, and today is the last day of the century...'

In another scene, the first person interviewed meets the film crew in a street on the hill and starts a conversation. She asks whether the 'old guy' (Coutinho) was pleased with the song she had sung for him at his request, and then starts to sing another one she believes will please him even better. Whatever spontaneity was suggested by this woman when she first appeared is now broken.

In *Santo forte*, cinema is also demystified when the camera carries on shooting when the fees are being paid to each participant, and their permission for the use of their images is being read. Character Braulino skims through the contract: 'Through the present instrument, I declare that I received... the amount of... concerning my participation... the cession of the copyrights of the image... verbal account... very well.' After her interview, Lídia receives her payment, and the following dialogue takes place:

Lídia: *You don't need to pay.*

Director's assistant: *But we did it with all the others. If we don't pay you it won't be right. Please accept.*

Lídia: *If you think so...*

Assistant: *I think it's fair.*

Lídia: *I don't need money to testify the word of God. It's my pleasure.*

Assistant: *I understand. But because this is a film, and we came into your house...*

Lídia: *When is this film going to be released?*

Assistant: *Probably by the end of the year, in December.*

Lídia: *I'd like to see it.*

A dialogue in progress

In the film *Babilônia 2000*, some 'failures' are apparent, for example, images out of focus or black slots due to accidental shutting of the diaphragm. Such images, that in any other film would be discarded, are kept by Coutinho, because their content was satisfactory. As he always states in his interviews, for him, the person focused on is more important than the form.

In *Santo forte*, from what Teresa says it becomes clear that there had been a selection of characters to be interviewed, which also reveals that there is a relationship between the characters and the film crew. This interaction becomes clear, for example, when Teresa asks for permission to talk about her surgery and starts telling how she managed to build her brick house, that she raised her children alone, that her husband was a 'plague' and so on. Nobody stops her. It is a homely kind of conversation.

In the closing scene of *Babilônia 2000*, it is already the New Year, and the following dialogue takes place:

Tomás (a character): *Will you allow me to say a word?*

Geraldo (executive director): *Sure.*

Tomás: *I invite society down there to enjoy a New Year as wonderful as we are having up here. The hill up here is open to them for a Christmas supper with us. They have wrong ideas about us, we're nothing of what they think.*

Geraldo: *What do they think of you?*

Tomás: *They think badly of us, that the hill only produces bandits. This isn't true. This is a friend's house. This is a family. If they would like to come up here, we'll prepare a special supper for them.*

...

Geraldo: *Would you like to move out of the hill?*

Tomás: *No, never. To sell my house? No money can buy my house.*

...

Tomás: *Would you change your house down there for one up here?*

Geraldo: *It depends...*

Tomás: *This is the first year you spend up here. How did you like it? Wasn't it very good?*

Geraldo: *Very good.*

...

Marcos (a character): *Cut this news report. You are all invited to a barbecue at our place. Let's go. Let's have a barbecue right now. Switch it off! Cut it, cut it! It's over! Bye!*

During the development of this conversation, Coutinho's helper is asked to speak. Roles are reversed. Tomás wants to hear what the crew have to say. The dialogue is courteous, precise, incisive. Tomás is allowed to say a word, and he invites society 'down there' to have supper with the *favela* people. After that, Geraldo, the crew member, is asked to give his opinion – would he change his house for a place on the hill? When the crew is identified with the ruling class, the dichotomy is made explicit. Geraldo answers evasively: 'It depends...' Coutinho does not try to dissimulate his embarrassment, he emphasizes the contradiction. In the end, a former character becomes the director himself: 'Cut it, cut it! It's over! Bye!', and at this inversion of roles Coutinho obeys this order and brings the film to an end. That is how he sent his message to the 'asphalt' society, who can, through his film, watch the fireworks from closer. By allowing, at the end of his film, that the characters determine how they wish to be seen, Coutinho accomplishes his realist method.

In Coutinho's *favela* films discussed here, it is indeed through the encounter of 'hill' and 'asphalt', which questions the capacity of cinema to reproduce reality, that the truth of cinema is produced.

Translation by Lúcia Nagib

NOTES

I would like to thank Eduardo Coutinho for his good will in providing material for my research and giving me interviews. I am also grateful for Lúcia Nagib's useful comments on this chapter.

1. Ismail Xavier, 'Cinema e Descolonização', *Filme Cultura* 40, August/October 1982, pp 23-27.
2. Jean-Claude Bernardet, *Cineastas e imagem do povo* (São Paulo, Brasiliense,1985), p 6.
3. Luiz Zanin Oricchio, 'Cineasta faz filme político sobre a esperança', 'Caderno 2', *O Estado de S. Paulo*, 5 January 2001, p D3.
4. Babilônia was the location of several films, such as *O primeiro dia*; *A fábula* (*The Fable*, 1965), by Arne Sucksdorf, quoted as *Uma fábula em Copacabana* (*A Fable in Copacabana*), by Cida, a character in *Babilônia 2000*, who says that her brother played a part in Sucksdorf's film; and *Black Orpheus*. Jorge, an inhabitant of Babilônia who played a part in *Black Orpheus*, tells, in *Babilônia 2000*, that it was an 'excellent experience' and that, after Camus' film, people started to call him 'Black Orpheus' and shopkeepers would give him presents. His son, another character in *Babilônia 2000*, has also performed in several films.
5. Bernardet: *Cineastas e imagens do povo*, pp 12-13.

Part four

Sertão and *favela*: the eternal return

8

The *sertão* and the *favela* in contemporary Brazilian film[1]

Ivana Bentes

Frontier territories and social fractures, mythical lands laden with symbolism and signs, the *sertão* (arid backlands) and the *favelas* (slums) have always been the 'other side' of modern and positivist Brazil. They are places of misery, mysticism and the disinherited, non-places and paradoxically places of picture postcard beauty, with their storehouses of 'typicality', where tradition and invention are extracted from adversity.

The north-eastern *sertão*, the *favelas* and the outskirts of the cities were the settings of important Brazilian films in the late 1950s and early 1960s: *Cinco vezes favela* (*Favela Five Times*, 1961), by various directors; *Rio 40 graus* (*Rio 40 Degrees*, 1955), *Rio Zona Norte* (*Rio Northern Zone*, 1957) and *Vidas secas* (*Barren Lives*, 1963), by Nelson Pereira dos Santos; *Deus e o diabo na terra do sol* (*Black God, White Devil*, 1964), *O Dragão da Maldade contra o Santo Guerreiro* (Antonio das Mortes, 1969) and *Câncer* (*Cancer*, 1972), by Glauber Rocha; *Os fuzis* (*The Guns*, 1963), by Ruy Guerra; *A hora e a vez de Augusto Matraga* (*Matraga*, 1966), by Roberto Santos; and *A grande cidade* (*The Big City*, 1966), by Carlos Diegues, among others.

They are both real and symbolic lands which to a large degree invoke Brazilian imagery; they are lands in crisis, where desperate or rebellious characters live or wander; they are signs of a revolution to come or of a failed modernity. In the films of that period, people from the *sertão*, travelling from rural to urban Brazil, become slum-dwellers and marginalized, 'ignorant' and 'depoliticized', but they are also primitive rebels and revolutionaries, capable of radical change, as in the films of Glauber Rocha.

Brazilian films in the 1990s radically change this narrative tone when focusing on these same lands and their inhabitants. I propose to map out some of these changes and explore the emergence of new arguments and ethical approaches in recent films. *Guerra de Canudos* (*The Battle of Canudos*, Sérgio Rezende, 1997), *Central do Brasil* (*Central Station*, Walter Salles, 1998), *O sertão das memórias* (*Landscapes of Memory*, José Araujo, 1996), *Crede-mi* (*Believe Me*, Bia Lessa and Dany Roland, 1997), *Baile perfumado* (*Perfumed Ball*, Lírio Ferreira and Paulo Caldas, 1997) and *Orfeu* (Carlos Diegues, 1999) are films that function as indexes of different styles and approaches.

What do the settings mean and how are characters represented in the films of the 1990s? Before mapping out the different forms of representing territories of poverty in contemporary Brazilian Cinema, we need to go back in time to understand how they appeared in the time of *Cinema Novo*, especially in the work of Glauber Rocha. It is important to establish the differences between those films and contemporary ones, in an attempt to understand the lack of political perspectives and aesthetic proposals in some of the latter. A key text to introduce this issue is the manifesto 'An Aesthetics of Hunger', written by Glauber Rocha for a congress in Italy in 1965.

In this text, Glauber proposed a radical twist, rejecting the sociological discourse of 'denunciation' and 'victimization', much in vogue in the 1960s and 70s, and giving an affirmative and transforming sense to the phenomena related to Latin American hunger, poverty and misery. He was trying to turn 'major self-destructive forces' into a creative, mythical and oneiric impulse. In his manifesto, Glauber talked with urgency, virulence and anger about the 'Europeans' paternalism towards the Third World'. He criticized humanism's 'language of tears', a political discourse and an aesthetics incapable of expressing the brutality of poverty.

It was a courageous text against a certain kind of humanism, pity and cliché images of misery that feed the international circuit of information up to today. Glauber raises an issue that, in my view, has not yet been resolved or overcome by Brazilian Cinema, television or even international cinema. It is both an ethical and an aesthetic question directly related to our theme of *sertões* and *favelas*. The ethical question refers to how to show suffering and represent territories of poverty and the excluded, without falling into folklore, paternalism, and conformist and lacrimose humanism. The aesthetic question is how to create a new means of expression, comprehension and representation of the phenomena related to territories of poverty;[2] how to lead the viewer to experience the radicality of hunger, the effects of poverty and exclusion, inside or outside of Latin America.

Glauber offers an answer to both questions by proposing an 'Aesthetics of Violence', meant to violate the viewer's perception, senses and thinking, and to destroy the sociological, political and behavioural clichés about misery. Glauber's 'Aesthetics of Violence' should result in images of unbearable power to the viewer. They have nothing to do with the aestheticized, explicit violence of action movies; instead they are charged with symbolic violence which leads to trance and crisis at all levels. That is what Glauber does in *Deus e o diabo na terra do sol, Terra em transe* (*Land in Anguish*, 1967), *A idade da Terra* (*The Age of the Earth*, 1980) and all of his other films. He moves away from critical realism and classical narrative, creating a kind of aesthetic apocalypse.

In an abrupt jump from 1964 to 2000, we find both the *sertão* and the *favela* inserted in another context and another imaginary, in which misery is more and more consumed as an element of 'typicality' or 'naturality' in the face of which there is nothing to be done.

A curious event illustrates this new imaginary. When Michael Jackson decided to shoot his new music video in a *favela* of Rio de Janeiro, in 1998, he used the *favela* people as extras in a visual super-spectacle. This is, in my opinion, the ultimate illustration of this situation: a pop star appropriates images of misery as a plus to his own image and throws the image of a *favela* into the international circuit as something 'typical' and original. All the while there is a vaguely political appeal in there, expressed in the video's title: *They Don't Care about Us*.

This discourse bears something extremely ambiguous that characterizes the new mediators of culture and politics in the scenery of poverty – and it is the subject of Carlos Diegues' *Orfeu*, which I will look at later in this chapter. The interesting aspect of Michael Jackson's strategy is the efficiency with which it gives visibility to poverty and social problems in countries like Brazil without resorting to traditional political discourse. The problematic aspect is that it does not entail a real intervention in this poverty, which results in a humanistic media discourse that turns poverty into another banality.

Another interesting event, also during Michael Jackson's visit, is the interview that the drug dealer Marcinho VP, an inhabitant of the *favela* where Jackson was shooting his video, gave to a respected Brazilian newspaper, *Jornal do Brasil*, explaining socio-logically 'why I am a drug dealer.' Both Michael Jackson and the drug dealer have become spokesmen of the *favela*, a theme to be developed at the end of this chapter.

The *sertão* as museum and history

It could be said that films such as Nelson Pereira dos Santos' *Vidas secas* and Glauber Rocha's *Deus e o diabo na terra do sol* invented a kind of metaphysical 'slum handwriting'. A handwriting of the dry and deserted land, and the cruelty of the white sun in *Vidas secas*; the *sertão* as a land in crisis and in trance, shown as violence and viola-tion in *Deus e o diabo*, with its scorched, rough, barren scenery, and its wizened, twisted, prickly flora.

This *sertão* emerges as a counterpoint to the tropical and para-disiacal civilization by the sea. It acts as a metaphor for an intoler-able situation and an imminent transformation. There, social vio-lence adds to geological violence, and ideas of rebellion against the intolerable germinate everywhere. The *sertão*, the barren and unruly land, with its exploited and destitute characters who have nothing to lose, is ready to undergo radical changes, moving from extreme aridity to extreme exuberance as it becomes the sea, a utopian and mythical place.

These classic films of the 60s created an aesthetics based on the dry cut, the nervous framing, the overexposure, the hand-held cam-era, the fragmented narrative which mirrored the cruelty of the *sertão*. This is the *Cinema Novo* aesthetics, whose purpose was to avoid turning misery into folklore. Those films proposed an ethics and an aesthetics for the images of pain and revolt.

However, the idea rejected by those films of expressing the intol-erable through beautiful landscapes, thus glamorizing poverty, emerges in some contemporary films, in which conventional lan-guage and cinematography turn the *sertão* into a garden or a muse-um of exoticism, thus 'rescuing' it through spectacle. This happens in films such as *Guerra de Canudos*, based on Euclides da Cunha's monumental book *Os sertões* (*Rebellion in the Backlands*), and *O can-gaceiro* (*The Cangaceiro*, 1997), a remake by Aníbal Massaini Neto of Lima Barreto's classic film of 1953, which in the middle of the 1990s aims to reinstate the values of Vera Cruz[3] of the 1950s, but lacks the brilliance and novelty of the original film.

It is a move from the 'aesthetics' to the 'cosmetics' of hunger, from the 'camera-in-hand and idea-in-mind'[4] (a hand-to-hand battle with reality) to the steadicam, a camera that surfs on reality, a narrative that values the beauty and the good quality of the image, and is often dominated by conventional techniques and narratives. The goal is a 'popular' and 'globalized' film industry, dealing with local, historic and traditional subjects wrapped in an 'international' aesthetics.

Guerra de Canudos seeks to reinstate the epic genre in Brazilian film by recounting the Rebellion of Canudos through the eyes of a lucid and ambitious heroine, played by actress Cláudia Abreu turned into a Scarlett O'Hara of the *sertão*. To introduce the heroine's family to the audience, Rezende resorts to the structure created by Rocha in *Deus e o diabo*, using a cowherd who rebels against the established order to become a sort of north-eastern saint. The difference is that Glauber forgets history and delves into popular imagery, the mystic trance, the pure state of rebellion of believers and *cangaceiros* (outlaws of the *sertão*), thus creating complex models of mise-en-scène and narrative that reveal a world in upheaval. Conversely, Rezende bets on realism, historical facts and period reconstitution, leaving popular imagery aside. The *sertão* then becomes the stage and museum to be 'rescued' along the lines of a historical-spectacular film, a 'folklore-world' ready to be consumed by any audience.

The romanticized *sertão*

The counterpart to the glamorization of the *sertão* and their characters as a grand cinematic showcase is the *sertão* of modest friendships and re-encounters with humanism. That is what happens in *Central do Brasil,* by Walter Salles. The film portrays an urban world and its relationships in rapid dissolution. It is a place of isolation and destruction of ethical values in contrast with the rural scenery of lasting relationships, a world of exchanges and talk, where individual experiences are still worth something, a world of memory, sacred images, photographs and letters that record promises.

The film recounts the protagonists' trip from the city of Rio to the north-eastern *sertão* in search of lost relationships and remains of solidarity, and is a Brazilian re-reading of *Alice in den Städten* (*Alice in the Cities*, Wim Wenders, 1973), for, like the German film, it tells the story of an adult who happens to be in charge of an unknown child.

The characters' rudeness is tempered with emotion, creating a kind of romantic and 'dignified' misery of the *sertão.* Many ele-

ments show an attempt to approach the *Cinema Novo* style: the
trance of Dora (played by Fernanda Montenegro) in the procession, with the camera spinning around her; the locations in
Milagres (site of *O dragão da malgade* and *Os fuzis*) and Vitória da
Conquista (Glauber Rocha's birthplace); the 'tourism' through the
same Glauberian *sertão*; and the fiction recounted in a documentary way. However, in *Central do Brasil* we do not find the violent and
unbearable *sertão* of *Cinema Novo*, but the innocent, rough but pure
sertão, where the brothers of Josué, the young protagonist played by
Vinícius de Oliveira, accept him back with benevolence.

It is a friendly *sertão*, where violence is internalized. This occurs
when Josué encounters the first family, who remain silent and hostile, but peaceful, until it is revealed that they are not his real family. In this key scene, the boy moves from euphoria to sobbing and
frustration at not having found his father. Nobody, nor the *sertão*
itself, corresponds to his ideals. Nevertheless, the *sertão* is a pacify-
ing place. The film seems to suggest that the *sertão*'s monotonous,
crude poverty and its mute violence is more bearable than the
urban inferno of Rio's central station, with its bandits and gangs.

Central do Brasil offers the romantic *sertão*, the idealized return
to the 'origins'. Its aesthetic realism, with citations of *Cinema Novo*,
offers a utopian wager like a fable. The *sertão* emerges as a projection of lost dignity and as the promised land of a reversed exodus
from the seaside to the interior, a return of the failed and disinherited who were unable to survive in the big city. It is not a
desired or politicized, but an emotional return, led by circumstances. Thus the *sertão* becomes a land of social reconciliation
and pacification, where the boy returns to the village with its
humble houses to join a family of carpenters.

The film closes with a melancholic and reconciliatory happy ending,
that distances itself from the utopian wager of transcendence and freedom
suggested by the final race of the cowherd towards the sea in *Deus e o diabo*,
and from the cruel, uncomfortable realism of *Vidas secas*, where the characters end up as they began, as prisoners in a cell without bars, the desert
sertão and its misery.

The *sertão* as a mythical-religious land or the transcendental realism

In *O sertão das memórias*, the *sertão* re-emerges as a paradoxical land
of misery transcended by a world of magic and religion. By fiction-
alizing the documentary, by staging the real daily lives of Miraíma's
population, and by turning his own history into fiction (Maria and

Antero, the protagonists, are the director's parents), the director re-encounters the *sertão* as a site where religion and myths emerge as a natural culture.

O sertão das memórias is the documentary of a religious imagery contained in the most prosaic of daily routines. Biblical characters abound in daily life, and the sacred is revealed in prophetic dreams and visions emerging from a barren and violent reality, monotonous in its horror. True to this special kind of realist cinema, the film's characters play themselves, like Maria and Antero or the believer who becomes a holy warrior and politico-religious leader, when he takes up the task of preventing the water from a dam in his village in Ceará (a state in north-eastern Brazil) from being diverted to a private farm.

'We'll drag ourselves like geckos across the rocky surface of life'; 'Life is an aimless crossing', say Maria and Antero, who find in religion the poetry and charm of a world bereft of direction. The film develops in a form of transcendental realism, simplicity and economy of gestures, camerawork and narrative. The arid, monotonous life bursts with happiness through the experience of the sublime and the mythical and enchanting world of religion.[5]

Crede-mi, by Bia Lessa and Dany Roland, follows the same vein, but works with a magical religious world heavily aestheticized through fiction and theatre. Here, Thomas Mann's novel *The Holy Sinner* is recreated with the reality of the Ceará *sertão* and local amateur actors. It is a multicultural *sertão*, where experimentation and stylization (tilted camera, soft focus images, etc) encounter folklore and tradition in a world re-enchanted through art.

The similarity between the European Middle Ages depicted in Thomas Mann's novel and the culture of the north-eastern *sertão*, a place of survival and transcription of that medieval culture in *cordel* (oral literature booklets) and in the oral and religious culture, provides *Crede-mi* with a multicultural ambience in which to establish a dialogue between different repertories. In the film, the documentary snapshots of the actors' workshops and of popular festivals celebrating the Epiphany become elements of fiction. This re-encounter of man with what is human in the divine – a theme of Thomas Mann's – echoes in the culture of *sertão*, where myth and the sacred permeate daily life, and the relationship with the divine is as an intimate and prosaic dialogue. 'God was there waiting for dinner. Dinner wasn't served, His belly growled...' is one of the speeches about God overheard by the filmmakers.[6]

The idea of an immemorial history which traverses the European Middle Ages as described in Thomas Mann's novel, and the north-eastern oral culture transposed to film as an experimental undertaking by theatre directors new to film, provide the tone for a possible re-reading of the north-eastern *sertão* in contemporary Brazilian culture. In *Crede-mi*, different actors play the same character on a pilgrimage through a *sertão* converted into cultural experimentation and aesthetic location. The use of clips of classical music unifies, homogenizes and smothers the various environmental sounds and noises, providing at the same time the exaltation and fusion of popular culture into high culture repertory.

Another multicultural construction of the *sertão* appears in the film *Baile perfumado*, by Lírio Ferreira and Paulo Caldas, a pop re-reading of the traditional *sertão*. What is in question here is less the violence of the *cangaço* (the outlaw life) than its mythical construction through the eyes of a stranger, the Lebanese photographer and filmmaker Benjamin Abrahão, who actually accompanied, photographed and filmed Lampião and his gang.[7]

The film, narrated by the photographer in Arabic with subtitles, focuses on the moment in which the *cangaço* comes into contact with a germinating mass culture and a technically reproducible art capable of eternalizing and mythologizing it. It is a cross between the archaic and the modern, a green, stylized and virtual *sertão*, energized by the contemporary pop music of Recife, the *mangue-beat* of Chico Science's band. The film is stylized through camera movements, framing, music and the actors' performances, showing the *cangaço* as a stylization of violence and an aestheticized existence, exemplified by Lampião's self-consciousness and concern with his own image.

This is a representation of the *sertão* that does not translate into a search for an identity or a unified 'Brazilianness', but opens itself up to different readings of the *sertão* through a 'foreign' eye. This *sertão* is an iconography that has already been appropriated by Brazilian urban pop culture.

Romanticism, exotic primitivism and *favelas* as media folklore

It is possible to make a direct link between *sertão* and *favela*. *Favelas* are like a *sertão* within the city, because *favelas* are where immigrants from the *sertão* moved to in search of a better life. The *favelas* developed their own culture, a blending of the rural legacy and the urban ethos of the new generation born on the *favela* hills.

14. A popular festival in *Crede-mi.*

Today, *favelas* are part of mass culture and its products, and their population is devoted to television, music, drugs and consumerism.

The *favelas* in the films of the 1950s and 60s were totally different. They were always the site for idealized dreams of a beautiful and dignified poverty. The clichés of the 'noble savage' were applied to the 'noble poor'.

The fascinating quality of the geography and landscape of the *sertão* finds its urban counterpart in the outskirts and slums. They cause fascination as well as horror and repulsion, contradictory feelings which films have never ceased to note and express.

Basically, we could oppose the films romanticizing the *favelas'* misery to their counterpart, the 'pedagogy of violence' typical of some *Cinema Novo* films. The starting point of this romanticization is the culture of samba in the slums of Rio as displayed in films such as *Favela dos meus amores* (*Favela of My Loves*, Humberto Mauro, 1935), *Orfeu negro* (*Black Orpheus*, Marcel Camus, 1959) and *Rio Zona Norte*. In these films, the *favela* (former *sertão*) population is 'pillaged' by the coastal, asphalt people, thus showing a kind of romantic masochism of misery that finds an escape through art, popular culture, carnival and samba.

Violence and misery acquired a different aesthetic sense in the early 1970s. From the martyrs of the revolution of the *Cinema Novo* we progress to the lyrical agents of violence and their lyrical victims. They form a political and social marginality now destitute of their references and slogans, in a movement that starts within *Cinema Novo* itself, in a film such as *Câncer*, directed by Glauber Rocha in 1968, continuing through *Cinema Marginal* (Underground Cinema), in which this lyrical sense of marginality symptomatically emerges. These films no longer show the humiliated and massacred people of *Deus e o diabo* or *O dragão da maldade*, who are granted a mythical redemption. Glauber moves away from his own pedagogy of violence and his revolutionary call to arms that would lead to a collective solution. With *Câncer* and other films of the end of the 1960s, violence, articulating with humiliation and misery, will never lead to revolution, but rather to a diffuse and anarchic death drive, a tension which becomes the typical trait of *Cinema Marginal*.

Câncer is the reference point for this new approach to violence in Brazilian Cinema, which evolves in a precarious scenario of theories, aesthetics and politics. The film's characters, from the lower middle classes, the outskirts and the slums, are deterritorialized, they no longer belong to a certain land, i.e. to the *sertão* and the rural world, but have not been absorbed by urban culture either. They express their pain and suffering anarchically, lyrically, or through the rationality and efficiency of the new media.

In Brazilian films of the 1990s, the theme of the popular composer living in the *favelas* and his relationship with both high and mass cultures makes a comeback, re-reading the films of the 50s and 60s, but also incorporating later developments. I present here a comparative analysis of three films: *Rio Zona Norte* (1957), directed by Nelson Pereira dos Santos, and *Orfeu negro* (1959), directed by Marcel Camus, on the one hand; and the new version of the latter, *Orfeu*, directed by Carlos Diegues in 1999, on the other. The aim is to map the way in which these three films transform a popular character – the *favela* composer, the musician, the *sambista* (the samba player) from the hills – into a kind of mythical national character who will find his redemption and his way out of misery through art, through myth and/or through the media. The popular composer will appear in the 1990s as a new mediator of culture, legitimized by media folklore.

The romanticization of the popular and the search for a lyricism in adversity and poverty is a mark not only of Brazilian cinema, but also Brazilian music, literature and soap operas. It is a symbolically strong 'project' or myth of national identity, according to

15. Patrícia França and Toni Garrido in *Orfeu.*

which Brazilian people possess a latent talent for producing an original culture and way of being.

Rather than questioning this discourse that naturalizes myth, it is interesting to analyse its consolidation, whose first consequence is the faith in redemption from misery through art – a theme as recurrent in cinema as other myths and discourses on Brazilian culture, such as the racial 'democracy' that, although not real, is important as a symbolic production and consumption or even as an 'integrationist' project. The culture of samba in the *favelas* is seen, over and over, as a niche, a kind of urban *quilombo*,[8] at once integrated with and isolated from the city. The *favela* becomes a territory of crises, of cracks, but also a niche of treasures and cultural and symbolic riches that open up and expose themselves to integration and pillaging.

This theme, in a paradigmatic way, appears in the three films. They all derive from a distinct historical context, holding a dialogue with other films of their period and among themselves.

Rio Zona Norte, by Nelson Pereira dos Santos, shot in black-and-white in 1957 and starring the black actor Grande Otelo, tells the story of a *favela* musician who gets one of his sambas stolen by a successful white singer. The film works as a kind of anti-*chanchada*,[9] while maintaining a dialogue with elements of *chanchada*: musical sequences, samba school rehearsals and the radio studio broadcasting live performances (in this film, singer Ângela Maria at the peak of her popularity performs at Mayrink Veiga Radio Station). At the same time, it relates samba to its origin in the hills, describing the atmosphere of the train station Central do Brasil and of the suburbs of Rio de Janeiro. Grande Otelo, renowned for his comic performances in the *chanchadas*, here plays a dramatic role. Thus, the film combines realism, melodrama and musical.

Another important element is the insertion of the geography of Rio and its settings, especially the hills, as a character. Nelson Pereira dos Santos had already aroused attention with *Rio 40 graus*, a predecessor of *Cinema Novo* that had put the hills of Rio on the map. With *Rio Zona Norte* he drew a new map of this urban *quilombo*, its characters and problems.

What kind of imaginary about the *favelas* was being constituted in the 1950s? Nelson Pereira dos Santos calls attention to the fact that drugs did not represent a problem at that time. The issue was of a different nature. Police blocked the access to some of Rio's *favelas* at 11pm. There were repression and restrictions to integration. One could not come and go at will. It was necessary to carry a badge at all times stating that the carrier was under a work contract; idleness was a crime punishable with imprisonment.[10] All these social circumstances are revealed in *Rio Zona Norte*. The problem for Grande Otelo's character, a samba composer and singer, is that he wants to own a *tendinha*, a little grocery shop in order to become a 'worker'. Samba singers are seen as *malandros*, unemployed outcasts.

On the one hand, samba was beginning to be legitimized by radio singers and stars in the 1950s. Samba schools still used to parade in Praça Onze, next to the poor areas of Mangue and to the red-light district. Carnival was not yet integrated into high culture. *Favelas* were seen as places of marginality, crime and prostitution. On the other hand, the 1950s were a decisive period for the construction of a 'mythological image' of Rio de Janeiro as the country's political and cultural capital, marking the golden age of the Copacabana Palace Hotel, international tourism, nightclubs and gossip columnists.

The film focuses on the hardships the 'pure' popular artist has to face and the perverse character of a still incipient cultural industry, for which the *sambista* is nothing but cheap raw material. As such he is bought and thrown into the circle of radio stars. The film exposes the relationship between the popular artist and high culture through a series of dichotomies. The *sambista* does not have any connections in the music world and therefore cannot record his own songs; he is not even able to write musical scores. Therefore he composes for other singers or white composers who will make profits from his songs.

Rio Zona Norte's narrative emphasizes the naivety of the composer from the *favelas*, who is black, semi-illiterate and dependent on the help of a classical musician to write down his scores. The film shows the uneven absorption of popular culture and folklore into mass culture through the influence of radio. It values anonymity, the embryonic stage of a popular talent not yet recognized outside its own circle. The narrative ennobles and romanticizes the sufferings of the *sambista*, his innocence and purity.

It is interesting to observe the way in which *Rio Zona Norte* presents the many stages of the process of legitimizing this popular culture through different mediators. Firstly, the *sambista* has to be accepted and recognized by the samba school of the hill where he lives. Then he needs to please the visitors from the South Zone (the middle class neighbourhoods of Rio) who show up on the hill for a sort of 'cultural feeding', searching for an 'authentic' experience – an expression often used by a refined couple delighted by the 'popular' ambience. Thirdly, he has to pass the scrutiny of singers, successful composers and the system of 'purchase' and airplay of his music created by radio stations and recording companies.

The film describes these mediators and centres the action in the opposition between the black composer, Espírito da Luz (Spirit of Light), and the sophisticated, tall, elegant white composer, who is shown with his wife, a blond, shapely painter – both examples of a literate and well-educated elite that appreciates the authenticity of the 'popular', embodied by the black *sambista*, while doing very little to help him out of his ghetto.

Another mediator or agent who appears in the film to legitimize the popular element is the *malandro* (crook) from the middle class, who acts as a go-between, hanging out on the hills and stealing sambas to be sold to famous singers. And yet a third agent of legitimization are the radio stars themselves, who can fancy a certain samba and decide to record it, provided the *sambista* is able to bridge the gap between the classes and be heard by these stars.

If the film places value on the experience of the popular artist and 'canonizes' him, it also maintains a critical stance, underlying the distance between the glorification of the character and his dismay and frustration in the face of reality. It also shows the ambiguity of cultural mediation. The *sambista* loses his son, who becomes a burglar; he is abandoned by his wife, loses his house and the *tendinha* which he was going to run, and has only one way out: to sublimate pain and misery through art, an artistic redemption dependent on oral memory and on the community of the hill who will carry on singing his songs, regardless of the market, until they catch someone's attention and are recorded.

In *Orfeu negro*, made after *Rio Zona Norte*, all historical and social context is abandoned. This is probably the reason why emergent *Cinema Novo* directors reacted so furiously against what they called the portrait of a 'mythical' Rio de Janeiro presented by the film.

Director Marcel Camus creates a crazy non-realistic geography. His Rio de Janeiro is a cinematic construction, a juxtaposition of postcards. The *favela* on the hill is presented in the film as a mythical and paradisiacal place where poverty is glamorous, even desirable, where nature and culture are one, where poor dwellings, the *barracos*, look charming and the backdrop is a touristy landscape of the Guanabara Bay. Work is shown as something pleasurable and liberating. Women dance and sway their hips while carrying water tins atop their heads. The Portuguese grocer, the sole white person on the hill, exchanges his products for little kisses from the local beauties. Sexuality is playful, joyful and the only threats are from violent jealousy.

Children, animals, women, the 'sun', everything comes to a standstill to hear Orpheus' seductive music. Rather than *favela* people, they are fantastic characters of a Brazil changed into a lost paradise, like the utopian lands described by the first European travellers to the New World. The actors (a former soccer player and other non-professionals), the use of colours and landscapes, all contribute to creating an imagined community, constructed by foreign eyes, a vision that still constitutes a certain imaginary of Brazil to this day: in an exuberant land there lives a humble, simple but happy people. *Favelados* (the *favela* inhabitants) become 'Indians', a people original to Brazil, triggering fantasies about racial democracy and sexual freedom.

Marcel Camus' film is not exactly 'naive'. It brushes history aside in order to stage the mythic aspect of things. Daily life is transformed into celebration and playful time. In the film, misery is transubstantiated into 'primitivism' and 'archaism'. In fact, misery is not an element in the film. The characters live in a 'primitive' way, but misery has disappeared under the veil of a non-problematic poverty.

Everything follows the logic of myth and the film is there to narrate myth. An *Umbanda*[11] session is used only so that the character of Orpheus can try and communicate with his dead Eurydice. Hermes, the mythological messenger, is a tram conductor. Orpheus dies, but a child with the gift of music and poetry takes his place. The lovers' death is a beautiful one, an aestheticized 'still life' with the bodies lying in symmetry on the branches of a tree.

Carlos Diegues' *Orfeu* holds a dialogue with Marcel Camus' film, even if the director tries to deny it, and also with Nelson Pereira dos Santos' *Rio Zona Norte*. In Diegues' film, the prevailing discourse is sociological, including power relationships, mediators of popular culture and the clash between mass culture and high culture. There is an attempt at a realistic or even naturalistic aesthetics. Thus, the film places itself at the crossroads between the mythological and sociological discourses described above.

To that end, the director makes use of different approaches to the *favela*. The script is a collaborative work between Hermano Vianna, an anthropologist specializing in popular music; Paulo Lins, a writer raised in a *favela*; and João Emanuel Carneiro, a professional scriptwriter. Despite retelling a mythical story, the film focuses on present-day reality, using myth as a pretext to present sociological, political and aesthetic questions.

Orfeu also creates a Dionysiac, highly positive discourse about a popular hero, employing a realistic narrative that paradoxically reaffirms the existence of magic and an aesthetics (including spectacular postcard images of Rio) that turns the city into a microcosm and allegory of the whole nation.

The distinctive trait of Diegues' film is that it presents the title-character already fully integrated in a consumerist culture, in a country entirely dominated by mass culture. He is not only a hero among his peers on the hill, but a national personality. He is aware of his quality as a sign of Brazilianness and conscious of his self-image. He is a 'myth' of mass culture. He offers himself as a role model, a possible alternative to that of Lucinho, the drug dealer. 'I won't move out of the *favela*; I want to prove that it is possible to succeed without being like you' – he tells Lucinho. Orfeu is also aware of the fact that he is respected by the police and worshipped by his neighbours because he has the media behind him. Orfeu is at the same time a mythic and a media character.

But Lucinho is also a media personality, representative of a new mythology of mass culture that transforms drug dealers into pop stars. His characterization in the film suggests that of a member of a rock, rap or funk band. He is as successful as Orfeu and both are businessmen: one deals drugs, the other, art. Lucinho explains the logic of his trade thus: 'Drug dealing is just like any other business. Instead of cleaning toilets or doing hard, humiliating labour, it is preferable to be in the drug business'. He sees himself as an entrepreneur.

The *favela* here is a territory of myth and social conflicts, tension and violence, but it is also a place for the creation of art and trends (samba, *pagode*, funk, rap). Orfeu and Eurídice's love story loses interest and moves to the background in the face of other, more relevant issues: the execution of a man who had slept with a pre-teenage girl; the conflicting religious beliefs of Orfeu's parents; a police commander torn between his duties of repressing or protecting a drug dealer tied to him by family bonds.

The film shows two possible ways of self-assertion on the hill: music as mass culture and banditism. If one is not respected as a citizen, then one will be respected as a media character or a criminal.

In both cases, the only way out, the only possible redemption, is through fame and popularity in the media. Television is omnipresent on the hill and, significantly, it is on television that the romantic couple appear resurrected at the end of the film.

Translation by Vladimir Freire

NOTES

1. This article is a heavily revised version of an essay previously published in the catalogue of the exhibition *Cinema Novo* and Beyond, at The Museum of Modern Art (New York, 1999).
2. See 'Eztetyka da Fome 65', in Glauber Rocha, *A revolução do Cinema Novo* (Rio de Janeiro, Alhambra/Embrafilme,1981), pp 28-33. An English version, 'An Esthetic of Hunger', was published in Randal Johnson & Robert Stam (eds), *Brazilian Cinema*, expanded edition (New York, Columbia University Press, 1995), pp 68-71.
3. Vera Cruz is a production company created in 1949, based on Hollywood models, in an attempt to improve the technical and aesthetic levels of Brazilian films. It lasted only five years and then went bankrupt.

4. The phrase '*uma câmera na mão e uma idéia na cabeça*' was a famous *Cinema Novo* slogan.
5. The theme of the world of the *sertão* enchanted by religion is analyzed by Martine Kunz in 'Religião, sonho e poesia', *Cinemais* 10, March/April 1998, pp 165-170.
6. Interview with Bia Lessa, 'A realidade como matéria-prima e a busca do interior', *Cinemais* 3, January/February 1997, pp 7-28.
7. See interview with Paulo Caldas and Lírio Ferreira, 'A Modernidade, o sertão e a vaidade de Lampião', *Cinemais* 4, March/April 1997, pp 7-39.
8. *Quilombos* were settlements created by runaway slaves from colonial farms, from the seventeenth century onwards. They constituted important centres in the struggle against slavery. The most famous among them was Quilombo dos Palmares.
9. *Chanchada* is the most popular genre in Brazilian film history, being a combination of slapstick comedy and musical, in many instances parodying Hollywood films. Most *chanchadas* featured songs related to Brazilian carnival. Its golden age occurred between 1948 and 1960.
10. See interview with Nelson Pereira dos Santos by Tunico Amâncio, in *Catálogo da Mostra de Filmes e Vídeos*, Centro Cultural Banco do Brasil (Rio de Janeiro, 1999), p 17.
11. *Umbanda* is a syncretic Afro-Brazilian religion.

9

The *sertão* in the Brazilian imaginary at the end of the millennium

Luiz Zanin Oricchio

To Maria do Rosário Caetano

In order to appreciate why the *sertão* or backlands occupy a privileged position in the Brazilian imaginary we must look back to the Battle of Canudos and the work of Euclides da Cunha. Canudos is a model, a prime example of Brazilian social rebellion. In the last decade of the nineteenth century, thousands of believers gathered around the mystical figure of Antônio Vicente Mendes Maciel, known as Antônio Conselheiro. They formed an autonomous community that rejected the Republic, proclaimed shortly before in 1889. They were wretched people who lived around the river Vaza-Barris, in the hinterland of Bahia. They named their community Arraial de Canudos.

The Republic saw Canudos as both a problem and a challenge. It sent successive military expeditions there with the aim of wiping out what was felt to be a focal point of resistance to central government. Each new military mission was in turn held back until in 1897 Canudos finally fell, at the hands of a very powerful and well-equipped army. At no time did the republican government recognize that what kept Canudos going was both the charismatic figure of Conselheiro and the hunger, drought and hopeless poverty of the *sertão*. Conselheiro was a guide, but he also represented hope for redemption, both in this world and in the next. On that occasion, as on others, the Brazilian social question was dealt with as if it were a criminal matter. But, in contrast to what has taken place on similar occasions in Brazil, Canudos bore witness to fighting, heroic resistance and death.

There was also someone at Canudos who could recount the episode, understand its fundamental importance and transform the rural tragedy into a social epic. That someone was Euclides da Cunha, who had been sent as a reporter by the *O Estado de S. Paulo* newspaper to find out what was going on in that backwater. Da Cunha left São Paulo with a preconceived idea that the Republic stood for progress while Canudos was the most obvious sign of backwardness. Light versus darkness. Civilization, clutching its sword, had to triumph. Once in Canudos, Euclides da Cunha began to realize the complexity of the situation, and as a result he changed his opinions. He recognized that he had been a witness, not to the enlightened victory of progress over superstition, but to a massacre. He published his newspaper reports together under the title *Diário de uma expedição* (*Diary of an Expedition*). Those texts form the basis of a fundamental piece of work that he published a few years later in 1902 with the title *Os sertões*, an absolute classic of Brazilian literature and one of its seminal works. Euclides da Cunha from then on has been regarded as a kind of Brazilian Homer, the great epic narrator of the nation's social tragedy.

The following lines from one of the final pages of *Os sertões* give an idea of the author's style:

> Canudos did not surrender. The only case of its kind in history, it held out to the last man. Conquered inch by inch, in the literal meaning of the words, it fell on October 5, toward dusk – when its last defenders fell, dying, every man of them. There were only four of them left: an old man, two other full-grown men, and a child, facing a furiously raging army of five thousand soldiers.[1]

This book is compulsory reading when it comes to discussing Brazil's social inequality, and the *sertão* in which it is set has become a space – a physical, imaginary and symbolic space – where the country's contradictions are expressed with the maximum intensity and impact.

The *sertão* and the films of the *Cinema Novo* movement
The *sertão* is the backdrop to three of the most important *Cinema Novo* films: *Deus e o diabo na terra do sol* (*Black God, White Devil*, Glauber Rocha, 1964), *Vidas secas* (*Barren Lives*, Nelson Pereira dos Santos, 1963) and *Os fuzis* (*The Guns*, Ruy Guerra, 1963).

They are classic examples of the movement – the so-called Holy Trinity of *Cinema Novo* that contain practically everything there is to know about the period. In all three the *sertão* is used in diverse ways to depict a nation in crisis. *Vidas secas*, an adaptation of the novel of the same name by Graciliano Ramos, draws attention to the lives of the poor migrants of the North-East who flee drought and hunger in search of survival. In *Os fuzis* the starving population of a town is prevented from pillaging a warehouse by the army. The rural opera *Deus e o diabo na terra do sol* follows the character Manuel, a cowhand, through different stages of his life, namely conflict with an exploitative landowner, the search for solace in religious fanaticism, senseless violence when he joins a group of rural bandits and finally the rejection of this path in preparation for the transformation of the hostile world which created him. *Vidas secas* is basically more documental, more physical so to speak. That is why the film's lighting and sound effects are so important. The flattened photography, 'blinded' by the aggressive light of the *sertão*, seeks to convey the dryness of the inhospitable environment, and it was aesthetically original in its day. In *Os fuzis* Ruy Guerra gets to the heart of Brazil's social contradictions: it is the common people serving in the army, who defend the interests of the warehouse owner. Seen as a microcosm of the nation as a whole, the film represents the essence of the gridlock that characterizes Brazilian society, or at least how it was perceived at that historical juncture.

Deus e o diabo na terra do sol is the most explicitly dialectical of the three films. Manuel, played by Geraldo del Rey, is a kind of Hegelian figure in search of his own consciousness. The catalyst for this journey is the exploitation that he feels in his very bones. He then experiences religious alienation, followed by equally alienating extreme violence, until he reaches the point of fighting for change. At this stage he takes on the elements of all the previous stages and synthesizes them. His point of departure is that of the exploited: from religion he gains faith, essential for any kind of action, and from banditry he takes violence that is also necessary for transformation to take place. Or at least a radical transformation of society – revolution, to use a word that in fact had poetic value in the 1960s.

What is curious is that these three films roughly follow the approach of Euclides da Cunha in *Rebellion in the Backlands*. Taking his inspiration from Taine, the writer divided his work into three parts: The land, Man, and The rebellion. He starts with the description of the environment, passing through anthropological analyses to finally reach the social question. Laden with positivism, this structure is masked by the literary quality of the text. Nelson Pereira focused his attention more on the physical and hostile environment and everything it produced. Ruy placed his emphasis on the people of the *sertão*, their class divisions and differing degrees of consciousness, traditionally overlooked. Glauber's film went straight to the historical process.

National developmentalism, the Left and the revolution, and the coup of 1964

The reader can thus have an idea of just how complex the films being made were at that time. But where did this cinema come from? From many places, but in general terms, from another paradox. Brazil was basking in the glory of the years of optimism in which the national developmentalism of president Juscelino Kubitschek was heralding a promising future for the country. Fifty years' development in five was his government's slogan. In this general context of democracy and supposed economic prosperity, the Arts flourished and innovations took place in music, theatre, literature, the plastic arts and in the cinema. Brazil had won the World Cup for the first time in 1958. A new capital had been unveiled, based on a modernist and cutting-edge project drawn up by Lúcio Costa and Oscar Niemeyer. The automobile industry had been established. Meanwhile poverty continued to exist in the underbelly of the country and even in the big cities. Most of the population did not enjoy the benefits of progress that the middle class assumed was widespread.

At the same time the power structure of the country began to show signs of instability. This was owing in part to the escalation of the Cold War between the two superpowers. Cuba and its socialist revolution served as the model for intellectuals and artists, convinced as they were that the socialist alternative would be the solution to Brazil's endemic problems. In domestic politics an unbalanced president, Jânio Quadros, had resigned seven months into his term of office and was replaced by João Goulart, who did not have the support of the Armed Forces who were fiercely anticommunist. All this had created an explosive cocktail that spilled over on 31 March 1964 with a right-wing coup. The military stayed in power for 20 years before handing it back to civilians.

The films mentioned above, made in 1963 and 1964, were conceived during this moment of great energy, tension and creativity. They reflect the originality of their creators, as well as a certain perception on the part of intellectuals that they were living in a society on the brink of insurgency, a belief that, as we now know, was proved wrong by the facts.

The death of cinema and its resurrection in the 1990s

Films made in the 1990s were, of course, inspired by a completely different environment. The revolution of the 1960s never took place. The tensions of the Cold War era subsided, and the world witnessed the fall of the Berlin wall and the collapse of an empire. In the 1990s the hegemony of the free market economy was already in place. This state of affairs has not failed to leave its mark on Brazil as a whole and on its cinema in particular. Elected president in 1989 over a candidate of the Left, Fernando Collor de Mello, in one of his first acts, did away with all the sources of State support for cinema.

This threw film making into crisis. Production practically came to a standstill and only picked up again in 1994 with new laws of incentive, which allow for a reduction in income tax for businesses that invest in cinema. This was how the new presidents of the Republic – Itamar Franco, who succeeded Collor (impeached on corruption charges) and Fernando Henrique Cardoso, elected thereafter – sought a compromise between State management of cinema, already considered passé, and the current obsession with market forces. The State makes fiscal contributions, via unlevied taxes, and private enterprise decides in which films it wants to invest the money that it would otherwise pay in taxes.

Needless to say, this situation is far from ideal because the selection process is based on economic factors, with the business class deciding which movie themes and styles it prefers to endorse. The disadvantages of this situation are so obvious as not to require comment. What is important for this study is that films were being made once again. And, of course, the *sertão* reappeared as a theme, as a location and as an imaginary space in the 1990s. It appears in various films produced throughout the decade, such as *Sertão das memórias* (*Landscapes of Memory*, José Araujo, 1997), *Baile perfumado* (*Perfumed Ball*, Paulo Caldas and Lírio Ferreira, 1997), *Corisco e Dadá* (*Corisco and Dadá*, Rosemberg Cariry, 1996), *A guerra de Canudos* (*The Battle of Canudos*, Sérgio Rezende, 1997), *Crede-mi* (*Believe Me*, Bia Lessa and Dany Roland, 1997), *O cangaceiro* (*The Cangaceiro*,

Aníbal Massaini Neto, 1997), *Milagre em Juazeiro* (*Miracle in Juazeiro*, Wolney de Oliveira, 1999), *São Jerônimo* (*Saint Jerome*, Júlio Bressane, 1999), *Central do Brasil* (*Central Station*, Walter Salles, 1998) and *Eu, tu, eles* (*Me You Them*, Andrucha Waddington, 2000).

For example, the theme of banditry, inextricably linked to the *sertão*, makes a return in *Corisco e Dadá* and *O cangaceiro*, the latter a remake of Lima Barreto's famous film shot back in the 1950s. In *Corisco e Dadá* the goal of the director was to resurrect the symbolism and the iconography of both the theme and the environment of the *sertão*. Massaini's *O cangaceiro* is a modern reworking of an old story of love and violence in the harsh world of the *cangaceiros*, but without any of the sparkle of the original.

Crede-mi takes the interesting idea of adapting Thomas Mann's novel *The Holy Sinner* to the environment of the north-eastern *sertão*. The work is eclectic in terms of recording images (they were recorded in video then transferred to 35 mm film) and in terms of the theatrical conception of the plot, which reveals the aesthetic background of filmmaker Bia Lessa, a successful stage director making her first movie. *The Battle of Canudos* by Sérgio Rezende tries to reproduce the saga described by Euclides da Cunha, but the director chose the narrative point of view of an individual (the young woman whose family had gone to the Canudos settlement, who becomes a prostitute, and so on), which weakens the collective dimension of the epic. *Milagre em Juazeiro* by Wolney Oliveira paints a charismatic portrait of the priest Padre Cícero Romão Batista, who transformed faith into political power in the region of Cariri in the north-eastern state of Ceará, but his approach is also flawed.

Key films

Four films in particular lend themselves to an analysis of the return to the theme of the *sertão* in the cinema of the 1990s: *Sertão das memórias, Baile perfumado, Central do Brasil* and *Eu, tu, eles*. The four films are of high quality and fulfil perfectly the objectives of their creators. Moreover, they express clearly, but each one in its own way, the ethos and the ideology of the decade when they were made.

One of the most significant works of the 1990s is *Sertão das memórias* by the first-time director José Araujo. Born in Ceará, Araujo returns to his native town, Miraíma, in the interior of the state. Although the tone of the film is nostalgic throughout, Araujo is not satisfied with merely capturing a piece of his childhood. In terms of direction, *Sertão das memórias* at first seems to

16. Maria Emilce Pinto in *O sertão das memórias.*

establish an active dialogue with *Cinema Novo.* This can be felt through the framing of shots, through the camera work, through the lack of concern for a linear narrative and through the search for a sensory perception of the rural experience – something that had already been notably achieved by *Vidas secas* and *Os fuzis*, in particular. Nevertheless it is in the 'political' dimension of the film that its greatest weakness is revealed.

Araujo seeks to show that people of the *sertão* are not only crushed by drought and by poverty. There is in Brazil a poverty industry that profits from the exclusion of others. Everyone knows this, but the characters that the director creates to discuss this Brazilian reality are such caricatures that in the end they lose their credibility. They weaken the content of the film. This type of weakness, as we shall see, does not happen by chance.

The opening sequence of *Sertão das memórias* illustrates the director's agenda. The camera wanders slowly over a series of old photographs displayed on the wall. It then lingers on a few simple objects, before introducing the characters. In only a few minutes the audience is tuned into the imagination of the director. As the title of the film suggests, it is a story of the return to a beloved land and to cherished memories. The film is full of Araujo's recollections. He was born in Miraíma, and later joined a seminary but did not become a priest. He took an arts degree at university, became aware of social problems and ended up leaving Brazil during the military dictatorship. He went to the United States, studied cinema and worked as a sound technician on several films, notably those directed by Percy Adlon and Gregory Nava. Between 1991 and 1996 he worked on this, his first fictional film (he had previously made the documentary *Salve a Umbanda*, 1987).

In *Sertão das memórias* Araujo uses his own parents, Antero and Maria, as fictional characters. Maria is a kind of Jesus Christ figure reincarnated as a woman, on a pilgrimage with a group of *rezadeiras* or women who pray. Maria is on an evangelizing mission in the *sertão*. Antero plays the archetypal man of the *sertão*, hardy and worn out by work; a descendant of the Old Testament prophets. On their journey they come across the devil incarnate, in the guise of a businessman who wants to divert the water from a lake for his own use. Politics and power relations thus converge with the mystical. In fact they always co-exist, since mysticism cannot exist in isolation and thus it even plays its part in local politics.

Araujo's idea is to gather together all these different loose ends: his own imagination, the setting of the *sertão* and the power relations that permeate them. Perhaps what Araujo is proposing here is that art should relate the individual to his circumstances, without casting aside his spirituality. *Cinema Novo* was secular; Araujo seeks to reinvent it, by giving it a religious dimension.

Thus, *Sertão das memórias* is, first and foremost, a return journey. A journey is a process of dislocation. The traveller is never the same person when he returns, and even the point of departure changes. For this reason, the classic symbolic journey is that of Ulysses. He returns no longer the same man; Ithaca has changed, but Penelope is still weaving her robe. When Araujo, the hidden narrator of the film, returns from the United States he finds that his parents have grown old. Nevertheless, everything around him seems strangely familiar. But this familiarity is unwelcome. Drought continues to wreak havoc and the conditions of exploitation of the poor have not changed. Populist politicians make their age-old speeches and lay the same old traps. The film's initial impulse seems to have sprung from this contrast between what has changed and what never seems to change.

It is a paradoxical impulse, because it oscillates between the will to preserve and the desire to modify. First there is memory, which seeks to capture something and defeat time. Such a task is doomed to failure, as we all know. But it is only human to refuse to accept the inevitable victory of the swift passing of time. It is an artist's lament for what is dead and gone. It is Villon's question about the 'snows of yesteryear', or Proust's literary cathedral to defeat time through artistic endeavour. On this subject, the treatment Araujo gives the images of his reunion with the *sertão* of his childhood is moving to watch. There is something almost tactile in the way that the camera approaches people, searching out their wrinkles, their hands roughened by hard work, but also how it approaches the dry earth, objects, his home. He reproduces the gaze of a child, seeing everything with a clarity that afterwards will be lost. There are some instances of heightened realism in the film, which convey the intensity of a reunion.

In this process, Naná Vasconcelos' film score plays a fundamental role. Naná is not a conventional musician. He incorporates sounds from various instruments, but also from everyday objects and from his own body. Sound, for him, is not just a physical or musical register, but it is also a world view. For this reason, no one is better placed to produce the film's music than him. Naná's sound does not illustrate images. It does not paraphrase or comment on them – it seems to originate from them. The sound comes from images like a statue from a block of marble, giving the impression that it was there all along, waiting to be revealed, and that the sculptor's job was merely to remove what is left over. It is rather telluric, but at the same time infinitely personal, almost a lullaby of the *sertão* – treated here as an autonomous character and not as the backdrop to the action.

The enchantment of the reunion is countered by the disenchantment provoked by the continuation of an unjust situation. This is the second element that characterizes the 'Holy Trinity' of films, referred to above. The personification of evil can be traced directly back to Glauber Rocha, but perhaps this conclusion is a little hasty. Rather than representing a return to some of the key figures of *Cinema Novo*, it appears to be a quest for something more archetypal, more remote, rooted in both tradition and the collective unconscious. Hence the evocation of the horsemen of the apocalypse, of the symbols of evil, that within the film are embodied in the figure of the exploitative capitalist.

This approach has been called naive, but perhaps it is unfair to suppose that Araujo wanted to present a sociological analysis of the conditions of exploitation. The film's intentions could not, in fact, be more different. It does not appear to be at all concerned with rationalizing social disparities or dissecting their causes. Poverty and oppression find their way into Araujo's discourse in a mythical form. Scenes seem to have been inspired by the canvases of Bosch or Brueghel, or by images straight out of *Det sjunde inseglet* (*The Seventh Seal*, 1957), in which Bergman takes death as his theme, but also the legendary poverty of the Middle Ages. This depiction of poverty is archetypal, rather than a graphic denunciation, analysis or call for social change.

It is no surprise that religion lies at the heart of this very personal film, and that it should constitute the third element of the 'Holy Trinity' mentioned above, but not because Araujo sees faith as a way out that political activity cannot provide. There is no escapism nor the usual reference to alienation in this spiritual dimension that permeates *Sertão das memórias*. The artist sees the relationship between the people of the *sertão* and mysticism as an intrinsic aspect of their lives. He does not judge or interpret, but simply observes. To portray this world without the spiritual dimension would be to disfigure it, to tell a lie, to create an incomplete picture. The landscape of the memory, such as is seen and retrieved by Araujo, is both body and soul.

Another film of great interest is *Baile perfumado*, by Lírio Ferreira and Paulo Caldas. This duo, also from the North-East (Lírio is from the state of Pernambuco, Paulo from Paraíba), have created one of the most stimulating films of recent years. It is based on the life story of the Lebanese Benjamin Abrahão. A photographer, travelling salesman and filmmaker, Abrahão succeeded in penetrating the very heart of the *sertão* and filming the legendary bandit Lampião and his followers. The only moving images of this mythical figure and his entourage that exist today were shot by Abrahão at the end of the 1930s. Although this film is based on a well-worn theme, everything about it is innovative. From the camera movements to the sound track (from the Recife-based musicians who performed with Chico Science's group) *Baile perfumado* is a hip film. Lírio Ferreira and Paulo Caldas show the bandits 'off duty', dancing, drinking and laughing. Lampião is portrayed as a complacent, 'bourgeois' bandit, who likes French cologne and White Horse whisky. The film is set when the banditry movement of the North-East was in a state of decadence, when the bandits simply lived off the rich landowners, from whom they levied a 'protection' tax. This indolence was to prove their undoing, and soon after they were decimated by government troops.

17. Lampião (Luís Carlos Vasconcelos) and Maria Bonita (Zuleica Ferreira)
in *Baile perfumado*.

The most notable feature of this film is not so much the story that it tells, although interesting in itself, but the portrait that it creates of an unfamiliar *sertão*. Lampião sets up camp on river banks, surrounded by lush vegetation. His *sertão* seems to be prosperous, fertile and happy. It is as if the sea (the film's directors do, after all, come from the coast) were embracing the dry earth and fertilizing it. In this way, and unintentionally, the film fulfils the prophecy of one of Glauber Rocha's characters, the miracle worker Sebastião (the alter ego of Antônio Conselheiro), who said that the *sertão* would turn into the sea, and that the sea would turn into the *sertão*. These words, that can be traced back to Antônio Conselheiro and to the Canudos rebellion, have dual significance. They refer to the millennarian vision of the Kingdom of Earth, of the milk and honey that will flow with the return of King Sebastian, of the poor that will inherit Heaven. But they also refer to revolution, to the radical inversion of the established order, when the exploited of the world will finally overcome their circumstances and usurp their oppressors.

However, this fertile *sertão*, this creative inversion of the stereotype, does not lead to any more profound social critique in *Baile perfumado*. It functions as an effective scenario for bringing up to date a genre considered hackneyed, but nothing more than this.

This does not weaken the film, per se, since a political agenda is more likely to have been an expectation among critics (or at least some of them) than one of the intentions of the film's two creators.

In addition to *Sertão das memórias* and *Baile perfumado*, there are two other films which are set in the *sertão*, two films that, in my opinion, are particularly worthy of analysis. These films are *Central do Brasil* and *Eu, tu, eles*. The former enjoyed tremendous success at the box-office in Brazil (more than 1.5 million people went to see it), and at the Berlin Film Festival it was awarded a Golden Bear for best film and the award for best actress went to its leading lady, Fernanda Montenegro. *Eu, tu, eles*, Waddington's second feature film, is an example of quality popular cinema. It was well received in Brazil and abroad (and was given a standing ovation in one of the parallel events of the Cannes Film Festival in 2000). The film is a fictional tale of the true story of a woman from the *sertão* who lives with her three husbands, all under the same roof, in the interior of the state of Ceará.

Central do Brasil is so rich in symbolic significance that it is impossible to tell whether this aspect of the film emerged spontaneously or whether it was planned by the director. The story begins in the city and from there it moves to the countryside. It is that rare kind of film that is capable of delighting both specialist critics (or at least a considerable number of them, because pleasing them all is impossible) and the general public. To do this it retains an emotional and affective tone, that involves the audience without needing to blackmail them with the easy option of melodrama.

For film buffs this film heralds a return to the great tradition of *Cinema Novo*, that in the 1960s was concerned with documenting a country that had not yet been discovered, at a time, unlike now, when Brazil was still relatively lacking in visual representations of itself. Television was just taking its first tentative steps, and everything that was happening far from Copacabana Beach, or from the centre of São Paulo, seemed as unreal and distant as images from Mars. As we have seen, cinema in the 1960s acted as a critical observer of Brazil, and filmmakers felt a duty to show the hidden underbelly of a euphoric country. They wanted to expose its poverty, show its inequalities and denounce its contradictions.

Central do Brasil draws on this noble tradition, at least in terms of its thematic inspiration, but its style and its cultural references are entirely different. The main character is Dora, played by Fernanda Montenegro, a woman who makes her living by writing letters for illiterate people. She does this in a railway station, a place synonymous with the forced migration caused by the huge disparities of development and thus unequal job opportunities that exist in Brazil. At this swarming interchange, people who do not know how to read or write pay her to write letters for them and to send them to relatives who live far away. One such character sends news back to his family, another rants about problems in his love-life, and another tries to patch things up with a wayward husband.

This woman is the mother of Josué, a young boy played by Vinícius de Oliveira, who was discovered by the director Walter Salles. She wants to get in touch with her errant husband to ask him to come to Rio de Janeiro to get to know his son. When a twist of fate brings Dora and Josué together, the film sets off in another direction. It then becomes a road movie, which allows the director to visit Brazil's backwaters, those places that are always ignored by a population that likes to cling to the coast. Dora experiences a crisis of conscience, as if she were the alter ego of the film's director, who uses cinema in order to get closer to his own country. For this reason, this film is not only a road movie in terms of spatial movement but it also takes the form of a journey of self-discovery.

Dora is an urban woman, albeit from the poorer outskirts of the city, who has no connection with the world that she gradually discovers, almost against her will. In one of the best scenes in the film, we see her at a religious pilgrimage, where she has lost Josué, and where the overwhelming presence of religious symbols, such as icons, candles, chanting, prayers and *ex votos*, cause her to faint. This is an effective way of depicting the dissociation of the conscience that occurs when she comes into contact with a radically unfamiliar world.

Dora is a cold-hearted woman, drained by her fight for survival, who has more than a little to learn from the young boy in her precarious charge. Salles does not resort to the usual, easy formula of melodrama, along the lines of 'child teaches adult about life and helps her to recover lost innocence'. Quite the reverse. The relationship between the two of them is tense, because both the woman and the boy are hard, long-suffering people; the former is disenchanted, the latter precociously mature. Their relationship is made up of a mixture of attraction and revulsion. They are always together but want to be apart, and yet when they are apart they go in search of one another. By creating these complex personalities, Salles avoids falling into the trap of shallow sentimentality. As a result of this mature choice, the audience is rewarded, because the story is told with real sentiments and not with false emotions of the kind that Hollywood loves to serve up.

For Josué the purpose of the journey is to look for the father that he has never known. The father represents a point of reference, as anyone knows, without having to call on psychoanalytical jargon. This aspect of the story plays with the existential question that Salles has tried to include in his work, particularly in his previous feature film, *Terra estrangeira* (*Foreign Land*, Walter Salles and Daniela Thomas, 1995). In that film he used a period of upheaval in Brazil's history, namely the Collor era, in order to go in search of a lost country that was becoming alien in the minds of its own citizens. It looked at Brazil from the outside, through the experiences of those who had gone to try their luck abroad.

In *Central do Brasil* he continues to search for his identity, but this time he is looking within the very soul of his country. He goes in search of the heartland, the *sertão*, the real Brazil, the core of the country. This is when Josué's quest for his father and Dora's quest for affection become blurred with the quest for a lost nation. One meaning is superimposed on the other.

There is one aspect that does not feature in this film, that is so successful in every way. *Central do Brasil* never engages with politics, in the widest sense of the term, and it is this which sets the film apart from the politically committed tradition of *Cinema Novo*, from which at first sight it appears to draw its inspiration.

Many elements of *Central do Brasil* are moving and sincere, such as the dignified portrayal of characters who live in dire poverty. The attitude of the individualistic Dora is absolutely in tune with the times, now that people no longer believe in collective solutions, in contrast to the 1960s and early 70s. On a certain level, the film is about Dora rediscovering herself, or rather, rediscovering her 'healthy' side, if we can call it that. From almost becoming a dealer in human organs (and thus a deplorable figure) she turns into, or reverts to being, a sensitive human being who wants to help a little boy to find his father. She then remembers her own childhood, cries for her father, whom she lost long ago, and so on. This role, it should be stressed, is played without any hint of sentimentality by Fernanda Montenegro, thus overcoming the risk of appearing melodramatic.

The film also brings out the opposition between the city and the countryside, which are places with very different symbolic resonance. The city is a violent place, where a person can be murdered in cold blood as people look on indifferently. It is a place where children are kidnapped for their organs, perhaps the most heinous crime that a human being can commit. The countryside, more precisely the *sertão*, functions as the polar opposite of the city, and perhaps as a place where the nation's morality remains intact. It is a place of dignified poverty, of solidarity, of fundamental values that have been lost in other places but which have survived in the countryside, as if it were an archaeological site for preserving the nation's ethics. It is here that the orphaned boy is reunited with his brothers. It is also here that the brutalized city-dweller, Dora, comes to terms with herself. In a globalized, postindustrial world, here in the *sertão* children's toys, like spinning tops, are made using traditional crafts. Here relationships are warm, brotherly and open. The *sertão* of *Central do Brasil* acts as a source of healing for a nation in need.

The *sertão* in *Central do Brasil* is essentially a place of reconciliation. Whereas *Cinema Novo* in the 1960s used the *sertão* as the most obvious expression of social divisions, conflict and discord, Brazil's new cinema associates this setting with a sense of community, the accommodation of opposites and the elimination of differences. There are no value judgements in these statements. This is not to say that previous films were better or worse, but that they simply represented different ways of coming to terms with the realities of Brazil. Some films go in search of fissures, others seek reconciliation. Some hope for revolution, others for reform; different points of view, different times, that are reflected in films which cannot be lumped together.

Eu, tu, eles is also set in the *sertão*, more precisely in the interior of Ceará, where a woman, Darlene (Regina Casé) lives with her three husbands under the same roof. Osias (Lima Duarte) is the owner of the house and the official husband; Zezinho (Stênio Garcia) is gentle and a good cook; Ciro (Luís Carlos Vasconcelos) is young. Darlene organizes her life by drawing on the best qualities of the three different men. Security, tenderness and sex, namely everything that you could want from a spouse. It sounds too good to be true, the product of a fertile imagination, but this really happened, and in rural Ceará, to a woman called Marlene Sabóia da Silva.

If you are one of those people who believe that life imitates art, you might think that Marlene had decided to build on one of

Jorge Amado's novels. In *Dona Flor e seus dois maridos* (*Dona Flor and Her Two Husbands*, made into a film by Bruno Barreto, in 1977, and to this day Brazilian cinema's biggest box-office success), the female protagonist longs for excitement (with Vadinho, the compulsive gambler) but she needs security (in the form of Teodoro, the pharmacist) in order to balance her life. Darlene needs three male props, but her feet are much more firmly on the ground than Dona Flor's. The latter is a talented cook, but the former is a rural worker, a farm hand. One belongs to Bahia's lower middle class, whilst the other is a landless peasant. One lives in the city, the other in the countryside, the *sertão*, that mythical place where the tragedy of economic oppression was played out in films from the 1960s.

The director of *Eu, tu, eles* has insisted that this is a universal tale, that could have been set in any part of the world. This is true, but I think that the film's particular strength stems from the fact that it is set in the *sertão*. In the heartland of Brazil, known for its moral conservatism, Darlene's story has much more impact than it would have had if it had been set in Ipanema, for example.

It is in this *sertão*, transformed into a symbolic but more neutral stage, that Darlene seeks to resolve the complex dilemma that has taken over her life. She is practical, as only a woman of the *sertão* can be. She has to live, or survive, raise her children, have some pleasure and peace and quiet, dream sometimes and feel reasonably secure. Any middle class housewife would aspire to the same things, so why not a humble woman, who has been mistreated and battered by the trials of life but is still cheerful and sensual? In this sense, *Eu, tu, eles* is a democratic film in that it affectionately shows us the steps taken by Darlene to make a harsh life more bearable.

The film addresses and engages with a particular self-image of Brazil, one that is also quite ambiguous. Sometimes it is a nation that does not like itself, with an inferiority complex, a perverse narcissist that spits at his own image, as Nelson Rodrigues would say. At other times Brazilians are on a permanent high, with forced smiles on their faces, citizens of that stereotypical sun-tanned and fun-loving nation. These mood swings, that range from one extreme to the other with no happy medium, from euphoria to depression, are perhaps what best characterize Brazilians. *Eu, tu, eles* proposes a compromise to correct this instability by means of a character who creates her own happiness in the midst of the most abject poverty.

Conclusion

Darlene, the narrator of *Sertão das memórias*, Benjamin Abrahão, Dora and Josué are rich, nuanced and interesting characters. However, they are very different from those of *Vidas secas*, *Os fuzis* and *Deus e o diabo na terra do sol*. Fabiano, in *Vidas secas*, is a humiliated man who progressively detaches himself from everything, even from his pet dog, in order to eke out a precarious existence with his family. He is dispossessed to such an extent that he ceases to be an exploited peasant. He could be any of us, such is the level of abstraction that he attains, as Jean-Claude Bernardet reminds us in his analysis of the film in the book *Brasil em tempo de cinema*.[2] Gaúcho, the character in *Os fuzis*, played by Átila Iório, who also stars in *Vidas secas*, represents division. He is familiar with the army, since he was once a soldier. He knows the crowd of starving people that want to storm the warehouse, because he was once one of them. He moves between these two opposing worlds and he experiences at first hand the gulf between them. When he tries to mediate between the two sides he pays for it with his life. Manuel, the cowhand played by Geraldo Del Rey, turns his back on religion and extreme violence. He takes a third path, that the audience can only guess at when he finally arrives at the ocean, having come from the heart of the *sertão*. They are characters in crisis, irredeemably torn between difficult choices.

They differ greatly from Dora, in *Central do Brasil*, who finds her way through the existential maze to reach a point of catharsis, and the narrator/director of *Sertão das memórias*, who combines his personal recollections with contemporary social critique, an unlikely but successful combination. They also differ from Darlene, in *Eu, tu, eles*, who 'constructs' her husband using the best qualities of three different men, and is rewarded, in the end, when her children are legally recognized. For Benjamin Abrahão, the marvellous travelling salesman-filmmaker of *Baile perfumado*, things turn out badly. He is a restless soul, the film tells us, and it is the restless who make the world go round. In this individualistic world, Abrahão embodies free enterprise, and pays for his daring with his life. He is not a political man and nor does he think collectively. No one thinks collectively in these films from the 1990s. The only direct reference to politics, found in *Sertão das memórias*, seems fragile and out of place, something that does not fit naturally with the rest of the film.

These films from the 1990s that return to the *sertão* interpret it in a new way. A place that was the harsh setting for insoluble contradictions in the 1960s emerges in the 1990s in a different guise. The rough, dry earth has been softened. Religious faith, previously thought of as nothing more than a distraction, is now part of the human landscape. Poverty may still exist, but it is dignified, more moderate and rectifiable. Pre-revolutionary fervour has been replaced by the quest for personal happiness. Where once the breakdown of society was depicted on screen, now we see problems that can be overcome with hard work and good will. What was once a battlefield has become a stage for cathartic reconciliation or existential redemption.

This conclusion does not question the aesthetic quality of the films but only their social standpoint, which depends on the historical context. In the past the enemy was easier to identify. The world was unjust and everyone knew what they were fighting against. Now, with the hegemony and omnipresence of globalized capital, everything is becoming less clear-cut. The world is still unjust, but the targets have disappeared into thin air, establishing what you could term the microphysics of exploitation. These films about reconciliation, in essence, can also be seen as involuntarily bearing witness to a moment of political confusion.

Translation by Stephanie Dennison and Lisa Shaw

NOTES

1.   Translation taken from Samuel Putman's *Rebellion in the Backlands* (Chicago and London, University of Chicago Press, nd), p 475. First published 1944.
2.   Jean-Claude Bernardet, *Brasil em tempo de cinema* (Rio de Janeiro, Civilização Brasileira, 1967).

10

Death on the beach – the recycled utopia of *Midnight*

Lúcia Nagib

The film *O primeiro dia* (*Midnight*, Walter Salles and Daniela Thomas, 1999) contains in its Portuguese title (literally, 'The First Day') a suggestion of the inaugural myth that distinguishes Brazilian history as much as Brazilian Cinema. Brazil is said to have been 'discovered' 500 years ago, although it had been inhabited for thousands of years before that, while Brazilian Cinema undergoes periodical births and rebirths and, after brief peaks, is afflicted by sudden deaths and prolonged silences. At each new awakening, the films seem to be the 'first' ones, disconnected from the past and history.

O primeiro dia was commissioned by the French television company ARTE to be a reflection on another beginning, the coming of the new millennium. However, the film does not seem to believe in its own proposal, for it speaks of beginnings only to deny or ironize them. Of its four main characters, three die in some violent way at the very beginning of the new millennium and the fourth escapes suicide by a hair's breadth. Even the firework apotheosis at the zero hour of the millennium is mixed with the terror of gunshots.

The film's story also denies its Portuguese title and rejects the inaugural myth by invoking a land of the past against the widespread idea of Brazil as 'the land of the future'. The *favela* (shanty town) and its problems, a favourite theme of Brazilian Cinema since Humberto Mauro's *Favela dos meus amores* (*Favela of my Loves*, 1935), is once again the subject here, appearing as the privileged repository of Brazilian society's contradictions. Although *O*

primeiro dia is one of the best achievements of new Brazilian
Cinema – said to have been 'reborn' in the mid 1990s, after so
many premature deaths – instead of inaugurating something, it is
aimed at making a synthesis of the historical – and cinematic –
processes in Brazil, proposing a sequel to them.

In this way, the promise of a new cinema gives way to a rever-
ence for the cinema of the past. This gesture, incidentally, is typical of the Brazilian Cinema of the 90s, which is constantly paying
homage to classics and veterans. As soon as the results of the
Audio-visual Law – the key factor in the recent cinematic 'rebirth'
– started to appear in the mid 90s, there came a torrent of films
about the north-eastern *sertão* (arid backlands) and the *cangaço*
(the activity of the outlaws in the *sertão*), a combination which constitutes the most recurrent genre in Brazilian Cinema in all periods. A few examples of this are: *Corisco e Dadá* (*Corisco and Dadá*,
1996), by Rosemberg Cariry, that explicitly quotes Glauber Rocha
and one of the latter's main literary sources, Guimarães Rosa; *Baile
perfumado* (*Perfumed Ball*, 1997), by Lírio Ferreira and Paulo
Caldas, who resort to the film images made by peddler Benjamin
Abrahão in the 1930s of *cangaceiro* (the *sertão* bandit) Lampião and
his band; *O cangaceiro* (*The Cangaceiro*, 1997), by Aníbal Massaini
Neto, which is a remake of Lima Barreto's classic of the same
name; *A guerra de Canudos* (*The Battle of Canudos*, 1997), by Sérgio
Rezende; *Sertão das memórias* (*Landscapes of Memory*, 1997), by José
Araujo; *Crede-mi* (*Believe Me*, 1997), by Bia Lessa and Dany Roland;
and the famous *Central do Brasil* (*Central Station*, 1998), Walter
Salles' incursion into the North-East.

The fact that Salles and Thomas now turn their attention to the
favela simply confirms their adherence to Brazilian Cinema's traditional concerns. It is common knowledge that *favela* and *sertão*
are two sides of the same coin and, although they had been
appearing since the early days of Brazilian Cinema, it was in the
1950s that they became the obsessive subjects that launched social
cinema, with Nelson Pereira dos Santos (*Rio 40 graus/Rio 40
Degrees*, 1955, and *Rio Zona Norte/Rio Northern Zone*, 1957), and the
Cinema Novo (in three fundamental films of 1963-64: Glauber
Rocha's *Deus e o diabo na terra do sol/Black God, White Devil*, Nelson
Pereira dos Santos' *Vidas secas/Barren Lives*, and Ruy Guerra's *Os
fuzis/The Guns*).

Free from the obligation to be novel, present day filmmakers
take a delight in re-exploring these themes, not only for their social

18. João (Luís Carlos Vasconcelos)and a jailer (Tonico Pereira) in *O primeiro dia*.

and political relevance, but also for their obvious visual and cine-matic potential. The *sertão*'s blinding light and large expanses of sun cracked earth had already characterized the aesthetics of early *Cinema Novo*; in recent films they sometimes result in landscapes of tourist appeal, such as the views of the *sertão* bathed in the smooth red light of the sunset in *Corisco and Dadá*. And the privileged loca-tions of the *favelas* on the Rio hills offer the most overwhelmingly pictorial views of the city, which is the reason why Nelson Pereira dos Santos used the city, with its tense proximity between rich and poor districts, as the 'main character' in *Rio 40 Degrees*; Santos' images, incidentally, would be quoted and re-elaborated in several later films, from Marcel Camus' *Orfeu negro* (*Black Orpheus*, 1959) to Carlos Diegues' *Orfeu* (1999), and even in *Midnight*.

Ivana Bentes in this volume notes the recurrence of these themes in contemporary Brazilian Cinema and states that, togeth-er, *favela* and *sertão* build the 'other side of positivist and modern Brazil'. Indeed, the *favela* is (or used to be until recently) as divorced from the 'asphalt' or the city as it is identified with the problems of the North-East – those relating to both the victims of drought and the legacy of slavery. Alba Zaluar quotes João do Rio, who says that in a *favela* he felt himself 'in the countryside, in the *sertão*, far from the city'.[1] This deep chasm between rich (from the 'city') and poor (from the hills), despite their proximity, can be observed even today. It gave origin to Zuenir Ventura's book

Cidade partida (*Divided City*), which clearly echoes in *O primeiro dia*.
It is known that the hills of Rio, even though they were inhabited from the end of the nineteenth century, became *favelas*
thanks to the soldiers who returned from the expeditions to
Canudos in the first years of the twentieth century. As Jane Souto
de Oliveira and Maria Hortense Carcier explain,

> the word favela evokes in its origins the place in the Bahia
> *sertão* where Antônio Conselheiro's followers concentrated,
> and its use became popular in Rio from the occupation of
> Providência hill by soldiers returning from the Canudos
> campaign. They were the ones who gave the name Favela to
> that hill.[2]

The word comes from the Favela range, in Bahia, the birth-place
of many of the *cabrochas* (dark mixed race girls) who came to Rio
with the soldiers. From the beginning of the twentieth century on,
the hills were also subjected to increasing occupation by former
slaves who had migrated from Bahia and then been expelled from
their homes in the harbour districts of Rio. More recently, the
favela has also been occupied by north-eastern migrants fleeing
the drought. These started to fight with the black population for
the scarce remaining space.

In short, the population of the Brazilian North-East is concentrated in the Rio hills, and is made up both of descendants of African
slaves and of poor Portuguese and Indians. In a certain sense, it
could be said that in the *favela* the remnants of Palmares and
Canudos, that is, the heirs of the greatest rebellions of slaves and
north-eastern peasants in the country, have survived and multiplied.

Thus, it was only natural that Brazilian Cinema, while searching in the 1950s and 60s for so-called 'Brazilian reality', would
turn to the *sertão* and the *favela*. In 1965, these themes had
already been so thoroughly explored that Gustavo Dahl suggested that they had been exhausted and proposed a progressive
move to an 'urban' cinema (significantly, he does not include the
favela in this latter category):

> As regards the old opposition between urban and rural cine-
> ma, it is clear to me that, when *Cinema Novo* started off with
> its first films, ... it evolved in the area where the problems
> were most radically presented and where, therefore, it could

evolve more swiftly and efficiently. This is why it concentrated on the North-East and the favela. Obviously, once these problems had been proposed, they were rapidly exhausted, thanks to their typical simplicity. Thus, there is a need to open up the range of problems, to extend the same approach established for the North-East and the *favela* to other regions, other environments, other social zones. [3]

The fact that such subjects, after more than thirty years, have not yet died and today are actually experiencing a revival, points to unsatisfied social and cinematic hopes, unfulfilled promises, miscarried utopias.

Favela fashion

This reassessment of past themes certainly does not mean a lack of interest in the present. This has been recently shown by the example of *Baile perfumado*, from Pernambuco, which gave a pop treatment to the images and sounds of the *sertão*, updating it in the light of a globalized world in which the *cangaço*, far from its traditional traits of brutality, ugliness and roughness, is provided with a glamour of creativity in terms of costumes, language, dance and gestures. If Lampião kills, he also spreads his perfume through the thorns of the *caatinga* (the rough vegetation of the *sertão*).

The handsome actor Luís Carlos Vansconcelos, the Lampião of *Baile perfumado*, has been exported as an icon of male beauty straight to the *favela* of *O primeiro dia*, which, thanks to his presence, acquires an attractive look, becoming almost fashionable. His seductive looks charm the no less attractive female middle class character, played by Fernanda Torres, who, for one night, leaves aside her fears of outlaws and gives herself to the most dangerous of them.

The antiquity of the theme does not imply an old fashioned approach. The interesting aspect of the recent films is that, although they do not believe in revolutions, innovations or novelties, they do succeed in shedding a contemporary light on their themes, which includes an historical perspective and an acute awareness of the specific conditions of the present.

O primeiro dia belongs to a 'family' of contemporary *favela* films, ranging from Murilo Salles' *Como nascem os anjos* (*How Angels Are Born*, 1996) through Eduardo Coutinho's *Santo forte* (*Strong Saint*, 1999). Its closest relation is certainly Carlos Diegues' *Orfeu* (1999), which is not only a homage to films of the past (*Rio 40 graus, Rio Zona Norte*), but also a remake of Camus' *Orfeu negro* (1959). In his film, Diegues tries both to correct the French director's sweetened imagery and to describe the *favela*'s present situation, updating its history. According to Sérgio Augusto, Diegues' idea is that

the *favela* is currently going through its third historical stage. Up to the 1950s, the form through which the hills of Rio were represented in the sambas, on the stage and on the screen was, at its best, lyrical. This happened in *Favela dos meus amores*, directed by Humberto Mauro in 1935, in *Tudo azul* (by Moacir Fenelon, 1951), in *Orfeu da Conceição* [Vinicius de Moraes' play that was the origin of *Black Orpheus*], *Rio 40 graus* and *Orfeu negro*. In the past, they used to publicize an idea of purity and even privilege connected with the *favela*, for 'those who live in the hills are close to heaven,' as Herivelto Martins' samba proclaims; today this is inadmissible, since the *favelas* have long ceased to be a scarcely inhabited, peaceful and bucolic place. After they became overpopulated due to urban growth and chaotic migrations, and their doors were opened to violence and crime, another stage started which Diegues named 'the complaining phase'; that is, people started to think that living on the hills was close to hell. In the 1990s, a new stage began, the fight for affirmation and for the pride of being a *favela* inhabitant, even if one has to live day by day with its adversities. *Orfeu* is intended as a faithful portrait of this stage.[4]

This understanding of the contemporary *favela*, which includes the 'pride of being a *favela* inhabitant', is also present in *O primeiro dia* (not least because both films have João Emanuel Carneiro as one of their scriptwriters). In both films the intention of separating the *favela* from the idea of an oppressed and ostracized place, submissive to the ruling powers, becomes apparent, for such an image would hardly correspond to the *favela*'s current status. Instead, they want to enhance its features of an alternative source of power. In these films, the hill looks like a trenched battlefield, and its inhabitants are like a heavily armed army, with their all-powerful commanders, their own rules and their own structured ethos.

Walter Salles had been working on such issues for some time before he made *O primeiro dia*. He had been assistant-director to his brother João Moreira Salles for the documentary *Notícias de uma guerra particular* (*News of a Private War*, 1998), a very interesting essay on the current situation of Rio *favelas*. The documentary alternates statements by *favela* inhabitants and policemen, descriptions of weapons by experts of both sides, and funerals of the victims also of both sides. Beyond the hatred between the adversaries, a mutual admiration and profound knowledge are visible, turning the opposing warriors into similar characters. The crude pragmatism of the *favela* soldiers, the matter-of-factness of their murdering gesture, the quiet awareness of certain death prove that the *favelas* have lost their last rural traits and entered modernity. 'When you kill your enemies, you light fireworks, you make barbecue parties. It's a victory, why wouldn't you commemorate it?', says an infant cocaine dealer, while another comments calmly: 'Everybody has to die one day'.

In *Notícias de uma guerra particular* the most evident aspect of urbanization is the industrial scale of the phenomenon. The swelling population on the hills is emphasized in the takes of piled huts stretching out of sight, in the similarity of the countless mixed race youths working in the drug-dealing army, in the kafkaesque accumulation of seized guns stored in a warehouse of the police department.[5] Incidentally, similar images of this gun warehouse occur in the opening scenes of *O primeiro dia* as a background to the dialogue between the blackmailer Chico (Mateus Nachtergaele) and the policeman (José Dumont), when the former tries to extort money from the latter in order to pay for his family's New Year feast.

Thin boys, armed to the teeth, seem to want to demonstrate that the rebellions of Palmares and Canudos were not concluded in the past; instead, they have grown and spread in the present, and the poor people now find themselves almost on equal terms with their opponents, for they are equipped with weapons identical to theirs. At the end of *Notícias de uma guerra particular*, the dispirited statement made by a *favela* character – 'The war will never end' – echoes the confession by one of the policemen that he is exhausted and indicates that the official power has never been so far from winning.

Leaving aside the usual warning campaigns directed at the middle class, aiming to inspire terror in them because of the violent *favela* inhabitants, *Notícias de uma guerra particular* emphasizes the change of status that occurred on the hills with the coming of the drugs and the guns. There seems to be no answer to an enemy so irrevocably oppressive and strongly armed other than fighting back. At a certain point, writer Paulo Lins – the author of a very important novel about the *favela* population in Rio, *Cidade de Deus* (*City of God*),[6] who is also a co-scriptwriter of Diegues' *Orfeu* – is interviewed in the film and states that the press and society started to pay attention to the *favela* only when the kidnappings and the cocaine business started. Another witness, the wife of singer and composer Adão, enumerates the advantages of a strongly armed *favela* and observes how successful the *favela* young men, armed with heavy guns, are among middle class girls

Boys in their early adolescence reveal, behind masks indicating that they are wanted by the police, their pride at being in the drug business. The charm of heroic, romantic soldiers, who bravely face a premature death, is stressed through an extreme consciousness of fashion. The care with clothes and hairstyle, and the outrageous exhibition of famous labels are detailed by Zuenir Ventura in *Cidade partida*, referring to the funk balls: 'Bermuda shorts, sneakers and caps are "trophies won in the war for survival". In other words, "the labels are symbols of inclusion in the consumer society".'[7]

The tragic future indicated by such a situation, the hell of an 'endless war' lives on equal terms with the charm of the bandit of modern times. *O primeiro dia* is aimed at describing precisely that transformation of horror into attraction on the part of a middle class character (Maria) for a character from the *favela* (João). The young woman who wakes up in fear in the middle of the night, thinking the fireworks are gunshots, ends up being rescued by and loving one of the outlaws she is so scared of.

Recycled allegories

O primeiro dia, in its realistic (often documentary) and sceptical approach, does not hide a certain nostalgia for the time when the desire to 'begin' and to 'build the future' was possible.

The urge to compose an encompassing synthesis in little more than one hour results in gaps – and this serves the film's purpose. The characters are not individuals; personal details are erased or dismissed. The protagonists are called João (John) and Maria (Mary), that is, they have openly fictitious, fairy tale names. They are a given man and a given woman from Brazil, exemplary figures of a certain society.

The remaining characters of the story follow a similar pattern of individual indeterminacy – they have the sole function of representing social types. This is not the scheme usually adopted by recent Brazilian films, in general more preoccupied with the composition of individual dramas even when dealing with major political issues. *Guerra de Canudos*, for example, dedicates much more time to describing the destiny of the members of a migrant family than to the war itself. And *Baile perfumado* describes the private life of Lampião and his band, rather than his public activities.

A detail that accentuates the mystery of the protagonists' private story is the fact that they live wrapped in silence. In an overcrowded prison, João has the privilege of an individual cell, until another old prisoner is transferred there. Even with company, he insists on keeping quiet, despite the other's attempts at a conversation, arguing that he 'only wants to sleep.' Maria, the middle class young woman, is more eloquent, but has the curious profession of teaching deaf and dumb people, which also gives her an aura of living with silence. Communication, for her, seems to be a problem: she even breaks her own telephone, the only possibility of contact with her departed partner. At a certain point in the narrative, after a long and quiet shower, Maria rejects all communication, like João, stating that she 'only wants to sleep.'

João and Maria are therefore representatives of their social classes. As is well known, exemplary characters were a distinguishing feature of Glauber Rocha's and other *Cinema Novo* directors' films. This was the time of the famous allegories, intended to materialize abstract ideas about Brazil in human characters.

João, incarnated by Luís Carlos Vasconcelos, participates at several levels in this schema, for he is the typical heroic cowboy/*cangaceiro* who migrated to a *favela* in Rio. This information is not restricted to the spectator who first met him as Lampião in *Baile perfumado*: his origin is also indicated by the typical laconic style of the arid *sertão* inhabitants, his markedly north-eastern accent and his foreign and almost superior attitude inside the *favela*.

This hard nosed bandit, good with a gun, is an updated version of the north-eastern cowboy of Carlos Diegues' *A grande cidade* (*The Big City*, 1966, performed by the emblematic Leonardo Vilar of *O pagador de promessas/The Given Word*, 1962) who goes to try his luck in Rio and becomes a ferocious criminal of the hills. And in his foreignness he is analogous to another emblematic character of Glauber Rocha's films, Antônio das

Mortes. Just as Antônio das Mortes (in *Deus e o diabo na terra do sol*) takes money from the 'colonels' and the church to kill the preacher Sebastião and the *cangaceiro* Corisco, João buys his freedom by agreeing to murder a friend of his. But he lets himself be seduced by Maria, the middle class character, with whom he has a brief vision of freedom – while she experiences through him a kind of revelation. His commitment to the ruling class combined with his solidarity with the oppressed makes João a tortured, lonely being, condemned to a tragic end, just as it had done with Antônio das Mortes.

However, it would perhaps be inexact to say that the characters of *O primeiro dia* are allegorical. In their incompleteness, they are rather nostalgic reminders of the allegories of the past, when beginnings were possible, cinema was really new and the characters, with their revolutionary impulses, dragged behind them great social forces. This nostalgic trait becomes apparent in the character called 'Vovô' (Grandpa), performed by the old samba composer Nelson Sargento (who also appears briefly in *Orfeu*). At a certain point, in the prison, he sings one of his most famous songs:

> *Samba – agoniza mas não morre*
> *Alguém sempre te socorre*
> *Antes do suspiro derradeiro*
> (Samba, you agonize but never die,
> somebody always rescues you,
> before your last sigh)

The nostalgic overtone is also noticeable in another character. This is Pedro, played by Carlos Vereza (made famous by his performance as writer Graciliano Ramos in Nelson Pereira dos Santos' *Memórias do cárcere/Memories of Prison*, 1984), a character who is so fragmentary and inexplicable that he seems to have entered the wrong film. In one of his rare utterances, he reacts to an observation of Maria's (his partner) that he is too old, by saying: 'And you are so young...' Pedro in fact does not seem to belong to Maria's contemporary reality, his function as a lonely writer does not fit in there, it is lingering on almost two decades later from the time of *Memórias do cárcere*. Eventually, he and his computer disappear mysteriously, leaving Maria puzzled and desperate. Actually, Pedro's presence in the film is so ephemeral that Maria's despair seems that of somebody who has no other problems in life, a 'bourgeois mood', and her suicidal desire is convincing only thanks to the actress' extraordinary performance.

These three characters allusive to past eras fade away, as if returning to their remote origins, leaving the present to those entitled to it: Grandpa dies of a stroke after learning that he will not receive the amnesty promised for the end of the millennium; Pedro leaves the scene in the same mysterious way in which he appeared; and João is murdered by those who sold him his freedom.

An empty utopia

The character of Grandpa in *O primeiro dia* is above anything else a homage to the old samba maker of the hills, Nelson Sargento. This was normal in the cinema of the past, when *sambista* Zé Ketti featured in *Rio Zona Norte*, or Cartola in *Ganga Zumba*, 1964, the first feature-length film by Carlos Diegues. Nevertheless, Sargento ends up performing a central role. His confusing speech is a kind of *samba do crioulo doido* ('samba of the mad nigger'), but it is full of clairvoyance. His predictions of future happiness alternate with disillusioned pessimism. While he awaits the amnesty, he repeats: 'It will turn, nine will turn into zero, another nine will turn into zero, another will turn into zero, and one will turn into two. The year 2000 is the year of freedom!' But then, realizing that he will be simply transferred to another cell, he cries out: 'Everything will turn to zero, nobody will remain to tell the story, you fucking guards!' Later, when he is dying, his prediction is shortened to a repetitive 'it will turn, it will turn'.

If there is a utopian prediction in Brazilian Cinema that still resonates in our ears, it is the one repeated in prose and verse in *Deus e o diabo na terra do sol*: 'The *sertão* will turn into the sea, and the sea will turn into the *sertão*.' This prediction had been conceived with a clear logic, as Glauber himself explained it:

> The *sertanejo*'s (the *sertão* man's) fundamental obsession is to see the sea, ... the phenomenon of migration always goes in the direction of the shore. As to the prophecy 'the *sertão* will turn into the sea, and the sea will turn into the *sertão*,' it was made by Antônio Conselheiro and became well-known; even if it does not contain a revolutionary proposal, it does give you the freedom of interpreting it in a revolutionary sense. I took the symbol and used it in my film.[8]

In *O primeiro dia*, the promise of wealth on a paradisiacal seashore and the revolutionary hopes of the oppressed do not make sense any longer. Thus, the subject and the complements of Grandpa's sentence are progressively eliminated – they did not make much sense anyway, for they were nothing but numbers, nine, zero, one, two – and only the verbs remain: *vai virar, vai virar* (it will turn, it will turn). This is how the prophecy turns into an uncompleted, empty utopia.

However, the sea, with all its utopian overtones, is present in the film. And this is not an isolated case: in several of the recent Brazilian films, particularly those connected to north-eastern themes, the sea or great water expanses are recurrent images. As if to give a sequel to the unforgettable scenes at the end of *Deus e o diabo na terra do sol*, when the *sertão* merges with the sea, or at the beginning of *Terra em transe* (*Land in Anguish*, Glauber Rocha, 1967), in which the sea, taken in aerial shots, acquires cosmogonic dimensions, the sea returns in current films so insistently that it could suggest a utopia come true. Good examples of this are *Baile Perfumado*, when it shows Lampião dominating the vast extent of the great São Francisco river from the top of a rock; or *Crede-mi*, which opens with the image of an old north-easterner narrating the Book of Genesis, while his figure merges with the blue wavy surface of the sea; or *Bocage – o triunfo do amor* (*Bocage – The Triumph of Love*, Djalma Limongi Batista, 1998), in which the minimal figure of the poet Bocage floats in a cage on the endless ocean; or *Corisco and Dadá* and its legendary sea... The list of examples is very long.

In *O primeiro dia*, the utopian sea has again a prominent role, as we shall see. Maria, abandoned by her partner, is prevented from suicide by João, who has found refuge on the top of the building from which she intended to throw herself. They end up commemorating midnight together, to the sound of fireworks and gunshots, the latter fired in the air by João himself, and then they spend a night of love. In this sole moment of exaltation and joy, skilfully staged with a camera turning around the two characters in each other's arms and edited with the light of fireworks and Antônio Pinto's music, utopia is again reborn and formulated precisely by the most sceptical character, João. Although he had previously replied to the old prisoner's announcement 'it will turn' with anger: 'It will turn to fucking nothing, year two thousand, three thousand, fifty thousand will be all the same shit,' he now becomes a provisional believer: 'Don't sleep', he tells Maria, 'it will

19. Maria (Fernanda Torres) in *O primeiro dia.*

turn, everything will turn. Nine will turn into zero, another nine
will turn into zero, another yet will turn into zero, and one will
turn into two. Everything will turn, right will turn wrong, wrong
will turn right, and the one who kills now will save.'

The morning after, the lovers discover that they do not yet have
names for each other, so Maria says, looking down at the sea: 'I want
to be baptized in that sea.' This is the point where both lovers could
have turned into real, individual characters and acquired their own
names and stories. But the utopia of freedom is not fulfilled: while
Maria bathes in a huge, peaceful green sea, João, who had been sitting on the sand watching her from a distance, is suddenly shot in
the head by one of the policeman who had been following him.

The *sertão* man almost reaches the sea, but he dies on the beach.
In this way it becomes clear that the ordinary sea of the wealthy
Brazilian classes, who enjoy it constantly as a week-end entertainment or even – in the case of Rio's southern zone – as a daily pas-
time, remains inaccessible to the north-eastern poor. Here different concepts of the sea are made visible through the film editing.
The frame is entirely occupied by the sea where Maria bathes; then
a reverse angle shows João sitting on the sand, watching from a distance. These two takes edited together are overwhelmingly dis-
crepant: the first one, from João's point of view, is an oneiric image,
the sea is too green, too peaceful, too clean to be true. The second
take, from Maria's point of view, gives a realistic, ordinary image of

a man sitting on the dirty sand on the day after New Year's Eve, among sleepy remnants of the party and other passers-by.

Images of a distinct nature separate distinct realities. At the point where the male character could perfectly well have joined his lover in the sea, he remains apart in his own world, just complacently gazing from a distance at a dreamlike image that does not belong to him. With the midnight utopian dream and its fireworks at an end, the natural daylight brings the lovers back to their original places.

Negative religion

The end of utopia for the north-easterner is not the end of *O primeiro dia*. After João's death, the film proceeds to a kind of mystic climax, as we shall see.

The religious solution, when reality denies utopia, was one of the favourite *Cinema Novo* themes. Although devoid of the old critical perspective, when religious fanaticism was seen as an obstacle to political awareness, several contemporary Brazilian films are also devoted to the analysis of religious behaviours, particularly – as one could expect – those of the north-easterners and *favela* inhabitants. The examples are countless and other chapters in this book, such as those by Verônica Ferreira Dias and Luiz Zanin Oricchio, look at them more closely. But it is perhaps worth noting a recent recurrent motif: evangelization as an alternative to the dissolute life or gangsterism in the *favela*, as presented in Diegues' *Orfeu*, echoing Paulo Lins' *Cidade de Deus*.

In *O primeiro dia*, evangelization is emphasized as an escape frequently adopted by *favela* criminals who want to abandon their illegal activities. Chico, the blackmailer who extorts money from policeman and prison guards threatening to denounce them as corrupt, returns to the *favela* and finds his wife evangelized, listening to religious chants. He also promises, somewhat ironically, that he will 'turn to the Bible' – and here the 'it will turn' refers to salvation in God, a similar utopia to that of the freedom of the sea.

When neither freedom nor salvation arrive, Chico, kneeling as he is about to be killed by his friend João, composes a prayer denying God:

> Thank you my Lord for this bullet
> that will come into my brains.
> Thank you God, son of a bitch,

Our father, who is watching me here like a beast,
Be sanctified for the shit life you gave to me,
Let your brothel come to us,
Screw us up,
Amen.

Another door is shut, another utopia denied.

However, the end of *O primeiro dia*, with equally religious con-notations, leaves open the utopian possibility for the middle class. Maria's failed suicide was intended to be a religiously inspired sac-rifice: she looks at the statue of Christ, lit up on the top of Corcovado mountain, opens her arms like him and gets ready to jump, when she is held by João who suddenly appears behind her.

On the next day, after watching the real sacrifice of her one-night lover, who is shot at point-blank range on the beach, she returns to her apartment and opens the window facing the *favela* on the hill. Then the frame is entirely taken by the sun's rays com-ing from outside and the film ends in a total blank.

Is this a religious illumination? Is it Maria's destiny to 'turn to the Bible'? What has changed for this middle class character who almost killed herself when she lost her intellectual partner and came back to life when she saw her *favela* lover die? Did Maria's ephemeral contact with a formerly prohibited class bring her any kind of knowledge? Or was it just a passing enthusiasm for the charm of the armed man from the *favela*, as often happens with other women of her class?

The film gives no answer to these questions. This new baptism, this enlightened 'rebirth' remains vague, another empty utopia.

Notes

1. Alba Zaluar, 'Introdução', in Alba Zaluar and Marcos Alvito (eds), *Um século de favela* (Rio de Janeiro, Fundação Getúlio Vargas, 1998), p 17.
2. Jane Souto de Oliveira e Maria Hortense Marcier, 'A palavra é: favela', in Zaluar and Alvito: *Um século de favela*, p 64.
3. '1965 – Gustavo Dahl, Carlos Diegues, David Neves, Paulo César Saraceni', in Alex Viany, *O processo do Cinema Novo* (Rio de Janeiro, Aeroplano, 1999), p 120.
4. Press book of *Orfeu*, p 22-23.

5. 'Gangs' (of bandits) and 'galleys' (of funk ball dancers) could be seen as epiphenomena of the urban multiplication, a theme largely explored in the literature of Paulo Lins and Zuenir Ventura, but not dealt with in the films discussed here.
6. The book was made into the film *Cidade de Deus* (*City of God*, Fernando Meirelles and Kátia Lund, 2000).
7. Zuenir Ventura, *Cidade partida* (São Paulo, Companhia das Letras, 1997), p 126.
8. '1964 – Glauber Rocha, Walter Lima Jr., David Neves, Leon Hirszman – *Deus e o diabo na terra do sol* ', in Viany: O processo do Cinema Novo, p 62.

Part five

Screen adaptations

11

Nelson Rodrigues in the 1990s: two recent screen adaptations

Stephanie Dennison

Nelson Rodrigues (1912-1980) debuted on the Brazilian stage in 1941 with the play *A mulher sem pecado* (*A Woman without Sin*) and by his death in 1980 he had produced 17 plays and countless *crônicas*[1] and serialized fiction which are capable of doubling newspaper sales within a week. Some critics accused him of the worst excesses of disposable and exploitative culture: titillation, pornography, bad taste, poor writing, rehashing of material, melodrama, sexism, political conservatism and immorality. Others, however, considered him to have invented modern Brazilian theatre, with the staging in 1943 of the play *Vestido de noiva* (*The Wedding Dress*), a 'cinematographic' work which has strangely never been adapted for the screen. Nevertheless, in an industry which has consistently put its trust in literary adaptations, Brazilian Cinema has unsurprisingly invested heavily in Nelson's work: a total of 19 feature films have been released since 1952, based on his plays, novels and short stories, making him the most adapted Brazilian writer of all time, beating even the prolific and popular Jorge Amado. Most of these films have been critical or commercial hits.

This chapter will analyse two recent feature-film adaptations of Nelson's work, *Traição* (*Betrayal*, various, 1998) and *Gêmeas* (*Twins*, Andrucha Waddington, 1999), in which the legacy of previous adaptations can clearly be seen. This vast body of work has been termed *cinema rodrigueano*, and for many it is almost a national cinematic genre. It is therefore understandable that contemporary filmmakers should turn to these adaptations, just as they turn to other genres, for inspiration.

Cinema rodrigueano

Cinema rodrigueano got off to a disappointing start in the 1950s. The first adaptation of Nelson's work appeared in 1952, *Meu destino é pecar* (*Bound for Sin*), directed by the Mexican Manuel Pelufo for the Maristela Studios of São Paulo. The film disappeared without trace on its release, and can therefore hardly be said to have contributed to the development of *cinema rodrigueano*. The film is now available on video (many more popular adaptations are still difficult to view in Brazil) and Nelson's fans can detect in the film, despite the poor performances and direction, a number of the thematic staples of the author's work: kitsch melodrama, dark forces colluding against supposedly pure characters, and a love triangle which ends in death. It was not until 1962 that an adaptation had an impact on the press and public. *Boca de Ouro* (*Gold Mouth*), based on the 1958 play of the same name, was directed by Nelson Pereira dos Santos, who took a break from filming his *Cinema Novo* masterpiece *Vidas secas* (*Barren Lives*) to accept an invitation from Nelson's brother-in-law Jece Valadão to film him as the eponymous hero whom he had played on stage with resounding success. In the film Jece plays a *bicheiro*, a gangster and illegal lottery organizer from the suburbs of Rio de Janeiro, thus establishing the first prerequisite of the so-called *cinema rodrigueano*: a *carioca* setting, with characters and events taken from the popular lore of the city of Rio de Janeiro.

It is on this level that the *Cinema Novo* overlapped with Nelson's work: both Pereira dos Santos and Leon Hirszman in 1965 with *A falecida* (*The Deceased Woman*) could lend a social realist reading to Nelson's ironically conservative plays through their depiction of the hardships of the lives of Rio's urban lower middle and working classes. Most of Nelson's subjects are from the *Zona Norte* or Northern Zone of Rio, with its traditional way of life which is in sharp contrast to the more modern and wealthier Southern Zone by the coast. These characters are not slum-dwellers, but come from traditional families of Portuguese descent. They range from the working-class Zulmira of *A falecida*, who longs to rid herself of the stain of her poverty by dying quickly so that she can be buried in style, to the wealthy businessman Herculano of *Toda nudez será castigada* (*All Nudity Shall Be Punished*, adapted to the screen by Arnaldo Jabor, in 1973), who wants for nothing but who is forced by his family's position to live a life of emotional frugality. Nelson's protagonists are never satisfied with their lot: in his fiction they rarely get what they want and the writer therefore uses them as a warning to those who seek to change the status quo. It is too easy, however, to read Nelson's work as reactionary and nothing else, despite what critics have maintained over the years. His work seems to seek out hypocrisy wherever it can be found in Brazilian society and hold it up to ridicule: the Northern Zone of Rio with its stifling morality is revealed to be a hotbed of lust, deceit, adultery and incest.

As well as social realist readings of Nelson's work, filmed before *Cinema Novo* began its attempt to communicate with the masses, in the 1960s two films appeared which would establish a link between Nelson at the cinema and popular culture. J.B. Tanko was a successful director by 1964 when *Asfalto selvagem* (*Wild Asphalt*) was released. He had enjoyed success in the 1950s as a director of *chanchadas* or light-weight, formulaic popular comedies whose roots lay in popular theatre and the radio. With the demise of the *chanchada* at the beginning of the 1960s, Tanko sought new directions, and chose two films based on one of Nelson's hugely popular newspaper serials.

In the *chanchada* films of the 1950s characters newly arrived in Rio de Janeiro from the countryside were at first enamoured with and then disillusioned by the modernity of urban life, and had often returned to their traditional lifestyle at the end of the film. A similar confrontation between the archaic and the modern, as has already been mentioned, frequently appears in Nelson's work, and the popular flavour of his settings is also shared by the *chanchada*. Tanko's contribution to *cinema rodrigueano* only exacerbated the belief that Nelson's adaptations were the inheritors of the *chanchada* tradition; a belief that would haunt directors for years to come. Critics despised the *chanchada* and paid scant attention to the genre in their newspaper columns. *Cinema rodrigueano* was quickly establishing itself as yet another commercial genre which, as many critics saw it, was pandering to the limited needs of the popular classes, but unlike the *chanchada* there was nothing wholesome about Nelson's fiction, and there was no uplifting message for viewers in the closing scenes.

Characters were often debauched. The female protagonist of both *Asfalto selvagem* and Tanko's second film taken from the same source, *Engraçadinha depois dos trinta* (*Engraçadinha in Her Thirties*, 1966), like many characters in the *chanchada*, had moved to Rio from another state, but in these films she embraces the social and

sexual contradictions of the city, in what was perhaps a more genuine reflection of the confusion of the times, a confusion which
had already been recognized by the military when they seized
power in 1964, claiming that Brazil was on the brink of revolution.
As a result of Tanko's and other adaptations released in the 1960s,
cinema rodrigueano, just like the fiction on which it was based,
became (and for many continues to be) synonymous with critical
outrage. This has only helped directors over the decades declare
that they have a moral and political duty to film such material, as
the critics themselves prove that there is still much work to be
done to rid Brazilian society of its ingrained hypocrisy.

There is no doubt that in his two adaptations, *Toda nudez será
castigada* and *O casamento* (*The Wedding*, 1975), Arnaldo Jabor used
the issue of moral outrage to his commercial advantage. Jabor was
the first cineaste to attempt an interpretation of Nelson's work
after the coup-within-the-coup of 1968 which heralded an era of
violent political oppression and censorship. While *Toda nudez será
castigada* was censored at home, it was busy picking up prizes
abroad, including a Silver Bear at Berlin for Darlene Glória's performance as the prostitute Geni. The work came to represent a
challenge to the military regime. Nelson himself at the time was
no longer frowned upon as a supporter of the Generals: despite
his right-wing credentials, he had publicly protested against censorship of the arts. Also, in the early 1970s, critics were more open
to the kitsch interpretation of urban reality at the heart of
Nelson's work, perhaps as a result of the influence of the
Tropicalist movement in terms of a re-reading of Brazilian reality
in the heady days of the dictatorship.[2] An allegorical interpretation of the ills of society based on the debauched world of Nelson
was now recognized by many as a legitimate subject to be tackled
by Brazilian Cinema. Traditional left-wing critics and cinema-
goers, however, still refused to accept any cinema that avoided the
Marxist motifs of class pride and organization, social critique and
the honesty and redemptive power of labour.

In Rodrigues' play Herculano is in pious mourning over the
death of his beloved wife. His son and sisters encourage his self-
sacrificial existence, but his brother, Patrício, tires of the dullness
of the family home and fears that his brother is putting at risk the
fortune which he happily lives off. He sets to bringing Herculano
back to the land of the living by introducing him to his old flame,
the prostitute Geni. After a drunken evening together, both Geni

and Herculano fall in love, but Herculano initially fights against the perceived immorality of his act. He had sworn to Sérgio, his son, that he would never be with another woman. He eventually gives in to his desires, but rather than making a decent woman of Geni, as she would wish, he shuts her up in his second home, and visits her occasionally while he plucks up the courage to confess to his son. His son, however, catches the two together, gets drunk and arrested, and is raped in prison by his Bolivian cell-mate. Encouraged by Patrício, Sérgio sets out to destroy both father and lover, by making the emotionally weak Geni fall in love with him. He then heads off for Europe with his Bolivian lover. Geni commits suicide, and leaves a tape for Herculano revealing all.

Jabor's great achievement in filming Nelson's work was that he was not afraid to handle the depraved characters and situations which the fiction invariably included, and he was able to use shocking scenes of depravity to challenge bourgeois hypocrisy; a courageous and fitting venture given the political climate of the times. He was also the first director to comprehend that Nelson's work falls flat if it is toned down. Jabor recognized that an element of deliberately tacky melodrama emanated from much of the author's work, and the fact that such melodrama could sit comfortably alongside genuinely serious discussions was one feature which made him an original and striking writer of his time. Nelson (and his adapters) were frequently accused of producing nothing more than the Brazilian equivalent of *dramalhões mexicanos*, or overblown Mexican melodramas, and until Jabor's adaptations most critics had failed to appreciate this indispensable self-mocking and relief-providing element in his work.

A third wave of *cinema rodrigueano* got under way in 1978 and lasted until 1983, during which time seven feature films were released based on Nelson's work. In the interim years *pornochanchada* had confirmed itself as the most popular national cinematic form. *Pornochanchada* is an exaggerated term used to describe the soft-core porn comedies which dominated the national film scene at a time when foreign hard-core films were banned. It was inevitable that Nelson Rodrigues' themes of sexual and moral deviation would be picked up by the cinema at that time, and what had often been implicit in Nelson's work would be made explicit in the new-found freedom of Brazilian films.

The most successful adaptation of Nelson's work in box-office terms was *A dama do lotação* (*Lady on the Bus*, 1978). It was directed by Neville d'Almeida, who had made a name for himself as a 'marginal' cineaste in the early 1970s. *Cinema Marginal*, or *udi-grudi* as it was also known, in a parody of the English term 'underground', had appeared in the wake of *Cinema Novo*, and differed in its deliberate violence and lack of political direction, as an expression of the ideological limitations of military oppression. *A dama do lotação* was one of the stories published by Rodrigues in the very popular column entitled 'A vida como ela é' (literally 'Life as it Is'), the same column from where *Traição* and *Gêmeas* took their inspiration. In *A dama do lotação* a sexually repressed and recently married woman, incapable of making love to her husband, finds solace on the buses, picking up strangers, like a *carioca belle de jour*. On discovering his wife's philandering, the husband retreats to his bed and remains there, in a kind of living death, while his wife dutifully assumes the role of nurse by night, and continues her sexual encounters by day.

The smash hit *A dama do lotação* appeared hard on the heels of Bruno Barreto's *Dona Flor e seus dois maridos* (*Dona Flor and Her Two Husbands*, 1977), to this day the biggest Brazilian box-office hit, being seen by over 10 million people at the cinema. It could be argued that it was thanks to the success of *Dona Flor* that *A dama do lotação* made so much at the box-office. Both films were sleek and expensive productions for their day, both were erotic movies and, more importantly, both starred Sônia Braga, who was arguably Brazil's biggest and sexiest film and TV star. *A dama do lotação* seems to have started a trend in *cinema rodrigueano* of placing the latest muse in the starring role, ensuring that a cinema-going public, used to plenty of sex scenes and nudity, is kept happy, and having high production values.

During the late 1970s and early 80s, films based on Nelson's work were increasingly read in the context of previous adaptations, lending weight to the notion that *cinema rodrigueano* was becoming a kind of national cinematic genre. Popular genres had no kudos at the time, and these adaptations were seemingly lumped together in the minds of most critics with other pseudo-genres which were successful at the box-office and systematically ignored by the broadsheets, namely the *pornochanchadas* and the series of light-weight comedy films starring Os Trapalhões and Mazzaropi.[3] All of the adaptations of this period were more sexually explicit than the texts on which they were based, but at the same time were promoted as being challenging films

with serious messages: a clear departure from the aforemen-
tioned commercial successes and their straightforward aims: titillation, humour, or both.

José Carlos Avellar was one of the few critics to consider the
relationship between these films and their audience and, as an
extension of this, he suggested the existence of a Rodrigan genre:

> Everything occurs in an already clearly defined set, every-
> thing occurs among people who are moved to act by already
> established desires, dramas and repressions. And it is rela-
> tively easy to follow the story being narrated.[4]

The number of remakes and second and third movies by the same
director in this third wave of adaptations no doubt contributed to
this interpretation. Braz Chediak's 1980 film *Bonitinha mas
ordinária* (*Cute but Vulgar*) was a remake of J.P. de Carvalho's 1964
feature of the same name. Chediak adapted two more of Nelson's
plays, *Álbum de família* (*Family Album*, 1981) and *Perdoa-me por me
traíres* (literally *Forgive Me for Your Betrayal of Me*, 1983). Haroldo
Marinho Barbosa added one more to the Engraçadinha saga in
1981 (*Engraçadinha*). And Bruno Barreto in 1980 adapted *O beijo
no asfalto* (*Kiss on the Asphalt*) which had been first filmed in 1966
by Flávio Tambellini with the title *O beijo* (*The Kiss*). However film
reviewers, with their appetite for intertextual references, were
themselves instrumental in creating this so-called genre.
Audiences who went to see the other adaptations from this time
had clear expectations fostered in part by previous reviews of
adaptations of Nelson's work.

Traição

The production company Conspiração Filmes proudly but erro-
neously declare in their press notes that *Traição* marks the return
of *cinema rodrigueano* after a fifteen-year absence. They fail to mention a remake of *Boca de Ouro* which was released in 1990, directed by the well-known soap director Walter Avancini. It is interesting that the producers omitted this film from their list of adaptations, as it is a well-enough known if not very successful film. This
oversight is interesting in that through it the producers suggest
that *Traição* represents a new generation of adaptation for a new
generation of viewers, a declaration that would have been ham-
pered by mention of the existence of an adaptation from the

beginning of the decade which was stylistically different to the previous wave of *cinema rodrigueano.*

Conspiração Filmes is a production company made up of a group of young producers and directors who have established themselves as makers of commercials, music videos and one-off TV specials. *Traição* is their first feature film. Three directors contributed to the filming of *Traição*, as the film is made up of film versions of three of Nelson's short stories. The episodic film had been tried successfully in the 1990s in *Veja esta canção* (*Rio's Love-Songs*, Carlos Diegues, 1994), a collection of filmed stories which take their inspiration from popular songs. The *pornochanchada* also frequently resorted to episodic films, for example the three sequences shot by different directors which make up *Como é boa nossa empregada* (*How Good Our Maid Is*) of 1973.

As the film title suggests, all three segments in *Traição* deal with the issue of adultery. The short stories were taken from the newspaper serial 'A vida como ela é' which Nelson published every day from 1952 to 1962. Nelson's original remit was to produce a daily column based on news events, but he soon tired of this and started to invent his own amazing tales, all of which were 120 lines long, took two hours to write and dealt with the issue of adultery, especially adultery carried out by women. Nelson justified the use of what was daring subject-matter for the times by arguing that ignorance was not a good enough excuse for being virtuous. He thus continued in this column his crusade against hypocrisy, and his lucrative 'education' and titillation of the public, but at the same time continued to suggest that people, especially women, given half the chance, are doomed to sin. Inevitably this was not a message that everyone wanted to hear, and it was thanks in particular to this mass-produced column that Nelson failed to secure recognition of his talents as a dramatist until later in life.

The first part of *Traição* is subtitled 'O primeiro pecado' ('The First Sin'). It is set in the 1950s when the short story was written – the days before the contraceptive pill and acknowledgment of female sexual desire, when a married woman who asks another man out and puts up no resistance to sleeping with him really was considered a sinner. In this episode director Arthur Fontes brings to bear his experience in producing slick, upbeat and good humoured television commercials aimed at twenty-somethings, and his use of tongue-in-cheek intertextual references is designed to win over spectators instantly. The male lead, Pedro Cardoso,

20. Alicinha (Ludmila Dayer) in 'Diabólica', an episode of *Traição*.

plays a timid man, Mário Brandão, who is given an amazing opportunity when he is approached at a bus stop by an attractive married woman, Irene, played by Fernanda Torres. After a couple of
dates he borrows the keys to his friend's apartment and sleeps with
her, only to discover that he has been part of an experiment. The
married woman had never slept with another man, and she was
desperate to find out what it would be like. As she leaves the apartment, she tells Mário that he has failed the test and, performance-
wise, he does not even come close to her husband (*'não chega aos
pés do meu marido'*).

   In terms of intertexuality, 'The First Sin' can easily be read as a
reworking of the film *A dama do lotação*. Irene, like Solange in the
1978 film, picks up her victim at a bus stop. She is married, loves
her husband and has never had sex with anyone else. When she
tells her victim, *'Não chega aos pés do meu marido'*, it is in a direct evocation of a line from the 1978 film. 'The First Sin' is a politically
correct reworking of the hugely popular *Dama* tale for the 1990s.
In Neville d'Almeida's film, a large number of 'dirty old men' are
sexually gratified by Solange, who remains sexually frustrated
throughout. Male spectators also participate in the sexual gratifi-
cation, given the large number of scenes of sex and nudity with
strangers: an essential feature of any *pornochanchada* with its remit
of sexual titillation. In the 1998 version of the tale, Irene sleeps

once with a decent enough man, gets what she wants from the experience, and returns, we understand, to her happily married life, never to err again. The conservative values of the 1950s are thus maintained, as the film's setting arguably warrants, while Nelson's sexist message on the eternal need of women to commit adultery is turned on its head. Not only has Arthur Fontes updated the *Dama* tale, but he has also produced a (*porno*) *chanchada* for the 1990s. He does this through his vivid depiction of the era: the stylish fashions of Irene, the use of popular music, particularly samba, to suggest a care-free mood, the popular speech of *carioca* males discussing how to pull a woman in the ambience of pool halls and traditional bars, and the backdrop of Rio de Janeiro itself, where women from the Northern Zone only come south to look for mischief.

In terms of style, Fontes taps into the highly successful alternative comedy productions of Globo Television, for example the similarly episodic series *Comédia da vida privada* (Globo, 1995-6), which dealt with the disastrous private lives (in particular love-lives) of Brazil's supposedly sophisticated urban bourgeoisie. For a start, he chooses Pedro Cardoso, one of the most successful comedy actors of his generation, who himself starred in *Comédia*, to play the quick-witted loser Brandão. Fontes' style is also reminiscent of a number of good-natured comedies set in Rio which have been produced since the so-called *retomada* or rebirth of the film industry in Brazil, for example *Como ser solteiro* (*How to Be Single in Rio*, Rosane Svartman, 1998) and *Pequeno dicionário amoroso* (*The Little Book of Love*, Sandra Werneck, 1997), both of which also deal with finding a partner in the city.

The second episode of *Traição* is subtitled 'Diabólica' ('She-Devil') and was directed by Claudio Torres. In this episode Fernanda Torres plays Dagmar, fiancée of Geraldo, played by Daniel Dantas, whose relationship and impending marriage are threatened by Alicinha, her pubescent younger sister. Believed by the family to be an angel, Alicinha is in fact a devil in disguise, who uses her budding sexuality to turn Geraldo into her slave. In a bid to free himself from the powers of this she-devil, Geraldo murders the young girl on the eve of his wedding. Dressed in her sister's wedding dress, Alicinha's body is brought to the police station, where the story begins and is told in flashback.

This episode is much darker than 'The First Sin', and is cleverly filmed in an evocation of classic gothic horror films. Nelson was always at his darkest when dealing with issues of love and sex within the extended family, and two sisters falling in love with the same man was a particular favourite theme of his. Cases of love among in-laws and step-parents and children crop up in all of Nelson's prose fiction, while incest lies at the heart of the films *Engraçadinha, O casamento* and *Álbum de família.* In fact only three sources of the filmic adaptations do not deal at least in part with inappropriate passions within the family.

As many directors had chosen to do before him, Claudio Torres sets his tale amid a storm. A power cut at the police station throws the players into semi-darkness, as Geraldo narrates the events which led to Alicinha's death. The eerie atmosphere is maintained at the sisters' house, a badly lit nineteenth-century building, again a favourite device of set designers for depicting the out-moded and decadent lifestyle of Rio's lower middle classes, determined to hold onto the past.[5] This sense of claustrophobia and oppression is further suggested by the identification in the film of Dagmar's father as a military officer. Nelson had used the figure of the *militar* as shorthand for an authoritarian domestic regime long before the 1964 military coup. The father here is the archetypical morally conservative suburban patriarch who has no idea what goes on in the bosom of his family. As the story is set in the 1970s, and considering, as we shall see, that *Toda nudez será castigada* supplies the main intertexual references in the work, it would not be unreasonable to think of the addition of this feature of the father's life as being a (token?) contextual comment on the military regime of the time. This social context is absent from the original short story, where forces greater than the characters control the action, and it is taken as read that Dagmar has no choice but to let events run their inevitable, tragic course.

Contemporary audiences might have found this tale hard to swallow (why does Dagmar not move out?), had the story been told in a straight, naturalistic, or purely expressionist fashion.[6] As it happens, Torres makes it clear that the tale is not to be taken seriously, by inventing a typically Rodrigan ending. After Geraldo has related to the police officers how he came to kill Alicinha, the family arrives and the mother, played by Fernanda Montenegro, reveals that her younger daughter was the product of a love affair with another man. Torres' episode closes with the mother hysterically shrieking the words, *'Eu tenho um amante'* ('I have a lover'). Her deliberate overacting is in contrast to the controlled performances of the rest of the episode. In his over-the-top melodramatic denouement Torres clearly takes a leaf out of Arnaldo Jabor's book. The humour produced by the overblown melodramatic elements is intentional, as it was in Jabor's *Toda nudez será castigada*, and such humour does away with the need for a way out for the characters. It is as if the film is declaring that Nelson is worth watching from the point of view of nostalgia, if for no other reason – this is all good fun but not terribly relevant nowadays.[7]

This episode, more than any other, reveals the extent to which the cinematic climate has changed in Brazil. Had this subject-matter been handled by one of Nelson's adapters from the 1980s, Braz Chediak for example, it would undoubtedly have received a throroughly distasteful treatment. In Claudio Torres' aesthetic there is nothing visually nasty, dirty or cheap on screen, as viewers had come to expect of *cinema rodrigueano* from *Toda nudez será castigada* onwards. One noticeable result of this aesthetic sea-change is the omission of nudity, sex scenes and scenes of sexual violence.[8] Nelson's material has been cleaned up since the 1980s, despite the subject-matter, which makes for a less uncomfortable viewing experience. Fans of Nelson's work might well argue that something has been lost in the 1990s aesthetic, as part of Nelson's mission was to shake readers and spectators from their hypocritical complacency with regard to what goes on behind society's closed doors; a world bursting with filth and sleaze.

Nastiness and viewing discomfort make a return in the third instalment of *Traição*, José Henrique Fonseca's 'Cachorro!' ('Dog!'). In this episode another twenty-year jump takes place in the chronology to a setting in a down-market hotel room in present-day Rio de Janeiro. Action begins with a dying hotel receptionist, Fernanda Montenegro, trying to ring for help, as she bleeds to death on the floor of the hotel lobby. Having shot his way past her, a man, played by Alexandre Borges, storms into one of the bedrooms and catches his wife, played by Drica Moraes, in a romantic tryst with his best friend, played by the director himself. The plot revolves around the wife's attempt to convince her husband not to kill them both. In the end a waiter, who had unwittingly disturbed the hostage situation, shoots the husband, but not before the best friend has been badly wounded and the wife has been mercilessly stabbed in the palm of the hand. What we are left with is a veritable bloodbath, but despite this, the episode is the funniest of the three. The debt owed to Quentin Tarantino by the director is clear.

The episode was written by Patrícia Melo, a one-time journalist who has established a reputation as an author of violent contemporary thrillers.[9] This is an interesting aesthetic choice to portray the morbid and tortured world of Nelson Rodrigues, the effect of which is not unlike the experience of reading Nelson's fiction or reading one of his plays.[10] The feeling of unease and tension in the episode is relieved by humour based on bizarre incidents, dialogue and twists of fate, in a similar way to Tarantino's *Pulp Fiction*. Take, for example, the sequence in which a petrified Drica Moraes pleads with a volatile Alexandre Borges to let her live, and just as he is about to forgive her a waiter arrives at the door with a bottle of champagne, singing the words from a well-known bolero: *'Champanhe, para brindar o encontro'* (champagne to toast your date).

Stylish thrillers and films depicting mindless violence are two significant trends in contemporary Brazilian cinema, and their raison d'être have been convincingly argued, for example, in Ivana Bentes' chapter in this volume. Fonseca's episode is very reminiscent of Tata Amaral's 1997 film *Um céu de estrelas* (*A Starry Sky*), in which action is confined to a lower middle class dwelling in São Paulo, where a violent man murders his girlfriend's mother and takes the girlfriend hostage, until, in a surprise ending, she shoots him dead. The one element, of course, which is missing from this and other violent films is humour and, once again, the humour in this film works to remind the spectator that s/he is indulging in a spot of nostalgia. The intertextual references are there, for example when the best friend asks the husband to spit in his face: one of Nelson's favourite images of self-loathing. Despite the ultra-modern setting and cinematic style, this is inescapably an exercise in Rodrigan kitsch, and there is evidently no place in late-nineties nostalgic kitsch for a 'dirty' aesthetic. Just as in Tarantino's films, blood and guts are given a glossy veneer.

Gêmeas

In *Gêmeas* Fernanda Torres stars as identical twin sisters Iara and Marilena. Marilena meets and falls in love with Osmar (Evandro Mesquita). Until that time, the two sisters had 'shared' boyfriends, playing practical jokes on them by pretending to be each other as they took it in turns to care for their sick mother. Marilena is serious about Osmar, however, and warns Iara that he is not for sharing. Iara refuses to heed her sister's warning, and continues, behind Marilena's back, to play at being her twin sister. A seamstress by trade, she offers to make her sister's wedding dress, but to Marilena's horror she makes two identical dresses. Marilena, a biologist, decides that her only chance at happiness is by making a poison and killing her sister. But there is a twist in the tale, as always: Osmar is shocked to discover, after consumating his marriage, that he has married Iara. Marilena's body is found in the wardrobe, having been stabbed with a pair of scissors.

The similarities in terms of style between *Gêmeas* and 'She-Devil' are more than coincidental, as both films share the same scriptwriter (Elena Soárez), director of photography (Breno Silveira), art director (Gualter Pupo Filho), and three of the same actors (Fernanda Torres, Fernanda Montenegro and Francisco Cuoco).[11] *Gêmeas* is also based on a story from 'A vida como ela é', and was originally conceived as one more episode to form part of *Traição*. According to the director, when he arrived in the studio, he decided on the spot to make a feature-length film (75 minutes, in fact) with the material he had. It is almost inevitable that as a result the film feels like a stretched-out short, but in it the technical and story-telling talent of Andrucha Waddington can be seen. In 2000 Andrucha went on to release *Eu, tu, eles* (*Me You Them*), a film hotly tipped for international success.

Like *Traição*, *Gêmeas* is loaded with intertextual references to Nelson's work, the most striking of which is the appearance of Fernanda Montenegro at the beginning of the film, playing the dying mother. Her name is Zulmira, also the name of the title character in *A falecida*. Fernanda Montenegro, who is Andrucha Waddington's mother-in-law, and has also starred in a number of Nelson's plays on stage, played the leading role in Hirszman's 1965 film (the Oscar-nominated actress' first film role). She also appears in all three of the episodes of *Traição*, and is therefore used as a vehicle by which the four directors recognize a cinematic debt to previous adaptations of Nelson's work.[12]

What is perhaps more interesting than Andrucha Waddington's competent but unexceptional first film is the way in which he actively portrays himself in the media as a spontaneous, self-indulgent, cool and funny guy, telling tales of a wild youth and new-found happiness with actress wife Fernanda Torres. All this is very reminiscent of a Guy Ritchie-style (new) laddism that has had such an impact of late on British Cinema and its spectators, whereby the act of seeing a movie by a certain director, rather than the movie itself, can endow the spectator with the label 'cool', as if cinema were the new rock 'n roll.[13] The deliberate cheesiness and political incorrectness of the work of the oft-censored Nelson Rodrigues were made for both the contemporary audio-visual era, and for this self-consciously trendy production company.

Conclusion

The critic Sérgio Augusto, writing in 1981, declared that for screen adaptations of Nelson Rodrigues' fiction to work, they had to be unpleasant, unbearable, but with the right balance of humour.[14] In the same article he wrote that most of the directors who had dealt with Nelson's work up until then had been incompetent. None of the directors involved in the two productions considered in this article can be accused of being incompetent, and all of them have kept an eye on the comedy factor in their adaptations. Whether their films are sufficiently unpleasant and unbearable depends in part on the expectations of the spectator. An appreciation of Nelson's work fostered by *cinema rodrigueano*, and in particular the series of adaptations released in the 1970s and 1980s, is sure to result in disappointment, while an appreciation nurtured by the unchallenging alternative comedy shows on television, including Globo's miniseries based on the same newspaper series, is likely to result in approval.[15] *Traição* and *Gêmeas* will not change the face of Brazilian Cinema, nor do they intend to, but they do indicate a determination, on the part of Conspiração Filmes, to produce a watchable, well-made, commercially viable cinema which will, hopefully, play its part in convincing the Brazilian Cinema-going public that national cinema is a safe bet, because it can be good, as well as great and very bad.

NOTES

1.   The term *crônica* refers to short and entertaining factual or fictional pieces which established writers traditionally published in newspapers to supplement their income. In this chapter I will refer to Nelson's *crônicas* as short stories.

2.   Tropicalism, linked to the musical movement of the same name of the late 1960s, emphasized the grotesque and bad taste, with its kitsch style and use of gaudy colours. Tropicalist films tended to work by political indirection, often adopting allegorical forms as a coded language of revolt: Randal Johnson and Robert Stam (eds), *Brazilian Cinema* (New York, Columbia University Press, 1995), p 38.

The movement as a whole was linked to the cannibalist rhetoric of the Brazilian modernist movement of the 1920s, as clearly evidenced in the tropicalist film *Macunaíma* (Joaquim Pedro de Andrade, 1969).

3. Between 1970 and 1984 the Trapalhões team, a Brazilian version of the Three Stooges, starred in 14 of the 25 commercially most successful national films; *Cinejornal* (Embrafilme) 6 (1986). The two surviving stars, Renato Aragão and Dedé Santana, continue to make popular movies, appealing predominantly to children. Amácio Mazzaropi also starred in and later produced a series of popular comedy films from 1959 until his death in 1981. In his films he played the country bumpkin Jeca from the interior of the state of São Paulo. Both the Trapalhões team and Mazzaropi had loyal audiences of millions, and their films stuck rigidly to safe comedic formulas which had their roots in both the circus and vaudeville.

4. 'Saco de pancada', *Jornal do Brasil*, 14 October 1981.

5. A similar building is used to the same effect in, amongst other films, *Toda nudez será castigada*, *Engraçadinha* and *Gêmeas*.

6. The last film to attempt an expressionist reading of Nelson's work, Flávio Tambellini's 1966 feature *The Kiss,* was a disaster. It is interesting to note that one of the producers of *Traição* is Tambellini's son.

7. When the police chief throws Geraldo in prison, he tells the guard to put him in with the Bolivian thief, a humorous direct reference to *Toda nudez será castigada*. Other intertextual references in this episode include the presence in the cast of Jorge Doria, who had starred in four adaptations of Nelson's work between 1964 and 1983. Daniel Dantas had previously starred in *Engraçadinha*. The reference in the story to Alicinha being expelled from her private school for making a death pact with a fellow pupil is not in the original short story, but is reminiscent of the plays *Os sete gatinhos* (*The Seven Kittens*), *Perdoa-me por me traíres* and the newspaper serial 'O homem proibido' ('The Forbidden Man').

8. Braz Chediak, for example, thought nothing of filming the rape of a pregnant teenage girl in *Álbum de família*, a scene which does not appear in the original, shocking play.

9. See for example *O matador*, published in English by Bloomsbury Press as *The Killer* (London, 1997). José Henrique Fonseca is preparing a film version of the book.

10. Violence, as in the case of sex, only ever took place off-stage in Nelson's work.

11. The presence of the famously wooden soap actor Francisco Cuoco serves to remind us that such an audio-visual nostalgic journey inevitably includes both the good and the bad.

12. Fernanda Montenegro's role in 'O primeiro pecado', 'Cachorro!' and *Gêmeas*, in terms of the plot, is in fact superfluous.

13. Nick James, editor of *Screen* magazine, made this suggestion at the conference 'Brazilian Cinema: Roots of the present, perspectives for the future', held at the University of Oxford in June 2000.

14. 'Nas telas, os dividendos do autor do óbvio ululante', *Isto é*, 21 January 1981, p 40.
15. *A vida como ela é* (Rio, Globo, 1996). In the film's press notes, Arthur Fontes, whose episode is very similar in style to the Globo mini-series, makes a point of saying that 'O primeiro pecado' was filmed before the TV show.

12

An oblique gaze: irony and humour in Helvécio Ratton's *Love & Co*

Maria Esther Maciel

There should be at least,
As long as the truth is false,
Something true
In a way other than
The impossible certainty or reality.

Fernando Pessoa

The exploration of doubt and uncertainty was not one of the aims of the Portuguese writer Eça de Queiroz in the first two decades of his literary career. As a faithful follower of the principles of realism-naturalism in vogue at the end of the nineteenth century, he did not refrain from criticizing the excesses of the romantic imagination and from granting literature the function of portraying what he believed was the crude reality of facts.

At least until the middle of the 1880s, Eça de Queiroz was consistent in these convictions. He composed in their name his most popular novels, such as *O crime do padre Amaro* (*The Crime of Father Amaro*) and *O primo Basílio* (*The Cousin Basilio*), among others. In all of them, he treated love according to the laws of biology and the clauses of social contracts. He brought to the surface, by dint of explicit irony and humour, the sordid side of human relations, 'the ugly reality of things', the hypocrisy that upholds social conventions. In short, he worked out for himself and for his generation a literary project in which conclusive, even didactic precepts left no space for the fluctuations of uncertainty, imprecision and conjectures of thought.

However, this inflexibility did not always remain with him. It is known that Queiroz, in the last two decades of his life, had a more conflicting relation with the realist-naturalist school and his fiction opened room for contradiction and ambiguity. Critic Carlos Reis calls the attention to explicit touches of ambivalence in many of Queiroz's late works, in which dialogic voices and ironic subtleties are incorporated as important narrative elements into the critical investigation of reality.[1]

Helvécio Ratton found the point of departure for his film *Amor & Cia.* (*Love & Co*, 1998) precisely in a short novel from Queiroz's late literary career. I say 'point of departure' because, although the film follows the novel's narrative model, it does so through a form of non-complacent complicity, as we shall see.

Significantly, instead of looking for raw material in Queiroz's most popular and explicitly realist novels, such as *O primo Basílio*, surely more in tune with the demands of the contemporary film industry, Ratton chose to establish a dialogue with a novel that Eça de Queiroz himself did not seem to care for and to which he did not even give a title – a task which fell to the writer's son after his death. This novel, known as *Alves & Cia.* (*Alves & Co*), was probably written between 1877 and 1889, but was only published in 1925, and even today its place within the writer's oeuvre cannot be precisely defined.

As the author's son explains in the preface to the book:

> *Alves & Cia.* has no story. It does not explain itself. Its origin and date are unknown. And so is the title the author intended for it. *Alves & Cia.* is anonymous and unknown. The author has never referred to it in a letter or in a conversation or in an article. He never offered it to a publisher; he never even mentioned it.[2]

The film is therefore a work of both re-creation and recovery: in oblique ways, Ratton's version places Queiroz's novel in a position it never had in the literary canon of Portuguese literature. At the same time, the film revitalizes it by setting it in the cultural context of Brazil at the end of the twentieth century. Furthermore, the film brings to light a lesser-known side of the Portuguese writer in the period when his realist view of the world became more flexible. Ratton faces this challenge with sufficient cinematic force to construct a viable film. The literary basis does not hinder the

21. Alves (Marco Nanini) and Ludovina (Patrícia Pillar) in *Amor & Cia*.

autonomy of his film, which has already become a considerable contribution to Brazilian film history.

According to the director, screen adaptations of little known works by classic authors have at least two advantages: 'there will be less criticism on the part of critics and scholars of the author; and, regarding the audiences, the film is granted greater independence from the original text, because it has been little read.' Furthermore, according to him, that the original text was considered 'minor' and in a certain way 'incomplete' made his work of adaptation freer and more flexible.[3]

With a script by Carlos Alberto Ratton, photography by José Tadeu Ribeiro and art direction by Clóvis Bueno, *Amor & Cia.* is set in Minas Gerais (a southeastern state of Brazil) at the end of the nineteenth century, in the historical cities of São João del Rey and Tiradentes. It tells the story of a successful businessman, Godofredo Alves, who, upon arriving home early on the day of his fourth wedding anniversary, finds his wife, Ludovina, in the arms of his business-partner Machado.

The film's main deviations in relation to its literary basis are in the story, since Ratton reconnects facts, recontextualizes backgrounds, suppresses and adds scenes and characters, besides incorporating elements from Queiroz's other works. Conversely, there are obvious points of convergence in the narrative linearity and in the critical way the conflicts between love and money, marriage and business, in the bourgeois society of the nineteenth century are displayed. Furthermore, certain literary marks of enunciation are transposed to the screen, involving Queiroz's ironic strategies in the deployment of the plot. If we compare the two narratives, considering both the factual aspects of the story and the strategies of irony and humour employed, we may perceive that Ratton's film contains much more ambiguity and subtlety than the novel. This is because he explores and intensifies the irony which is apparent in a less obvious form in Queiroz's late production, which I called, earlier in this chapter, 'the exploration of doubt and uncertainty'.

Indeed, the book *Alves & Cia.*, while focusing on the issue of adultery, does not do so in the same way as the novel *O primo Basílio*, for example, whose tone is given by what Machado de Assis called the 'minute, almost technical description of adulterous relations';[4] instead, adultery is depicted through an ingenious play of deceptions. Even though Ludovina's act of infidelity is explicit, since the narrator's omniscient voice leads to this certainty, the plot deploys an intricate play of contradictions involving all the characters. If, on the one hand, they are moved by self-interest and self-advancement as they try to dismiss the proofs of adultery and convince us to the contrary, on the other hand, the narrator disavows them through humour and irony. Thus certainty is not given directly but is mediated by artifice and contradiction.

In the case of the film *Amor & Cia.*, those who fall into the trap of contradiction are not only the characters, but also the audience. This is because the 'eye' of the camera shuffles the points-of-view and the references, choosing a paradoxical and elliptical focus on the events. It may be said that Eça de Queiroz's irony in the novel has the function of unmasking, between the lines, what the characters try to falsify in the story, while Ratton's irony has the role of maintaining the said and the unsaid, the seen and the unseen, in a state of tension and mobility. This kind of irony fits into the category described by Linda Hutcheon as 'inclusive', that takes place simultaneously in conjunction and disjunction between the *this* and the *that*; when confronted with the choice between two mutually exclusive things, one chooses both of them, which means in the end that one chooses neither.[5] On this point, I also see in the film a concealed, almost underground, dialogue with Machado de Assis' novel *Dom Casmurro*. Indeed, some echoes of the artifices of ambiguity used by the nineteenth century

Brazilian author in treating the theme of adultery are apparent in the construction of the film's narrative. These procedures, as pointed out above, appear in Queiroz's second phase, but with a less structural function than in Machado de Assis' work.

Let us take some factual examples from the story. When in the novel *Alves & Cia*. the narrator describes the moment in which Alves catches Ludovina 'leaning on the shoulder' of gallant Machado, some of the details already give evidence of adultery. The fact, for example, that she is dressed in a *robe de chambre*, suggests a degree of intimacy between them. The first words Ludovina speaks to her husband through the narrator's voice, referring to her relationship with Machado, will reinforce these clues. I quote Eça de Queiroz:

> Avidly, as one who holds on so as not to fall, she accused Machado. It had been he, only he who had been guilty. It had begun four months ago... And then... she spoke to him, and wrote to him, and he tempted her, and went there when Godofredo was at the office, and one day, finally, almost by force... [6]

Besides this impulsive 'confession', the letters written by Ludovina, found by her husband, also begin to contribute effectively to the set of clues. In the novel, the exchange of love letters is confirmed both by her and by Machado, even though they are considered by both as 'foolish letters' and the husband finds only those his wife wrote, which, strangely, were not in the possession of their addressee. Even when Alves' friends – moved by self-interest – try to falsify the context in which the letters were written, the fact of their having been addressed to the presumed lover is at no time questioned in the book. The doubt that remains is whether these are the actual letters that were exchanged by the two.

Within this framework, some points related to the fluctuations of Alves' temperament may be observed, which serve to reinforce the play of deceptions Eça de Queiroz built around his characters. According to the narrator – and here Queiroz's usual contempt for romantic stereotypes makes an appearance – Alves had a core of romantic sentimentality inherited from his mother, which comes to the surface at the end of the first chapter and is explored through humour: challenges to a duel, suicidal thoughts, impulsive gestures, all these disrupt, in a comic and melodramatic way, the character's life throughout the novel. This is more evident when he gradually gets involved in the game of self-interest set up by the other characters, such as the maid-servant who knows too much, the friends agreeing on 'problems of honour', the self-interested father-in-law, and Machado himself, who cares about saving the business more than anything else. But the fact is that in the name of 'prudence' Alves ends up convinced that the adultery did not really take place. He thus erases, or pretends to erase from his memory, the words spoken by Ludovina right after she is caught, and he accepts a second version given by her and reinforced by his counsellors: that that had been the first time. In the ironic narration of all this, Queiroz humorously criticizes a hypocritical society motivated by money and personal interests.

The film *Amor & Cia.* follows more oblique paths in dealing with these same matters. If we take, for example, the strategies used in the composition of the *mise en scène* of the moment when Alves surprises the two presumed lovers, we can already detect some of the peculiarities of Ratton's approach.

If the variations of the narrative point of view proper to literary prose generally make up the greatest challenge to anyone undertaking adaptation, regarding *Amor & Cia.* it may be said that the director succeeds in making variations of the narrative point of view and cinematically translating some of the details present in Queiroz's description of the scene just described. The character's movement towards the room where the supposed lovers are to be found, for example, visually follows, together with the rhythm of Tavinho Moura's cunning music, the same pace of stealthy footsteps described in the novel. In order to recreate in images Queiroz's narrative point of view, which in this case is free indirect discourse, Ratton uses a subtle strategy: instead of the semi-drawn curtains from where, in the novel, Alves views the scene, he places between the character and the room a large glass door. The camera then captures the scene from two rapidly alternated, nearly simultaneous, positions: from outside the parlour, at the angle from which the husband (played by Marco Nanini) sees everything; and from the inside, focusing, also through the mediation of the glass door, on the livid face of the husband. This is swiftly followed by a new angle, that could be interpreted as the angle of omniscience and objectivity, through which the 'eye' of the camera, now without the mediation of the glass, is displaced to the scene of the two startled characters getting up.

In my opinion, the glass door has a fundamental role. As the glass is thick and divided into several sections by wooden frames, the image seen by the husband appears, for a few seconds, distorted and fragmented. I believe that it is precisely here, in the combination of clearness (third person) and cloudiness (subjective angle), where the subtle play of ambiguities begins. Besides working as a metaphor for the camera lens itself, the glass points to the hazy and fragmented vision of the character, especially because in other parts of the film he will appear to be gazing at reality diffusely 'through a glass darkly'. As the critic José Geraldo Couto says, 'everything is shown, but nothing is very clear – and this absence of certainty intensifies the torment of jealousy'.[7]

If, for the spectator, the question of adultery is taken as irrefutable in this scene, considering the physical closeness of the presumed lovers and the context in which everything happens, this certainty will be gradually toned down by moments of doubt regarding an *effective* (sexual) relationship between Ludovina and Machado. In contrast to the character in the novel, Ludovina (played by Patrícia Pillar) does not wear a *robe de chambre* when she meets Machado (Alexandre Borges), but a low-cut summer dress. Nor does she make any impulsive and compromising confession. The love letters make an appearance, but without a visible addressee. Besides, neither of the two involved in the supposed affair admits there has been any exchange of correspondence.

Indeed, Ratton takes advantage of the letters to entangle the references even more, taking from another novel of Queiroz's, *O Primo Basílio*, new elements for his plot. In this novel, an adulterous wife is described as a devoted reader of Alexandre Dumas' *Camille*, and this detail is transposed to the film in a sly way: when the seconds for Alves and Machado meet to discuss the terms of the duel, one of them reads (slightly falsifying the words in order to make them serve his intentions more than anything else) the fragment of some of Ludovina's love letters, followed by another who reads identical passages from *La Dame aux Camélias*, supposedly copied by her, on the pretence of passing the time. In the plot, this strategy contributes to place under suspicion the authorship of the letters; the doubt about the sincerity of the characters involved lingers on. To this is also added the hilarious fact that Machado swears, on the life of his sick mother, that there was no 'physical intercourse' between him and Ludovina, and, at the end of the film, his mother actually dies. This is a typical case of 'irony of fate', which in the story functions not only as a comic element but also as an additional artifice for the entanglement of the evidences.

Another point to be considered regards the treatment given to Ludovina's pregnancy – which does not exist in the novel. This pregnancy, which provides the story with a romantic flavour, generates another doubt: who is the child's father, Alves or Machado? Ludovina categorically asserts to her father that the child is her husband's, but is apprehensive because she knows that, in these circumstances, he will not believe it. What follows is all a game of dissimulation on her part to conceal the situation from Alves and society. At the end of the film, when the son is 'adopted' by the couple, as if he were not one of their own and belonged to all three at the same time, we witness the legitimization of this very doubt and ambiguity, especially because everything has been happening to the accompaniment of the characters' oblique glances, smiles at the corners of the mouth, dissembling and unsaid words. At the end, it falls to the audience to ask, *à la* Machado de Assis: 'Well, and the rest?'

It can be said that the end of the film, which does justice to the deliberate play of contradictions pervading the plot, confuses questions of money (the company) and questions of feeling (love) in a different way from Eça de Queiroz's novel, where the financial considerations predominate. If the reconciliation of the couple is basically justified, in the literary text, by capitalist logic, the final scene shown on the screen points to a double movement: the attempt to preserve both the good business of the firm (a realistic solution to the problem) and the couple's love relationship (a romantic solution for Alves' suffering). In this sense, as Abas Kiarostami (president of the jury of the Mar del Plata Film Festival, which gave Ratton the prize for 'Best Latin-American Film') pointed out, *Amor & Cia.* is a mixture of farce and melodrama: a farce for its burlesque features and critical view of the customs of the period; melodrama, for the way the film treats the relationship of Alves and Ludovina.

Furthermore, at the end of the film, it is possible to consider Alves' attitude in relation to the child and Ludovina as one which disregards both the standards of the nineteenth century novel and the masculine stereotype of the time. As Ratton explains, by adopting Ludovina's son (who may or may not be his own), Alves acts like a modern man, anticipating a certain type of masculine behaviour of the twentieth century.[8] In the off screen space, Alves and Ludovina make a secret pact regarding the problem of the child (the audience is not informed about the nature of the 'truths' that Ludovina tells her husband) in spite of the inevitable comments and critical looks of society, represented by those attending the christening. If, in Eça de Queiroz's book, Alves is not capable of any generous gesture, concerned as he is with his own financial interests and social reputation, this gesture is present in the film, which shows, once again, the non-complacent sense of complicity with the novel and its variegated, unorthodox focus on bourgeois marriage.

By means of such strategies, Ratton has made an amusing, outstanding film, both for its formal and technical qualities. The plot is a successful balance of drama and comedy. Ratton uses precise metaphors to create comic scenes around the awkward, bewildered figure of the jealous husband. He manages to transfer the story, in a natural way, to the context of Minas Gerais in the period immediately after the end of slavery. The mountainous landscape and colonial architecture of São João del Rey (which at the time was going through an economic boom thanks to the arrival of the railroad) are also significant visual elements in the composition and setting of the film. One might also mention the song 'Quem sabe' ('Who Knows'), by the nineteenth century Brazilian composer Carlos Gomes, which, both in Ludovina's voice and in the arrangement of the Minas Gerais born composer Tavinho Moura, is heard throughout the film, with the purpose of underlining these moments of the plot. Behind and throughout the whole, a critique of the false virtues that sustained (and still sustain) the provincial bourgeois society of Minas is also suggested.

Even if there is no radical attempt at deconstructing the narrative model of the original text, *Amor & Cia.*, as an adaptation, proves to be what Octavio Paz would call a subtle 'exercise of otherness' in relation to the literary text. Through its oblique look at the Queiroz novel, Helvécio Ratton is constantly telling, through the gaps of that look, that every work of translation/re-creation implies an act of infidelity.

Translation by Tom Burns

NOTES

1.   Carlos Reis, 'The Last Novels of Eça de Queiroz: Realism as a Problem', *Portuguese Studies* 14 (1998), p 86.
2.   Eça de Queiroz, *Alves & Cia.* (Lisboa, 1958), p 421.
3.   Helvécio Ratton in a letter to the author.
4.   Machado de Assis, 'Eça de Queiroz: *O Primo Basílio*', in *Obras completas III* (Rio de Janeiro, 1985), p 913.
5.   Linda Hutcheon, *Irony's Edge* (London/New York, 1995), p 51.
6.   Queiroz: *Alves & Cia.*, p 435.
7.   José Geraldo Couto, 'Amor & Cia. traduz em cinema ironia de Eça', *Folha de S. Paulo*, 6 November 1998, p 2.
8.   Ratton in a letter to the author.

Part six

History and film history

13

Cabral and the Indians: filmic representations of Brazil's 500 years

Robert Stam

In the year 2000, Brazil commemorated the 500 years of national history since the arrival of Pedro Álvares Cabral on the shores of what the Portuguese then called 'Vera Cruz'. In this chapter, I would like to examine filmic representations of the European/indigenous encounter in Brazil. I will discuss the more salient avatars of the figure of the Indian – the romantic Indian, the patriotic Indian, the tropicalist Indian and so forth – leading up to the documentary and fiction films of the 1990s. Strategically chosen films drawn from successive periods of Brazilian cinema will illustrate the various incarnations of 'Indianness' constructed by Brazilian cinema, against a comparative backdrop of North American cinema and culture. I will be taking a 'cultural studies' approach, seeing film as part of a larger discursive continuum that includes other arts and media such as popular music and television. Needless to say, I will not provide a comprehensive survey or even in-depth analyses of single films, something I attempt in my book *Tropical Multiculturalism: A Comparative History of Race in Brazilian Cinema and Culture*.[1]

In both Brazil and the USA, the Indian became a symbol of national resistance to European domination. Yet the national contexts were also different. While North American ideology tended to promote myths of separation, and the doomed nature of love between White and Indian, the romantic poets and novelists of the 'indianist' movement of the mid nineteenth century, for example, saw Brazil as the product of the fusion of the indigenous peoples with the European element, a fusion figured in the marriage of the Indian Iracema and the European Martins in José de Alencar's novel *Iracema*, or the love of the indigenous Peri and the European Ceci in the same novelist's *O guarani*. Brazilian ideology promoted myths of fusion, transmitted by what Doris Sommer calls 'foundational romances' of love between European and indigene.[2] And while Brazilian literature promoted heterosexual romance – Indian men loving white women (*O guarani*) or Indian women loving white men (*Iracema*) – seen as generative of a mestizo nation, American literature stressed homosocial bonding between white frontiersmen and the native American male.[3] Nonetheless, it is hard *not* to discern the transnational resemblances of such figures as Pocahontas in the United States, and Paraguaçu and Iracema in Brazil.

Even now, the cultural industries of both countries return obsessively to the theme of European/indigene romance. Recent years brought us not only the Disney *Pocahontas*, but also films like *O guarani* (*The Guarani*, Norma Bengell, 1996) and TV series like *A muralha* (*The Wall*, Carlos Araújo and Luís Henrique Rios, 2000) in Brazil. The Globo miniseries *A invenção do Brasil* (*The Invention of Brazil*, 2000), by Guel Arraes and Jorge Furtado, in this sense, commemorates the 500 years through a witty mixed-genre study of Brazilian identity. Most of the miniseries is devoted to telling a foundational fiction which precedes even those of nineteenth century romanticism, to wit the story of the romance between the Portuguese cartographer and portrait painter Diogo Álvares Correia (renamed 'Caramuru' in Brazil) and the Indian princess Paraguaçu, the daughter of the chief of the Tupinambás in Bahia. Unlike Indianist novels like *Iracema*, the Caramuru story is based on a real relationship, subsequently embroidered with legend. What we know about Diogo Álvares is that he arrived in Brazil in a wrecked ship at the beginning of Portuguese colonization, after which he resided in Bahia for many decades, always in sporadic contact with the Portuguese. He learned the languages and customs of the Indians and participated in local wars, thus gaining the respect of Indian chiefs. He married Paraguaçu in France on 30 July 1528, in the presence of the King, and subsequently had children with her (and probably with other indigenous women). According to the legend, Diogo Álvares subsequently became 'King of Brazil', reigning over the Tupinambás for over 50 years. As Janaína Amado points out, Caramuru and Paraguaçu represent symbolic parents of Brazil, which is why all the versions of their story reference their many descendants.[4] The TV series is just the latest twist in a multi-century intertext. The story of Caramuru has been worked and reworked by many authors of diverse nationalities – Gabriel Soares de Sousa, Gregório de Matos, Sebastião da Rocha Pita, Francisco Adolfo de Varnhagen, Arthur Lobo d'Ávila, João de Barros, Claude d'Abbeville, Robert Southey – but it became part of Brazilian popular imaginary thanks to Frei José de Santa Rita Durão's epic poem *Caramaru* (1781). Caramuru and Paraguaçu have formed the theme for samba school presentations, and they were celebrated at Salvador's quincentennial carnival.

Invenção do Brasil opens with a counterpoint of perspectives concerning the arrival of the Portuguese – alternating the Portuguese view from the ships with the Tupiniquim view from the shore – in order to discover 'who we – we Brazilians – are.' The series' narrator relates how the Portuguese, looking through telescopes from the ships, were astonished by the paradisiacal qualities of the land and the naked beauty of the women, while the Tupiniquins, looking from the shore, were astonished by the overdressed and foul-smelling Portuguese. Each group brought its intertextual mythologies to the encounter: the Europeans imagined the Garden of Eden and Eldorado, and the Tupiniquins the 'Land without Evil'.

Invenção do Brasil brilliantly interweaves maps, paintings, archival footage, digital simulacra, staged scenes, all backed up by highly syncretic music which evokes the 'multi-nation' cultures at the roots (routes) of Brazil. Throughout Arraes/Furtado deploy anachronism as a device, linking Cabral to Neil Armstrong, Renaissance maps to satellite TV, and the Voyages of Discovery to a theme park ride. At one point, the narrator appears in a helicopter over the coast of Brazil trying to rescue Diogo, but laments that we can't help Diogo since 'we're 500 years too late.' Diogo's status as a portrait painter becomes a pretext for reflexive discussions about art and censorship, the nature of artistic realism and so forth. Throughout, the series is densely, but charmingly, informative, telling us, for example, that while Portugal in 1500 had roughly a million inhabitants, Brazil had six million Indians (Tabarajas, Tamoios, Tapuias, Tupinambás, Aimorés, Carijós, Caetés and so forth). The Portuguese language, we are told, incorporated four thousand Tupi-Guarani words, and Tupi remained the *lingua franca* up until the middle of the eighteenth century.

The attempt at a contrapuntal, polyperspectival approach sketched out in the overture sequence is compromised, unfortunately, by a number of features of the miniseries: (1) the predominance of a Eurocentric perspective throughout; (2) the 'redface' convention whereby non-Indians play Indian characters; (3) the white narrator who relays *all* the perspectives; (4) the ultimate falling back into a venerable 'foundational fiction', to wit the idyllic story of the marriage between Diogo and Paraguaçu. The historical/legendary love affair of Diogo/Paraguaçu recapitulates the gendered trope whereby European man plus indigenous woman equals Brazil. (Missing are both the indigenous man and African men and women.) The whole series is imbued with a sexualized telos – one which obviously nourishes high ratings – whereby everything moves toward a predestined erotic encounter. The story even becomes a kind of harem fantasy since Diogo enjoys access not only to Paraguaçu but also to her equally beautiful sister, thanks to the Indians' convenient lack of sexual jealousy. But this lack of jealousy benefits only the European man; Indian men in the series have no erotic agency whatsoever. The series is also interesting in terms of class mobility. It presents Diogo as a *degredado*, a transported convict, while Paraguaçu is a 'princess' who becomes the 'queen' of the 'King of Brazil'. Diogo also illustrates the perennial tendency to allegorize the Americas as female, as encapsulated in the moment where the protagonist describes Paraguaçu's body in geographical terms – remember he is a cartographer – so that her head is Europe, her breasts are North Africa, and so on within a voyage of sexual/anatomical/geographical discovery.

The romantic Indian
Invenção do Brasil prolongs a tradition that goes back to the very beginnings of Brazilian cinema. From its start at the turn of the century, Brazilian cinema has often performed variations on the themes first set down by literary *Indianismo* in the nineteenth century. The silent period of cinema offers a marked contrast between American and Brazilian Cinema. American cinema developed a schizophrenic discourse, positing the Indian both as noble victim and as bloodthirsty savage, within the discourse of conquest and 'manifest destiny'. Brazilian filmmakers, many of them immigrants, in contrast, did not stress conquest. Rather, they gave cinematic prolongation to the romantic Indianist tradition, while shying away from representations of black Brazilians, who become a

kind of structuring absence in silent cinema. Although no
Brazilian film of the first few decades advances an explicitly racist
perspective – there is no Brazilian *Birth of a Nation* (David Wark
Griffith, 1915) – one is struck by the frequent, almost obsessive
adaptation of Indianist novels such as *O Guarani* (four versions in
the silent period), *Iracema* (three versions) and *Ubirajara* (one version), in contrast with the general slighting of Afro-Brazilian
themes. The mythification of the Indian, unfortunately, involved
an element of bad faith toward both Indian and Black. By celebrating the fusion of an idealized noble Indian with an equally idealized noble European, such novels as *Iracema* and *O Guarani* prettified conquest and neglected the Black, seen at that time purely
as a source of labour, without rights of citizenship.

Silent cinema celebrated the Indian as 'brave warrior', as the
naively good and deeply spiritual source and symbol of Brazil's
nationhood. But this exaltation of the Indian was dedicated to
the very group being victimized by a process of literal and cultural genocide. While the actually existing Indian was destroyed,
marginalized, or eliminated through miscegenation, the remote
Indian was idealized. The ambiguous 'compliment' toward the
Indian became a means of avoiding the vexed question of slavery.
The proud history of black *quilombos* (settlements created by runaway slaves from colonial farms) was ignored; the brave Indian, it
was subtly insinuated, resisted slavery while Blacks did not. The
white filmmakers of the early decades of this century, in sum,
chose the safely distant and mythically connoted Indian over the
more problematically present Black, victim of a slavery abolished
just ten years before Afonso Segreto filmed the first Brazilian
'views' in 1898.

In Brazilian Cinema, Indians, who had the legal status of
'wards of the State', were not allowed to represent themselves.
Indeed, during the filming of the second adaptation of *O Guarani*
in 1926, the director Vittorio Capellaro was interrogated by the
police for showing Indians in his films, when 'there has been so
much progress in this region.'[5] Some Indian roles were performed
by black actors like Benjamin de Oliveira, the first Afro-Brazilian
film actor. While in the USA white actors like Al Jolson performed
in blackface, in Brazil black actors performed, as it were, in 'redface'. Thus Blacks played Indians in a situation where neither
Black nor Indian had power over self-representation.

The documented Indian

There is a marked tension, in the silent period, between the 'indi-anist' adaptations and the 'documentary' record provided by film-makers like Major Tomás Luiz Reis and Silvino Santos in the 1910s and 1920s, and even those of Claude Lévi-Strauss in the 1930s. In these films, we see actually existing semi-nude Indians, observed by white men in suits, shooting arrows, grinding corn, breastfeeding and dancing. Here it is important to underline a historical contrast between the USA and Brazil. Unlike the US, the Brazilian government rarely sent armies to crush the Indians; instead, it sent positivists, pacifiers and the Indian Protection Service. The discourse, if not the practice, furthermore, was paternalist, benev-olent, cordial. Instead of violent figures like Custer and Andrew Jackson, Brazil produced benevolent figures who presided 'cor-dially' over processes which, in the end, still worked to dispossess the indigenous people. The 19teens and the 1920s were the era of the Rondon Commission, named after the young Army officer who became famous as the 'pacifier' of Indians. The Army and Rondon were very much influenced by positivism, and their goal was to catapult Indians from what the positivists perceived as a state of 'barbarism' into the scientific stage. The most famous of Rondon's pacifications were those of the Bororo and the Nambiquara. Despite his generous discourse – crystallized in his famous slogan 'Die, if need be, but never kill!' – Rondon's goal was ultimately to turn Indians into Brazilians, so that they would choose 'civilization' of their own free will.

Photography and cinema played a major role in memorializing these pacification campaigns. Major Tomás Luiz Reis was the head of the photographic division of the Rondon Commission in Mato Grosso, and his films were designed to garner funding for the Commission. Reis even arranged screenings of his films at Carnegie Hall in 1918, presided over by ex-President Theodore Roosevelt, who had accompanied Rondon on scientific expeditions in the Amazon.[6] In *Rituais e festas bororo* (*Bororo Rituals and Feasts*, 1916), Reis focuses on funeral rites, always emphasizing the Indians' difference from Western society. The final title indirectly invokes Cabral: 'We had the sensation of witnessing the remote times of the Discovery.' In *Os sertões do Mato Grosso* (*The Backlands of Mato Grosso*, 1916), a record of the installation of telegraph lines in the interior of Brazil, Reis depicted what he called 'the pacification of numerous Indian tribes encountered in a primitive, Stone Age state.'⁷ *Ao redor do Brasil* (*Around Brazil*, filmed between 1924 and 1930), meanwhile, documents the flora, fauna, and social practices of the region, usually presenting the Indians directly to the camera, or in profile, as if Reis were cataloguing them.

The modernist Indian
The 1920s also featured another version of the Brazilian Indian, that of the modernist movement in literature and the arts, a movement which unfortunately never linked up with Brazilian Cinema. Instead of the 'bon sauvage' of the Romantics, the *modernistas* preferred the 'Bad Indian', the cannibal, the devourer of the white colonizer. The modernists made the trope of cannibalism the basis of an insurgent aesthetic, calling for an 'anthropophagic' devouring of the techniques and information of the developed countries in order the better to struggle against domination. Modernism articulated cannibalism as anti-colonialist metaphor in its 'Cannibalist Reviews' and 'Anthropophagic Manifestoes' and its famous slogan: 'Tupi or not Tupi, that is the question,' i.e. whether Brazilian intellectuals should 'go native' by symbolically imitating the putatively cannibalistic Tupinambás or alienate themselves into European domination. *Modernismo* also took a critical position toward Cabral and the *Conquista*, calling for the 'de-Cabralization' and the 'de-Vespucciazation' of the Americas (the reference being to Amerigo Vespucci).⁸ Radicalizing the Enlightenment valorization of indigenous Amerindian freedom, it highlighted aboriginal matriarchy and communalism as a utopian model for a society free of coercion and hierarchy, without police or capitalism. As it did for the European *philosophers*, philo-indigenism enabled a deep anthropological critique of the political and moral bases of Eurocentric civilization. (The movement reached the cinema, as we shall see, only with *Cinema Novo* in the 1960s.)

The patriotic Indian
In the late 1930s, Humberto Mauro's *O descobrimento do Brasil* (*The Discovery of Brazil*, 1937) was sponsored by the Cocoa Institute, a large landowners' organization, i.e. in a sense by the latter-day heirs of the *capitanias*. *Descobrimento* relays the official version of the European-indigenous encounter. First proposed as a project by Roquette Pinto, the film draws on various intertexts. First, Mauro chooses that version of history which sees Cabral's 'discovery' as intentional rather than accidental. Mauro bases his por-

trayal on the famous letter, often called the 'birth certificate of Brazil', that Pero Vaz de Caminha, official scribe of the Portuguese fleet, sent to the Portuguese monarch. Focalized even more than Cabral, Caminha is the protagonist-narrator of the film, the scribe whose écriture gives birth to the scene displayed. But the staging of the encounter in *Descobrimento* was also inspired by a famous painting by Victor Meirelles, entitled 'The First Mass', painted in Paris in 1860 and itself inspired by a French painting set in North Africa, Horace Vernet's 'Première Messe en Kabilie'. The Meirelles painting places the Portuguese centre frame in a shady grove under a canopy of tall trees. The climactic 'First Mass' sequence of the Mauro film clearly picks up on the cues provided by the painting, as seen most conspicuously in the repeated long shot of Europeans and Indians gathered around the cross.

A discursive palimpsest, the Mauro film 'embeds' multiple discourses drawn from diverse historical periods: the Christianizing mentality of the *Conquista*, the romantic idealizations of nineteenth century *Indianismo*, the scientistic optimism of positivism, and the populist nationalism of Vargas' New State. Like the Hollywood films devoted to Columbus, the Mauro film idealizes the European 'discoverer' and sacralizes conquest. The choral, religiously connoted music by Villa-Lobos 'blesses' the conquest with a religious aura, while at the same time incorporating some indigenous motifs. Unlike the 1949 Hollywood version, where the Indians have no voice whatsoever, the Mauro film has the 'Indians' actually speak Tupi-Guarani, although the lack of subtitles makes their words incomprehensible both to the Portuguese characters and to non-Tupi speaking spectators. The Indians are not seen as menacing as in the Hollywood versions, but rather as innocent, harmless, and not completely in control of their own bodies. Their scripted behaviour mirrors their official legal status as children in need of protection. Although they happen to reside on the land, it is suggested, they do not really deserve to dominate it. Despite linguistic self-representation, the film has its native mimic men applaud what must have been an alien ceremony, while the actor playing Caminha gently covers the nakedness of an Indian woman. The Indians abandon their own beliefs and culture, it is implied, in order to embrace Christianity and the culture of Europe as irresistibly true. Their genuflexions translate into veristic audio-visual representation the fantasy of the conquistadores: that reading a document in a European language to uncomprehending natives signifies a legitimate transfer of ownership. In short, the Indians are perfectly good candidates for European disciplining, Christianization and dispossession. This paternalist undercurrent did not go unremarked at the time. Novelist Graciliano Ramos, in one of his chronicles, denounced the film for idealizing what was ultimately nothing more than a violent conquest which prettified the 'invaders who came to enslave and assassinate indigenous peoples.'

Glauber Rocha's *Terra em transe* (*Land in Anguish*, 1967), a baroque allegory about Brazilian politics, offers a contrasting, 'unofficial' representation of Pedro Álvares Cabral. While *Descobrimento* was a kind of superproduction, with caravelas constructed for the film and the proverbial cast of thousands, *Terra em transe* is a low-budget exemplar of what Rocha himself called the 'aesthetics of hunger'. While the Mauro film deploys an aesthetic of realistic reconstruction, the Rocha film is trans-realist, interested less in reconstruction than in making us reflect on the historical process. While in no way a film 'about' Indians, the film does feature a remarkable sequence which alludes to the 'First Mass'. In a fantasy sequence dreamed by the narrator-protagonist Paulo Martins, the right wing figure of the film (named Porfirio Diaz after the Mexican dictator), arrives from the sea, in a scene suggesting a myth of origins. Much as Walter Benjamin spoke of 'memories flashing up in a moment of danger,' whereby repressed aspects of history take on fresh meaning in the light of contemporary crises, here Rocha, in the wake of the traumatic 1964 coup d'état, conjures up the memory of Cabral. Diaz's ritual raising of the chalice, and the outsized cross, references Cabral's 'First Mass', and even Mauro's filmic version of it, but in an anachronistic manner which stresses the continuities between the conquest and contemporary oppression; the contemporary putschist is portrayed as the latter-day heir of the conquistadores. Diaz, with his religion of violence, has replaced the priest, with his religion of love. And while both the 1937 Mauro film and the 1949 Hollywood Columbus film show the natives in postures of servility and worship, here there is neither genuflexion nor submission.

Rocha further destabilizes meaning by making Africa a textual presence. The very aesthetic of the sequence, first of all, draws heavily from the Africanized forms of Rio's yearly samba pageant, with its zany forms of historicism, its polyrhythms, and its delight in extravagant *alegorias* and *fantasias* (costumes); indeed, the actor who plays the conquistador is Clovis Bornay, a historian specializing in carnival pageantry and well-researched 'allegories', and a well-known figure from Rio's carnival; secondly, the mass is accompanied not by Christian religious music, but by Yoruba religious chants, evoking the *transe* of the Portuguese title. Rocha's suggestive referencing of African music, as if Africans had been in Brazil prior to the arrival of Europeans, reminds us not only of the 'continental drift' theory that sees South America and Africa as once having formed part of a single land mass, but also of the theories of Ivan van Sertima and others that Africans arrived in the New World 'before Columbus'.[9] (Needless to say, I am not positing conscious intentionality on Rocha's part.) The sequence even resonates with the recent discovery of Luzia, a skeleton thought to be over 11,000 years old and said to have Negroid features. (A 1992 samba pageant presentation by Vila Isabel, interestingly, also staged a pre-Columbian African presence in the Americas by including simulacra of the Mexican Olmec statues as part of the *alegoria*.) Africans, the music suggests, as those who shaped and were shaped by the Americas over centuries, are in some uncanny sense *also* indigenous to the region.

The sequence displays a dazzling aesthetic originality. It exemplifies what I would call a 'trance-Brechtian' aesthetic, through which Rocha manages to Tropicalize, Africanize, and carnivalize the theories of Bertolt Brecht. While Brechtianism deploys contradiction and disjunction between image and sound, here Rocha goes farther by a staging of the historical contradictions between vast cultural complexes existing in relations of subordination and domination, where the Chalice (or *Cale-se* – Shut up – as Chico Buarque would put it) of Catholicism is superimposed on music which incarnates precisely the religion historically suppressed by Christianity. Here music represents not merely a factor of disjunction but also the return of the historically repressed. Instead of the austerity and minimalism which characterizes a certain Brechtian tradition in the cinema, we find a multi-layered saturation of image and sound, a hysterical Trauerspiel linked both to carnival and to *Candomblé* (an Afro-Brazilian religion). The scene's fractured and discontinuous aesthetic stages the drama of life in the colonial 'contact zone', defined by Mary Louise Pratt as the space in which 'subjects previously separated' encounter each other within 'conditions of coercion, radical inequality, and intractable conflict'. Rocha's neo-baroque Afro-avant-gardist aesthetic here figures the discontinuous, dissonant, fractured history of the multi-nation through equally dissonant images and sounds.

The tropicalist Indian

Terra em transe was a strong influence on the films of the third 'oral-cannibalistic-tropicalist-allegorical' phase of *Cinema Novo* (1968-1971), where filmmakers turned for inspiration to the modernist writers of the 1920s and especially to Oswald de Andrade's notion of 'anthropophagy'. While cannibalism was also a common trope among European avant-gardists, only in Brazil did anthropophagy become a key trope in a cultural movement which was to prolong itself over many decades, ranging from the first *Cannibalistic Review* in the 1920s, with its various 'dentitions', through Oswald de Andrade's speculations in the 1950s concerning Anthropophagy as 'the philosophy of the technicized primitive', to the pop-recyclings of the metaphor in the Tropicalist movement of the late 1960s. As exploited by the Brazilian modernists, the cannibalist metaphor had a positive and negative pole. The positive pole posited aboriginal matriarchy and communalism as utopian model, while the negative pole made cannibalism a critical instrument for exposing the exploitative social Darwinism implicit in 'savage capitalism' and bourgeois civility.

Mario de Andrade's 1928 novel *Macunaíma* formed the epitome of the modernist movement and the powerful precursor of what later came to be called 'magical realism'. The novel's author, himself of mixed racial ancestry, culturally and phenotypically embodied the indigenous, African and European inheritance, giving him a proleptic sense of what later was to be called 'nomadic' and 'palimpsestic' identity. Of the two poles of the cannibalist metaphor, Joaquim Pedro de Andrade's 1969 adaptation of *Macunaíma* clearly emphasizes the negative pole.[10] Fusing what he knew of Oswald's anthropophagical movement with the theme of cannibalism which runs through the Andrade novel, the director turns cannibalism into the springboard for a critique of repressive military rule and of the predatory capitalist model of the short-lived Brazilian 'economic miracle'.

While *Macunaíma* does not stage the Europe/indigene encounter per se, it does stage the results of nearly 500 years of conquest and miscegenation. The names of the family members –Macunaíma, Jiguê, Manaape – are Indian, but the family is at once Black, Indian and European. The décor and costumes are oxymoronic, syncretic, culturally miscegenated. A sequence of racial transformation, in which black/Indian Macunaíma (Grande Otelo) turns into the white Macunaíma (Paulo José), ironically alludes to the Indianist movement. After Sofará's magic cigarette turns Macunaíma into a handsome prince, we hear an old carnival song (*'Ai Ceci, nunca mais beijou Peri'/* 'Oh Ceci never kissed Peri again') which references the characters from *O Guarani*. As Randal Johnson points out, the sequence is a satirical barb directed at the Brazilian 'economic miracle' of the late 1960s.[11] Sofará, the European 'Ceci' of the allegory, is dressed in an 'Alliance for Progress' sack. Her magic cigarette, i.e. American intervention, has turned Macunaíma, the Peri of the allegory, into a papier maché prince, just as the 'economic miracle' touted by the junta supposedly turned Brazil into an apparently prosperous nation.

The tropicalist allegorical phase of *Cinema Novo* resurrects, on a more critical register, the Indianist theme, expressed not only in *Macunaíma* but also in a number of other 1970s films. Dos Santos' *Como era gostoso o meu francês* (*How Tasty Was My Little Frenchman*, 1970-72), meanwhile, performs an 'anthropophagic' critique of European colonialism. The film is set in the sixteenth century, at a time when France was trying to found the colony of France Antartique in Rio de Janeiro bay. It was in this period that the French brought scores of Tupinambá Indians back to France to perform in a kind of proto-Disneyworld in Rouen, where the Tupinambás staged their daily practices for the delectation of French observers, among them the French philosopher Montaigne, who subsequently wrote his famous essay 'Des cannibales'. Although the film cites many writers of the time – Jean de Léry, Villegaignon, José de Anchieta – the film is largely based on Hans Staden's travel tale, the title of which bespeaks its sensationalist nature: *Hans Staden: The True History and Description of a Country of Savages, a Naked and Terrible People, Eaters of Men's Flesh, Who Dwell in the New World Called America*. (Although some scholars, such as W. Arens, are sceptical about claims for cannibalism, Santos assumes that such accounts have a basis in truth.) The film concerns a Frenchman captured by the Tupinambás and sentenced to death in response to massacres inflicted upon them by Europeans. (Santos transforms Staden's protagonist into a Frenchman because the French, unlike the Germans, participated directly in the colonial exterprise in Brazil.) Before he is ritually executed and eaten, however, he is given a wife, Sebiopepe (widow of one of the Tupinambás massacred by the Europeans), and is allowed to participate in the tribe's daily activities. As he is taken to his execution, the Frenchman refuses to follow the prepared ritual in Tupi, and instead says in French: 'my people will avenge me, and no Indian will remain in the land.' Shortly thereafter, the camera zooms into Sebiopepe's face as she devours her Frenchman, with no apparent regret despite her close relationship with him, an image which segues to a quotation from a report on genocide committed by Europeans.

In *How Tasty*, Santos attempts to subvert the conventional identification with the European protagonist of the captivity narrative. The title – *How Tasty Was My Little Frenchman* – implies an indigenous/anthropophagic perspective, while inverting the trope of ownership so that the European is now the slave. But more generally, the film offers a didactic lesson in cultural relativism, indirectly posing Montaigne's question: 'who are the real barbarians?' Ironically inverting the homogenizing convention by which Europeans perceive only generic Indians – they all look alike – here the Indians are unable to distinguish the French from the Portuguese. Relative nudity – relative because the Indian characters still wear ornaments, body paint and tangas – becomes the cultural norm during the film. (Indeed, the film was rejected by the Festival in Cannes, land of bikinis and semi-nude starlets, precisely because of its non-voyeuristic normalization of nudity.) The film systematically cuts off the conventional escape routes, maintaining an ironically neutral attitude toward the protagonist's deglutition. Here the European is the protagonist, but not the hero, and romantic love is less important than tribal loyalty. Unfortunately Santos underestimated the dumb inertia of Eurocentric identification; many spectators identified with the Frenchman despite the film's ironic intentions.

The title of the Bodanzky/Senna film *Iracema* (1975) references the Alencar classic, but turns the novel's Pocahontas-like story of romance between virginal Indian and Portuguese nobleman into a brutal encounter on the Trans-Amazonian highway, one which brings together a cynical white trucker and an Indian adolescent forced into prostitution. Here the 'virgin with the honey lips' has become a roadside whore along the Trans-Amazonian Highway. The authors go beyond reportage to compose a multilevelled text which is at once specific and general, documentary and allegorical – a synthetic view of the entire process of 'conservative modernization'. Given the centrality of documentation to the film's project, the filmmakers carefully authenticate images and sounds registered on the ground. An interminable tracking shot records a gigantic man-made forest fire, showing that the fire's dimensions on the screen do not depend on manipulative editing.

In *Iracema*, ecological disaster and social exploitation configure an institutionalized hell. The highway provides a privileged setting for the 'free investment' of distant capital (from southern Brazil and abroad) that organizes an intensified exploitation of the labour force, illegal land seizures, contraband in precious hardwoods, and new circulations of goods and human beings. One scene parallels migrant workers, prostitutes, and cattle as 'pieces' which are 'hauled' in trucks and sold to a foreign-owned plantation. Rather than use collage or discontinuous editing, Bodanzky/Senna deploy incongruous documentary strategies derived from the *Cinéma Verité* tradition, here made strange through the cynical interventions of the lead actor (Paulo César Pereio) in the 'real world'. (The actor pretends to be a truck driver around people who do not know him to be an actor.) The confrontation, in this allegory of modernization, crystallizes around the relation between the jingoistic truck driver Tião Brasil Grande (Big Brazil Sebastian) played by Pereio, and Iracema, the Indian girl played by the non-professional Edna de Cássia. The alienation effect works within the shot, as Pereio provokes ordinary people to words and action, contaminating brute experience with theatricality. As simultaneously the character Tião Brasil Grande and a *Cinéma Verité* interviewer, Pereio plays in and comments on the scenes. And within the asymmetrical couple Tião/Iracema, Tião is active agent, initiator, entrepreneur; Iracema is acted upon, prostitute, commodity. Tião is associated with the pet project of the dictatorship, the Trans-Amazonian Highway, and the modernizing nationalism it represents. He speaks in the jingoistic slogans of the period: 'Onward Brazil!'; 'There's no stopping this country!'; and 'Love it or leave it.' He embodies the arrogance of the 'economic miracle' and the ill-advised Pharaonic ambitions which led to the Third World's largest foreign debt. His grotesquerie forces the 'patriotic' spectator to acknowledge his/her complicity in the deplorable invasion of the Amazon. The film develops, then, a structural contrast between two filmic approaches: first, that of cinema reportage with hand-held camera, registering the ecological devastation and human exploitation in the Amazon, and second, that of fictional and allegorical procedures involving the relationship of Tião and Iracema. In a total interpenetration of documentary and fiction, the film understatedly denounces the human toll of frontier 'development'. And if Iracema in José de Alencar's novel embodied the noble savage, the native woman who responds to colonization by offering her love to a European knight, her contemporary namesake is clearly the victim of a twentieth century conquistador, ambulatory emblem of imperializing ambition.

Oswaldo Caldeira's *Ajuricaba: o rebelde da Amazônia* (*Ajuricaba: Rebel of the Amazon*, 1977), in this same vein, stresses historical continuities by shuttling between Indian resistance in the eighteenth century and resistance to neo-colonialism in the present. It tells the story of Ajuricaba, an eighteenth century chief of the Manau tribe who fought against his people's enslavement by organizing a pan-Indian Confederation against the Portuguese. (The story is well-known in the Amazon region but virtually unknown in the rest of Brazil.) After a four-year struggle, he finally leaped to his death rather than surrender. The film's pre-credit sequence, set in the present, deploys aerial shots to depict the discovery of an Indian corpse in the river. The media record the event as part of their daily routine of registering sensational violence. Then the narrative backtracks into the past, with another killing of an Indian, this time by eighteenth century Portuguese adventurers. Ajuricaba (Rinaldo Genes) is already chained and on his way to prison. From this point on, the film shuttles between past and present, between Ajuricaba as heroic rebel and Ajuricaba as present-day Indian, proceeding down the river past the slum housing in which Indians now live. Throughout the film, both as an eighteenth century and as a contemporary character, Ajuricaba says almost nothing; the word belongs to the colonizer. The film suggests the historical continuities, not only between the diverse incarnations of Ajuricaba, as a trans-historical figure, avatar of indigenous suffering and resistance, but also between the colonizing Portuguese and the contemporary multinational corporations which have turned the *zona franca* (free-trade zone) of Manaus into a glittering image of neo-colonialism. But rather than force the parallels, Caldeira leaves it up to the spectator to make the inference. At the finale, the film has Ajuricaba become a metalworker – perhaps reflecting a classical leftist class-over-race strategy – i.e. the kind of worker who led the revolts in the late 1970s. The film's ending begins the story once again, as the voice-over repeats '... once upon a time there was an Indian,' as if to say that the legend survives not only thanks to popular memory but also thanks to the cinema, one of whose functions it is to become the repository of myths, renewed again with each projection.

The Indian theme in the 1990s
We return to the Indian and the Amazon in Hector Babenco's *At Play in the Fields of the Lord* (1991). Although American-financed, the film employed a Brazilian producer (Francisco Ramalho Jr.), a Brazilian director of photography (Lauro Escorel) and a number of well-known Brazilian players (José Dumont, Nelson Xavier). The Babenco film used hegemonic financing circuits in order to make what looks at first glance like a Hollywood-style super-production. But as what Eugênio Bucci calls an 'anti-American blockbuster', *At Play in the Fields of the Lord* offers disillusioned subtlety, social contradiction, and spectatorial ambivalence instead of Hollywood's usual Manichean resolutions.[12] Despite the film's high production values, its use of stars (Daryl Hannah etc), its spectacular scenery, and its source in a best-selling novel by Peter Matthiesen – the film unsettled many First World audiences by its hostile portrait of the role of Brazilians and Americans in the Amazon.

The film makes an interesting comparison case, in this sense, with another film released in the same year, Bruce Beresford's *Black Robe*, which treats the same topic – the role of European-brought religions in relation to native peoples – but which, unlike *At Play in the Fields of the Lord*, was immensely successful in the North American market. The differential response to the two films has everything to do, one suspects, with the fact that while *Black Robe* was set in the safely distant past (the sixteenth century), the Babenco film is set in the explosive present. And while *Black Robe* is mildly critical of the Jesuit actions in Quebec, it forgives them because they 'did it all for love.' *At Play*, in contrast, portrays the Protestant missionaries specifically, and Europeans and Euro-Americans generally, as neurotic, arrogant, puritanical, insensitive, and ultimately dangerous to the general well-being. (The missionaries never really succeed, furthermore, in their project of converting Indians to Christianity.) The Brazilian policeman tells the two aviators (played by Tom Waits and Tom Berenger) to bomb the Niaruna village 'just to scare them.' Contact with whites, even with well-intentioned whites, the film suggests, almost always means death for the Indians. The pilots and the missionaries are symbolically linked in their mission; as they fly over the Amazon, the plane casts its reflection on the water in the form of a cross. Despite the tensions between them, the missionaries, the pilots, and the gold prospectors mutually reinforce one another within a common project of domination. Even the well-intentioned can provoke calamity. The genocide of the tribe results from the fact that Lewis Moon, the Berenger character who is supposedly half-Cherokee, kisses both Andy (Daryl Hannah) and his native 'wife' Pindi. Martin Quarrier (Aidan Quinn) tells Lewis Moon that 'as an American he would be proud to have Indian blood,' to which Lewis responds sardonically 'And just how much Indian blood would an American be proud to have?' Everyone projects their own ethnocentric vision onto the Indians; even the Jewish character Wolf sees them as 'the lost tribe of Israel, Jewish just like me.' At the same time, the Indians are not noble savages but rather ordinary people faced by a devastating challenge.

Most of the changes that Babenco made from the Matthiesen source novel had to do with his attempt to present indigenous conceptions of the world. In an interview with Neil Okrent, Babenco explained:

> Everything the Indians say or do in the movie... was suggested by them. They told me how they would react if a white man dropped from the sky into their village. They did the mise-en-scène. I just took my scissors and shaped it, but the inner concept, the core of everything came from workshops we did with them. They told stories from their families and relatives, including old people who remembered when they were first contacted.[13]

Thus Babenco on one level seeks a collaborative representation based on indigenous participation. In this spirit, Babenco makes a crucial alteration in the plot of the novel. In the Matthiesen novel, when Moon kills Aeore, the dying Indian says 'You are Kisu Mu.' But Babenco chooses instead to have the Indian denounce Moon, calling him a 'son of a bitch': 'You are not one of us. You are a white man.' Babenco also criticizes the hippy romanticism that believes that taking hallucinogenic drugs in the jungle magically turns white people into spiritual Indians. On the Indian side, Babenco shows active, diverse indigenous people, who debate how to react to the incursions by outsiders. Aeore, as leader of the Niaruna, sees through Moon's constructed identity as a cultural transvestite. The apparently 'pacified' Tiro people, meanwhile, use a kind of 'sly civility' to outwit the conquerors. They merely pretend to pray, acting out white expectations of them, in order to gain food and presents. They interpret Protestant Christianity through their own cosmological filter, and finally refuse to give up their own practices and beliefs.[14] Ultimately, however, Babenco's vision is elegiac, rooted in the trope of the inevitably vanishing Indian. The natives fight, but for a cause that is doomed in advance. Indian arrows cannot compete with the bombs of the invaders.

With the 'renaissance' of Brazilian cinema after the mid-1990s, the Indian theme re-surfaces. Aurélio Michile's *O cineasta da selva* (*The Jungle Filmmaker*, 1997), tells the story of Luso-Brazilian filmmaker Silvino Santos (1886-1970). Santos made hundreds of films in the Amazon after he settled in Manaus at the height of the rubber boom. In 1912, he was invited by the Peruvian Consul to do a photographic study of the Indians living in the lands held by the Peruvian rubber baron Julio Cesar Arana. Unlike filmmakers like Major Tomás Luiz Reis, who were linked to the paternalist positivism of the Rondon Commission, Santos was linked to famously brutal rubber companies. Indeed, some of Santos' early films were made in order to counter accusations of exploitation against the Peruvian Amazon Rubber Company, accusations made by the English Society for the Protection of Aboriginal Peoples and the Abolition of Slavery.

Santos, and his Amazônia Cine-Film, became especially famous after screenings of *No país das amazonas* at the 1922 Centennial Celebrations in Rio. The film was subsequently screened around the world in Portuguese, English, French and German versions. *O cineasta da selva* interweaves footage from Silvino Santos' films about the Amazon with a staged biography (in flashbacks) based on Silvino Santos Memoirs, *O romance da minha vida* (*The Romance of My Life*). Michiles alternates black-and-white and colour footages, clips from Santos with present-day interviews, archival material and staged sequences, with José de Abreu playing Santos, representing high points of Santos' life. We see astonishing footage of Trans-Atlantic ocean liners in the Amazon, of the mass destruction of Amazonia fauna, and of native celebrations. The image is

22. Silvino Santos in *O cineasta da selva.*

ultimately idealizing however, since the key metaphor organizing Santos' structuring of his materials was the trope of the Amazon as a 'new Eden'. And *O cineasta da selva* itself is somewhat torn between idealization and denunciation, divided between its nationalist desire to promote a pioneer Brazilian cineaste, and its duty to tell the truth about the filmmaker's links to powerful interests.

Sylvio Back's compilation film *Yndio do Brasil* (*Our Indians,* 1995) presents a wide spectrum of representations of Brazilian Indians superimposed on his own poems denouncing genocide. The film is prefaced by the phrase 'The Only Good Indian Is the Filmed Indian,' an intertextual variation on a well-known exterminationist slogan. Sequences from the most diverse sources – Brazilian features like *Iracema* (Jorge Conchin, 1931), *O caçador de diamantes* (*The Diamond Searcher,* Vitório Capellaro, 1933) and *A lenda de Ubirajara* (*The Legend of Ubirajara,* André Luiz de Oliveira, 1975), German films like *Eine brasilianische Rapsodie* (*A Brazilian Rapsody,* Franz Eichhorn, 1935), and American films like *Jungle Head Hunters* (Lewis Cotlow, 1950) are laid end to end without apparent rhyme or reason. 'Alien' music, such as ironic sambas, is superimposed on pre-existing image tracks, with the result that uninformed spectators (i.e. those unfamiliar with the films) are in doubt about the status of what they are seeing and hearing, although the anti-racist drift is always clear.

In 1996, Norma Bengell directed a completely uncritical version of Alencar's 1857 Indianist novel *O Guarani*, one which relayed once again the old 'foundational fiction', the gendered myth of the 'good Indian' Peri, who prizes his beloved Cecília above all else. One Portuguese noble in the film describes Peri as having the soul of a Portuguese nobleman, but wrapped in the body of a savage. The usual colonialist binarism separates off the good Peri from the bad Aimorés, the enemies both of Peri and of the Portuguese. The language of the film is stilted like that of the novel, and Ceci and Peri address each other in the third person – 'Is Ceci angry with her Peri?' Imbued with very contemporary ecological sentiments, Peri dialogues with the jaguars. The film adopts the 'redface convention' of having non-Indians (Ipanema Indians, as it were) play Indians, even though the new Constitution freed Indians from the infantilizing status of 'wards of the State'. The soundtrack, by Wagner Tiso, spins out electronic variations on Carlos Gomes' *O Guarani*, while also incorporating some indigenous sounds and instrumentation. As a Guarani, Peri is isolated from his own group, and in the end he converts to Christianity for Cecília's sake. Peri repeatedly saves Cecília from danger. As the pair play childlike games, erotic tension is constantly maintained, with their lips usually in close proximity but without ever touching; their love remains Platonic. While the Alencar novel ends with Peri's death as he is swept away by an apocalyptic deluge, the Benguell adaptation ends with Peri carrying away Ceci in his arms.

Luiz Alberto Pereira's *Hans Staden* (1999), meanwhile, tells the story of the German artillery man who was shipwrecked in 1550 off the coast of Santa Catarina. In January 1554, while in search of a slave who had disappeared, Staden was captured by Tupinambá Indians. Brought to their site in Ubatuba, he claimed to have narrowly escaped being devoured in an anthropophagic ritual. The film's point of departure is Staden's 1557 sensationalist account of his two trips to Brazil. While French Protestant writers like Jean de Léry and André Thévet (and later Montaigne) tended to defend ritual cannibalism (while denouncing Spanish Catholics as the real cannibals), Staden sees cannibalism as just one more trial which can strengthen his faith. At the same time, he does not depict Tupi cannibalism as purely an act of revenge but rather a way of acquiring 'beautiful names'.

The Pereira film displays scrupulous reconstitution of language, décors and costumes, but not much imagination. Indeed,

23. *Yndio do Brasil.*

Pereira seems to be the last person alive who actually believes it possible to show 'exactly what Brazil in the sixteenth century was like.'[15] According to its author, 'the film tells what happened, nothing more,' all within a spirit of journalistic objectivity. But such a view assumes that Staden himself only told what happened, without ideological filters or generic emplotments, when in fact Staden's writing is an exercise in allegorical homiletics designed to demonstrate the superiority of the Christian religion. Pereira revisits the theme of *How Tasty Was My Little Frenchman*, but only to render it more conventional and Eurocentric. While Nelson Pereira dos Santos synthesized the stories of the German Hans Staden and the Frenchman Jean de Léry, the Pereira version concentrates solely on the German, while explicitly rejecting allegory as a 'modernist syndrome which drives away the public.'[16] While Santos was ironic toward his 'hero', Pereira identifies with Staden's struggles, and tries to get the spectator to identify as well. While the Frenchman is ultimately devoured in *How Tasty Was My Little Frenchman*, the German tricks his captors and escapes. While the Frenchman is integrated into the tribe, the German returns to his real German family.[17] Eduardo Morettin points out that Pereira improves on Staden by showing him as more curious and sympathetic than he was in the book.[18] While Santos' film was an exercise in cultural relativity, whereby European languages, customs and assumptions were questioned and ironized, *Hans Staden* straightforwardly identifies with the European protagonist and his values of pragmatic realism combined with Christian religiosity. While scrupulously 'accurate' on one level, the film represents a missed opportunity on the other. It fails to dialogue with a rich multi-century discussion of cannibalism that includes Thévet, Montaigne, Oswald de Andrade, Florestan Fernandes, Caetano Veloso and many others, dismissing all these analyses in favour of a naive 'just-the-facts' verism.

The quincentennial year of 2000 brings us not only *Invenção do Brasil* but also two fiction features. The children's adventure film *Tainá: uma aventura na Amazônia* (*Tainá: An Adventure in the Amazon*, Tânia Lamarca and Sérgio Bloch) revolves around an eight-year-old orphaned Indian girl named Tainá, who lives with her grandfather Tigê in the Amazon forest. A feminine version of the Indianist *bravo guerreiro*, this time she comes equipped with ecological consciousness, as she confronts the smugglers who steal and sell threatened animals for genetic research abroad. She acts in solidarity with the Indian woman Tikiri, the pilot Rudi, and the Brazilian biologist Isabel and her son Joninho. In a new version of an *Iracema*-style romance, one clearly inflected by the spirit of Steven Spielberg, Tainá loves Joninho and helps him see the wisdom of Indian life and values.

Lúcia Murat's *Brava gente brasileira* (*Brave Brazilian People*, 2000), meanwhile, is set in the year 1778, when another Diogo (played by Portuguese actor Diogo Infante), a cartographer like Diogo Álvares, is marking borders claimed by both Portugal and Spain. In conflicts with the Guaicuru Indians (played by Kadiweu people), Diogo abuses and then falls in love with an indigenous woman played by Luciana Rigueira. *Brava gente brasileira* tells a kind of anti-*Iracema* story, where love between the Portuguese man and the indigenous woman is rendered impossible by the violence of the *bandeirantes* (the mestizo conquerors of the Brazilian equivalent to the North American 'frontier') in the colonial 'contact zone'. Even the most sensitive of the colonizers, men like Diogo, cannot have their dream of peaceful co-existence. Nor are the Indian characters without agency, for in the end they devise an ingenious plan of retaliation, involving seduction followed by massive destruction of the Europeans.

We have here surveyed the various incarnations of the Indian through a century of cinema: the romantic Indian, the ethnographic Indian, the allegorical Indian, the activist Indian and so forth. Lamartine Babo once said in a song that Cabral discovered Brazil on 22 April, just two months after carnival. It is no accident, therefore, that carnival too has appropriated the figure of the Indian, with *blocos* named the 'Apaches', the 'Comanches', and 'Cacique de Ramos'. Popular music too has constantly referenced the Indian in post-modern, recombinant ways, often permutating the tropes of romantic Indianist literature. I am thinking, for example, of the Chico Buarque de Hollanda song 'Iracema', where the Alencar heroine is reinvisioned as a woman from Ceará who has emigrated to the United States, or the Caetano song, 'O índio', which suggests that 'after the last Indian tribe has been exterminated,' a new Indian hero will emerge: not only 'fearless like Muhammad Ali', and 'agile like Bruce Lee', but also 'passionate like Peri'. Brazilian cinema and popular culture, as we have seen, have both prolonged and critiqued the myths and fictions inherited from *Indianismo*.

In the twenty first century, one hopes, the native Brazilian will emerge to speak in a more full-throated manner, as an integral part of the cultural polyphony which is Brazil.

NOTES

1. See Robert Stam, *Tropical Multiculturalism: A Comparative History of Race in Brazilian Cinema and Culture* (Durham, Duke University Press, 1997).
2. See Doris Sommer, *Foundational Fictions: The National Romances of Latin America* (Berkeley, University of California Press, 1991).
3. For a discussion of trans-racial male bonding in American literature, see Leslie Fiedler, *Love and Death in the American Novel* (New York, Criterion, 1960).
4. See Janaína Amado, 'Mythic Origins: Caramuru and the Founding of Brazil', *Hispanic American Historical Review* 80: 4 (November 2000), pp 783-811.
5. See João Carlos Rodrigues, 'O índio brasileiro e o cinema', in *Cinema Brasileiro: Estudos* (Rio de Janeiro, Embrafilme/Funarte, 1980).
6. See Carlos Roberto de Souza, *Nossa aventura na tela* (São Paulo, Cultura Editoras Associadas, 1998).
7. Quoted in Fernão Ramos (ed), *História do Cinema Brasileiro* (São Paulo, Arte Editora, 1987), p 74. Excerpts from some of these docu-

mentaries form part of Sylvio Back's 1995 documentary *Yndio do Brasil/Our Indians*.

8. Oswald de Andrade, 'Conversando com Oswald de Andrade', *Gazeta do Povo* (1950), cited in Maria Eugênia Boaventura, *A vanguarda antropofágica* (São Paulo, Ática,1985), p 31.

9. See Ivan van Sertima, *They Came before Columbus* (New York, Random House, 1975).

10. Joaquim Pedro de Andrade is the Brazilian filmmaker with the clearest links to the Modernist movement, in the sense that he made many films related to the movement: *O poeta do castelo* (1959) is a short about the modernist poet Manuel Bandeira (with whom Mario de Andrade exchanged letters); his first feature, *O padre e a moça* (*The Priest and the Girl*, 1965) adopts a poem by another modernist, Carlos Drummond de Andrade; *Macunaíma* is taken from Mario de Andrade; and *O homem do pau brasil* (1981) is inspired by the other monstre sacré of Modernismo, Oswald de Andrade.

11. For a thoroughly researched and closely observed textual analysis of *Macunaíma*, see Randal Johnson, 'Cinema Novo and Cannibalism: *Macunaíma*', in Randal Johnson and Robert Stam, *Brazilian Cinema* (New York, Columbia University Press, 1991), pp 178-190.

12. See Eugênio Bucci, 'Do filme brasileiro que parece americano (e do americano que parece brasileiro)', *Revista USP* 19 (September/October/November 1993). See also Lúcia Nagib, 'Nota em favor de um filme internacional' in the same issue.

13. See Neil Okrent, '*At Play in the Fields of the Lord*: An Interview with Hector Babenco', *Cineaste* 19/1 (1992), pp 44-47.

14. Anna M. Brigido-Corachan, in an unpublished paper on 'Indigenous Resistances: Representations of the Native in Contemporary "Brazilian" Films', compares the indigenous survival tactics to Gerald Vizenor's notion of *survivance* as an 'active repudiation of dominance, tragedy and victimry'. See Vizenor's *Fugitive Poses: Native American Indian Scenes of Absence and Presence* (Lincoln, Nebraska, University of Nebraska Press, 1998), p 15.

15. Interview with Paulo Santos Lima, '*Hans Staden* mostra os dentes nos cinemas', *Folha de S. Paulo*, 17 March 2000.

16. Santos Lima: '*Hans Staden* mostra os dentes nos cinemas'.

17. For an insightful comparison of *How Tasty* and *Hans Staden*, see Guiomar Ramos, 'Como era gostoso o meu Hans Staden', *Sinopse* 5 (2000).

18. See Eduardo Morettin, 'Hans Staden: o indivíduo e a história', *Sinopse* 5 (2000).

14

For all and traditions of popular musical comedy

Lisa Shaw

The opening credits of *For all: o trampolim da vitória* (*For All*, Luiz Carlos Lacerda and Buza Ferraz, 1998), are accompanied by the song 'Chiclete com banana' ('Chewing Gum with Banana') by Gordurinha and Almira Castilho, the title and lyrics of which provide a fitting metaphor for the screen encounter between two alien cultures, as well as for the film's aesthetic fusion of elements of both the classic Hollywood musical and the intrinsically Brazilian *chanchada*. This 1998 musical comedy wistfully recreates recognizable features of both cinematic traditions, thus appealing to a contemporary audience's sense of longing for the vogues and values of yesteryear.

In this respect *For all* forms part of a recent trend in Brazilian Cinema, which has seen filmmakers such as Helena Solberg (*Carmen Miranda – Bananas Is My Business*, 1994) and Rogério Sganzerla (*Tudo é Brasil/All Is Brazil*, 1998) turn their attentions back to the 1930s and 1940s. Sganzerla's work takes up where Orson Welles' ill-fated and unfinished documentary *It's All True* left off, and centres on the sentimental and clichéd radio broadcasts made by the American cultural ambassador to Latin America from Rio de Janeiro's Urca casino back to the USA in 1942. Like Solberg's biopic of Carmen Miranda, Sganzerla's work explores the manipulation of cultural stereotypes, and offers contemporary audiences a reassuring reminder of an era when issues of identity were openly articulated, and images of *brasilidade* (Brazilianness) were easily recognizable and readily devoured. *For all*, in common with these two other Brazilian films from the 1990s which draw heavily on popular music for their evocation of a golden age, invites the audience to turn back time and momentarily return to an age of innocence when anything seemed possible.

The film is set in Natal, in the north-eastern state of Rio Grande do Norte, Brazil, in 1943. The action centres on Parnamirim Field, an American military base, where 15,000 US servicemen were stationed after President Getúlio Vargas (in power in 1930-45) declared war on the Axis.[1] Although the troops' mission was to defend the South Atlantic coast and expel the Germans from Senegal, the film focuses primarily on the interaction between the North Americans and the 40,000 local inhabitants, and on the latter's fantasies of romance and material progress. Against a backdrop of air-raid sirens, black-outs, radio broadcasts announcing the sinking of Brazilian ships by Axis submarines and other military losses, sabotage, poverty and sexual exploitation, *For all* is essentially a light-hearted tale that revolves around the Brazilian characters' seduction by, and ultimate disillusionment with, the handsome strangers and their cultural baggage. The film's directors were inspired by the idea of two very different cultures coming into close contact and the subsequent transformation of a small, provincial Brazilian town in the underdeveloped North-East. *For all* thus homes in on the popular cultural products that the servicemen brought with them, and which dazzled the local community, ranging from consumer goods to musical influences. In the course of their research for the film, the directors discovered that a host of leading Hollywood entertainers had visited or performed at the base, including Tyrone Power, the Glenn Miller orchestra, and the film star Kay Francis, and they were inspired to create a musical comedy which celebrates the heyday of moviemaking and looks with nostalgia to a bygone age of Hollywood glamour.

The historical setting of *For all* naturally aligns it with the Hollywood wartime musicals of the 1940s, and the film is deliberately couched in the tradition of the 'show' or 'entertainment' musicals produced in the war years and beyond. The film actively engages with Hollywood by making constant reference to the Brazilian population's fascination with movie stars and to the impact of the cinema. This chapter will consider the elements that *For all* borrows from Hollywood traditions, and the theoretical implications of this choice of aesthetic template for a Brazilian movie made in the late 1990s. Before doing so, however, it will give due mention to the home grown brand of light musical comedy, namely the *chanchada*, which dominated Brazilian film production throughout the 1940s and 50s, and enjoyed unprecedented success at the box office. Although the *chanchada* owed much to Hollywood models itself, it was nevertheless intrinsically Brazilian in its adaptation of stock tropes and motifs, and *For all* clearly pays tribute to the genre's conventions. The intertextual and self-reflexive aspects of *For all* thus will be analysed within the wider context of the paradigms established by both Hollywood and the Brazilian musical film.

Citation of the Brazilian musical comedy or *chanchada*

One of the directors of *For all*, Buza Ferraz, explained in interview that the *chanchada* genre 'markedly influenced the directors in spite of the citation of classic American musicals', and it is the comic characters of the film that particularly resemble the stock types of earlier Brazilian musicals.[2] One of the protagonists of *For all* is Sandoval, a rather simple-minded local who, by dint of his tenacity, is taken on as a cleaner in the military base. This good-hearted, camp buffoon, who daydreams of meeting the Hollywood siren, Jay Francis, and of being serenaded by naked airmen in the showers that he cleans, has much in common with the comic lead characters, typically played by the actor Oscarito, of countless *chanchadas* produced by the Rio de Janeiro-based Atlântida studios in the 1940s and 50s. Indeed, Sandoval bears more than a passing physical resemblance to Oscarito, with his diminutive stature and wide-eyed innocence. Like the clowns of the *chanchada*, Sandoval is a naive, uneducated hick, who is awe-struck by his encounter with first-world glamour and the 'exotic'. (In the case of the *chanchada*, the yokel usually found himself in the big city of Rio, among other rural-urban migrants, where he was tempted by bourgeois hedonism).[3] The humour of Sandoval's character stems from his facial expressions and his clumsy attempts to better himself, and in both respects he has much in common with Oscarito's archetypal anti-heroes. In spite of his claims to the contrary, Sandoval has only a minimal grasp of the English language; when he is reminded by a sergeant at the base that a forthcoming dance is 'black tie', he exclaims, in a heavy accent, 'Black tie to you too!', and when he overhears a US soldier curse in English he repeats the phrase, remaining oblivious to its meaning. He has no sense of propriety and freely interrupts a Portuguese class being held at the base in order to ask for help in translating a letter to the star Jay Francis. When he is made to feel stupid he resorts to spouting a string of Brazilian proverbs and set phrases, regardless of their meaning. In the well-known *chanchada O homem do sputnik* (see note 3) Oscarito's character, an uneducated country bumpkin, has similar difficulties with more formal registers of his native tongue when he comes into contact with high society, and such communication difficulties are a common feature of these films, in which humble migrants come into contact with another world in the capital city.

The fool characters of the *chanchada*, like Sandoval, are gawky weaklings, the antithesis of the handsome Brazilian *galãs* or heart-throbs of the *chanchadas* and of the broad-shouldered, fair-haired US military heroes of *For all*. In spite of his lack of physical presence or attractiveness (not to mention his closet homosexuality) Sandoval 'gets the girl' in the climax of *For all*, when the Hollywood icon Jay Francis comes to perform at the base and invites her great fan to join her on stage for a dance. This is a typical case of the inversion of norms, an intrinsic feature of the *chanchada*, in which established hierarchies of class, race and gender were overturned in a spirit of carnivalesque irreverence. The most striking example is probably the attempted seduction of a yokel, played by Oscarito, by a Brigitte Bardot look-alike in the *chanchada O homem do sputnik*, but one is also reminded of Oscarito playing the gauche civil servant Felismino in *Esse milhão é meu* (*That Million Is Mine*, Carlos Manga, 1958), who is pursued by the scantily-clad showgirl, Arlete. In the same vein, in the *chanchada Garotas e samba* (*Girls and Samba*, Carlos Manga, 1957) the diminutive Zé Trindade, who frequently played an unlikely skirt-chaser in such films, enjoys a romantic tryst with the statuesque 'French' goodtime girl, Naná, played by Renata Fronzi. Male desire is often ridiculed in the *chanchada* and the genre is full of examples of emasculated, anti-macho males. Although the case of Sandoval is more extreme, since he confesses to his homosexuality, it nonetheless draws on this tradition of farcical male anti-heroes in Brazilian popular film, as does the figure of João Marreco in *For all*, who is rejected by his sweetheart, Iracema, in favour of a blond American, and who wears his emotions on his sleeve.[4]

There are many examples in *For all* of Brazilian characters who try to turn the presence of the American troops to their material advantage, such as the immoral barber who lures local young women into prostitution, the black shoeshine boy, and the prostitutes themselves, all, like the indomitable Sandoval and the Portuguese teacher at the base, João Marreco, keen to earn a few dollars from the servicemen. Throughout the *chanchada* tradition there are countless characters from society's lower echelons who attempt to turn their fortunes around by means of a slightly shady ruse or simply by using their wits, espousing what is known in Brazil as the counter-cultural lifestyle of *malandragem* and subverting the law and hierarchical authority via the unofficial Brazilian institution of *jeito* or *jeitinho*.[5] The female protagonist of *Samba em Brasília* (*Samba in Brasilia*, Watson Macedo, 1960), for example, sets out to win herself a rich husband, as does one of the three female leads of *Garotas e samba*; the character played by Zé Trindade in Cinedistri's *O camelô da rua Larga* (*The Street Vendor from Larga Street*, Eurides Ramos and Renato Restier, 1958) has no qualms about admitting that he is waiting for his aunt to die so he can get his hands on his inheritance; and in *De vento em popa* (*Wind in the Sails*, Carlos Manga, 1957) a young woman stows away on a cruise ship to gain access to the world of show business. The typically Brazilian comic aspects of *For all* centre on the film's more picaresque characters, who embody both *malandragem* and *jeitinho*, two of the principal tenets of popular identity in Brazil, but tacit citation of the *chanchada* genre is also evident in the film's closing sequence.

The finale of *For all* takes place at a dance at the base, to which both locals and military personnel have been invited. As an officer informs Sandoval, 'It's for all'. This is an archetypal Hollywood celebratory climax, involving all the main characters, however incongruous their presence. Nevertheless, the denouements of Hollywood musicals tend to see only the male and female leads paired off, and Rick Altman has studied the musical's typical romantic resolution, which depends on the harmony of a couple originally at odds.[6] In *For all*, however, the match-making is replicated among all the characters on screen, as all are paired off with a member of the opposite sex and dance happily together. Near the end of the film, three unknown couples pose for a photograph at the dance to reinforce the idea of closure via romantic union. Tensions are smoothed over and problems are resolved, and even those previously at odds, such as João Marreco and his future mother-in-law, are brought together in a festive mood. Even the comic villain of the piece, the repugnant pimp, Mr Bola, is there, dancing with a female partner. In contrast to US musicals, here everyone 'gets the girl' and they all celebrate in a utopian carnival atmosphere, in which all status and hierarchy are overturned. The respectable Miguel has bought his sweetheart, Jucilene, out of prostitution, and his family has accepted her. The star, Jay Francis, pairs up with the lowly Sandoval, and harmony, in this case between Brazilians and Americans, prevails.

There is even a close-up shot at the end of the film of a print of a painting by Raymond Neilson hanging on the wall, itself based on a famous photograph of Presidents Roosevelt and Vargas. This is a quintessential *chanchada* finale, and the return to a Brazilian cinematic tradition is mirrored by the introduction of a north-eastern musical style, *forró*, which replaces the earlier Hollywood-style big-band numbers.[7] Although the samba rhythm tended to dominate in the *chanchada*, the incorporation of a Brazilian musical genre here is significant. In the *chanchada Quem roubou meu samba?* (*Who Stole My Samba?*, José Carlos Burle, 1958), the final scene takes place in a hospital ward, and sees both the villains and their victims, together with the patients and doctors, dancing and singing together to a samba beat. All is forgiven and the music wipes away the problems of everyday life. Typically of the genre, the principal characters face the camera head-on, inviting the spectators to participate in the festivity. By all accounts it was not unusual for the cinema audience to join in the singing and to generally interact vocally with the antics on screen, reinforcing the sense of identification and equanimity fostered by such films. The musical finale of *For all* clearly bows to this established convention in Brazilian popular cinema, fondly evoking the community spirit and optimism engendered by the *chanchada*.

For all and Hollywood's cinematic models

For all repeatedly acknowledges the pervasive influences of US cinema in the story line, as well as borrowing from Hollywood's conventions in both overt and subtle ways. When Sandoval pretends to speak English in order to secure employment at the base, he tells the American officer that he learned his English from watching films and confesses to being crazy about the movies; the teenage Miguel masturbates while gazing at a photo of a Hollywood siren, and addresses her image with the English phrase 'Come on, baby'; when the Portuguese teacher at the base, João Marreco, is playing pool with his Brazilian pals one of them says

24. *For all.*

that his shot will be better than anything they will see in an American movie; Miguel meets his girlfriend in a movie theatre because he overhears her crying at the end of what is presumably a melodramatic love story; Sandoval is obsessed with and fantasizes about US-Cuban star Jay Francis, to whom he sends a letter in which he outlines what her films mean to him; and the camera catches sight of a poster for the film *Four Sons* in a bar, and of another on a wall in the military base advertising a movie called *Marine Raiders*, and so on.

For all clearly takes its cue from the Hollywood musical, particularly its wartime variant, and sets out to capture the spirit of the golden age of the genre. The film is a nostalgic tribute to the old-style, big-band show musicals, with its Glenn Miller-style musical arrangements, and it appears to nod in particular to what Altman calls the 'military entertainment film'.[8] The musical numbers in the film are generally performed for a screen audience as entertainment for the servicemen. (The exceptions are the dream sequences featuring Jay Francis perched on the wing of a plane and the homoerotic shower scene, both products of Sandoval's vivid imagination, and which will be discussed below). The fictitious US-Cuban star Jay Francis, for example, seductively sings 'Naughty Baby' (with a pronounced foreign accent) on stage, clad in a green lamé evening dress and surrounded by dancing sailors.

The choice to focus on a 'Latin' star in the film reflects Hollywood's fascination with stars from south-of-the-border during the war years.[9] The soundtrack of *For all* also draws heavily on classic wartime styles, particularly swing, and well-known numbers, such as 'The Glory of Love', which was sung by Jacqueline Fontaine in the role of a cabaret singer in the film *Guess Who's Coming to Dinner?* (Stanley Kramer) of 1967, but which dates back to the 1930s. The swing era is convincingly reproduced in the film via the inclusion of actors playing Tommy Dorsey and his orchestra, who featured in countless musicals in the 1940s, such as *Girl Crazy* (Norman Taurog) and *Du Barry Was a Lady* (Roy Del Ruth), both of 1943, and in the evocative musical numbers set at the base, which capture the mood of the times. (In Martin Scorsese's nostalgic pastiche of 40s musicals, *New York, New York* of 1977, referred to in more detail below, a Tommy Dorsey lookalike similarly helps to recreate the swing era.)

The finale of *For all* is a clear example of dual filmic citation. On the one hand it incorporates the key elements of the *chanchada* climax, as discussed above, but it also belongs to the US wartime musical paradigm. As Woll writes:

> While the plots of these musicals concentrate on the importance of group unity in times of stress, the musical numbers present undying praise for Roosevelt and the American war effort. The 'big show' at the end of each film becomes a symbolic display of youth's support for the United States.[10]

The climax of *For all* can be interpreted as an affectionate pastiche of the classic Hollywood musical's denouement, and in particular as an ironic comment on the values implicit in the wartime musical. The superficial, exaggerated harmony between the Americans and the Brazilians in the final scene, and the kitsch image of the two nations' presidents on which the camera focuses, glamorize the realities depicted in the film, such as the sexual exploitation of local girls for the benefit of the troops. Rick Altman says of the stock Hollywood musical finale, 'the ecstatic, uplifting quality of the musical's final scene permits no doubt about the permanence both of the couple and of the cultural values which the couple simultaneously guarantees and incarnates.'[11] In *For all* the lighthearted parody of this convention serves to poke fun at the ideological presumptions of the musical genre. The finale of the film is a tongue-in-cheek retort, on the part of the marginalized Brazilian film industry, towards the hegemonic cinematic model. In this respect, the musical climax to the film maintains a tradition of ironic pastiche vis-à-vis Hollywood that can be traced throughout the history of the *chanchada* genre. Perhaps the most obvious examples are *Nem Sansão nem Dalila* (*Neither Samson Nor Delilah*, Carlos Manga) and *Matar ou correr* (*To Kill or Run*, Carlos Manga), both of 1954, the first of which parodied the grandiose historical or Biblical epics produced by the likes of Cecil B. de Mille and Samuel Goldwyn, and most directly *Samson and Delilah* (Cecil B. de Mille, 1949), whilst the latter was a self-confessed burlesque of the western *High Noon* (Fred Zinnemann, 1952), released in Brazil with the title *Matar ou morrer* (*To Kill or Die*).[12]

In the USA 'soldier musicals' continued to be produced for some ten years after the end of the war, and this tradition was recalled in Martin Scorsese's *New York, New York* of 1977, which imitates a 1940s show musical, complete with a Tommy Dorsey lookalike big-band leader. A review of the film by Christopher Porterfield in *Time* magazine stated: 'What Scorsese is evoking is an epoch of moviemaking: the heyday of lavish studio musicals ... Half the time Scorsese is sending them up, and the other half trying to cash them in at face value for a dividend of unearned nostalgia.'[13] Penelope Gilliatt's review in *New Yorker* referred to the film as an *hommage* to all the musical films from the 1940s and 50s in which a boy and a girl fall in love, and as a bow to an age.[14] A review in *The Times* by David Robinson described it as 'a nostalgic tribute to the Hollywood musical, and an attempt to extend the expressive range of the form.'[15]

By deliberately situating itself in mainstream Hollywood traditions, *For all* is similarly seeking to induce nostalgia for a bygone age and aesthetic, but at the same time it is giving certain cinematic clichés an ironic and comic twist. Boy meets girl in the form of the young Miguel unwittingly falling for the charms of a prostitute, and more irreverently, the big climax to the film sees a Hollywood siren paired up with a homosexual clown. *For all* is above all a fond and cheerful recollection of a former epoch and style, and whilst never approximating the harshly critical view of Hollywood escapism contained in Scorsese's film, it does turn some of the stock conventions of show-business musicals on their heads.

In this respect *For all* also has much in common with the 1981 musical *Pennies from Heaven* (Herbert Ross), of which Jane Feuer writes: 'The film quotes widely from its musical comedy heritage, favouring the 1930s traditions contemporary with the film's setting.'[16] She goes on to call this film an example of a modernist rewriting of the film musical genre, and her assessment of the use of period music in it elucidates certain scenes in *For all*. Early on in the latter, the camera cuts to two female singers in uniform who are dancing and obviously miming to the well-known 'Beer Barrel Polka', sung by the Andrews Sisters. This song then becomes the background music for scenes at the base, the dialogue of which is spoken in English. Although the two women are miming to a record being played on a jukebox, this instance of lip-sync, together with Sandoval's sudden spouting of fluent English when he is introduced on stage to his idol, Jay Francis, are significant because they act as a kind of 'distancing effect' which serves to critique the clichés of the musical genre.[17] Such an effect is intended throughout *Pennies from Heaven*, as Jane Feuer explains:

> The sound-image relationship in 'Pennies from Heaven' exemplifies the 'distancing effect' that comes from separating the elements. When, instead of singing the numbers in the film, the characters lip-sync to old recordings from the 1930s, we are rendered aware of the constructed nature of the text rather than 'hypnotized', 'intoxicated', or 'fogged' out. The separation of the elements also seems to represent a critique of the traditional use of diegetic music in the musical genre. The idea that one spontaneously, naturally sings is exposed through this technique.[18]

In *For all* the only occasion when characters burst into song without warning is in the communal shower scene (albeit in Sandoval's daydream). Although not safe within the confines of a stage setting, the scene gets away with its high camp quality by being a product of the closet gay's imagination and a reflection of the impact that Hollywood has had on his visualization of fantasy. With a wink to the conventions of the show numbers of countless US musicals from the 1930s and 40s, particularly the spate of 'latino' movies made during the Good Neighbour Policy era, burly naked airmen, singing in Spanish, carry a reclining Sandoval in the air to a mambo beat, a dance move that is mirrored in the number performed by Jay Francis at the base, in which she is also held aloft by dancing sailors. The intention here lies somewhere between nostalgia and pastiche, and the camp excess is clearly self-parodic.

At key instances, such as in the shower scene described above and in the 'paradise' sequence featuring the lovers Iracema and Robert discussed below, *For all* deconstructs the classic syntax of the musical genre, and is both intertextual and self-reflexive. Feuer argues that 'self-reflexive musicals are "modernist" in that they systematically deconstruct those very elements that give the genre its regularity.' She believes that it is appropriate to look at the film musical in terms of its historical evolution, but that quotation does not necessarily imply a deconstruction of the genre, since most of the time late-studio and post-studio musicals merely borrow from already existing sources and reaffirm continuity with past traditions.[19] Thus *For all* could be viewed as a 'nostalgia film', in the same vein as *The Boy Friend* (Ken Russell, 1971) or *That's Entertainment* (Jack Haley Jr, 1974), whose very raison d'être is the act of conservation. The latter only quotes the musical numbers, not original narratives, rather like *For all*, and unlike reissues or revivals that quote entire films. But at times *For all* is a pastiche of the musical genre itself, and not only uses period songs, but cites the 'style' of Hollywood production numbers. The dream sequences in the film, for example, belong to a long tradition of multiple diegesis in film musicals. As Feuer writes:

> Musicals suggest that this dream work acts as a kind of exorcism, leading to the actual fulfilment of desires. In dream sequences the parallel between the dream in the film and the dream that is the film is rendered most explicit. The Hollywood musical creates dream sequences within musicals in order to obliterate the differences between dreams in films, dreams in ordinary life, and dreams as the fulfilment in ordinary life of the promises offered by the movies.[20]

The dream sequence was prevalent in the 1940s, and is therefore apt for the setting of *For all.* As Rick Altman says, 'the dream device is an important one in the history of the musical, particularly during the 40s, when the extended dream sequence reached the status of accepted alternative to the backstage musical's production number.'[21] Although the two dream sequences (Sandoval's fantasies about Jay Francis in a gold lamé dress sitting on the wing of a plane as she sings a snippet of 'The Glory of Love' and about naked servicemen singing to him when he gets a promotion) are relatively brief, their structural presence is a clear example of generic citation.

Although few wartime films introduced audiences to the South Seas – the notable exceptions being *Hollywood Canteen* (Delmer Daves) and *Up in Arms* (Elliott Nugent), both of 1944 – subsequent musicals have called on the 'south sea island' motif in an effort to recount 'wartime' tales against an 'exotic' backdrop. In this sense *For all* taps into a classic tradition of the Hollywood musical, albeit on the Atlantic coast. On Iracema's first visit to the base the bus travels along the shoreline, which provides an idyllic backdrop of palm trees and rolling surf, and there is a lingering close-up of a palm leaf silhouetted against a setting sun. Later we see a montage of shots of the beautiful heroine posing for photos on a sun-drenched beach, speeding down the dunes in a jeep, kissing her American lover, the navy pilot Lt Robert Collins, and making a garland of flowers for him as the sun sets in a hackneyed recreation of a cinematic 'paradise'.

Similarly, when Robert dies there is a flashback sequence showing the two of them making love on the beach. The 'tourist gaze' is very obvious in these photogenic scenes in which Iracema is the archetypal exoticized local beauty, and the parallels with the 1958 cinemascope movie version of *South Pacific* (Joshua Logan), amongst other musicals with 'south sea islandesque' settings, are striking. Rob Wilson has described 20th Century Fox's lavish production as 'a militouristic fantasy of Edenic enchantment, shirtless bodily bliss, [and] oriental seductiveness', which depicts a 'playground of Euro-American romance, commodity worship, sexual contamination, volcanic danger, miscegenational passion and (above all) hegemonic military might.'[22] The opening sequence of *South Pacific* features swaying palm trees and a spectacular tropical sunset, and the island of Hawaii was similarly portrayed as a lush garden of exotic/erotic delights in *Blue Hawaii* (Norman Taurog, 1961). In interview, Buza Ferraz acknowledged that the scenes of a mythical, 'island' paradise contained in *For all*, together with the homoerotic shower scene, are intended to parody the generic formulae of the classic Hollywood musical. These instances of visual quotation in *For all*, along with the celebratory climax of the film, toy with the filmic conventions of Hollywood's romantic melodramas and musicals, emphasising the illusionism out of which plots, with their obligatory happy endings, were traditionally constructed in the war years and the post-war era.

In this respect, *For all* seems to have much in common with a cycle of Hollywood films from the mid-1970s which could be called 'Hollywood on Hollywood', such as MGM's *That's Entertainment* of 1974 and *New York, New York* already mentioned. As Richard Lippe writes,

> the significance of these films wasn't just that they dealt with Hollywood's Golden Age. Rather, their appeal and potential value was that they offered 'nostalgia' to the American public who, supposedly, at the time, preferred reviving their past glory to confronting the decaying and corrupted present.[23]

Like these films, *For all* comments on and rehashes outdated generic formulae, and invites the audience to share in the recognition of the clichés and of the artifice of Hollywood, as well as to indulge in a comforting escapism by revisiting past times and lifestyles, and the most escapist of cinematic forms, the musical.

As a film about nostalgia and cultural difference, *For all* shares many of the concerns of *Yanks* (John Schlesinger, 1979), set in the period between 1942 and 1944, and which centres on the interaction between American servicemen stationed in the North of England and the local population. In addition to the obvious thematic similarities, *Yanks* is also characterized by an anachronistic use of genre, namely that of social realism, and betrays a longing for the implications of that genre. As Marion Jordan says, 'the film's real portrayal is a nostalgia for a moment when this meeting of cultures promised the possibility of different stereotypes, a nostalgia for the moment when social change seemed possible, a nostalgia for ... optimism.'[24] It is perhaps a nostalgia for optimism which best describes the tone of *For all*, which puts the clock back to a time when, in spite of the world war, Brazilians unwittingly had their first real taste of consumerism and cultural imperialism, and yet still enjoyed their own traditions, value system and innocence.

NOTES

I would like to thank both Buza Ferraz and Luiz Carlos Lacerda for their support and assistance in the writing of this chapter.

1.   With the outbreak of the war in Europe, Brazil, with its Fascist-style *Estado Novo* (New State) trade links with Germany, Italian and German immigrant populations, and strategic location, became a focus of international attention, particularly from the USA. If Brazil had sided with the Axis powers it could have threatened the supply of raw materials to the USA and British shipping in the South Atlantic. The possibility that some of the continent's nations might support the Axis led President Roosevelt to persevere with military agreements and with the Good Neighbour Policy, which promoted cultural exchange with Latin America in order to foster greater understanding and support for the USA's foreign policy. Brazil was officially neutral at the start of the war in Europe. However, German-Brazilian relations were upset by the drive to 'Brazilianize' the German immigrant communities of the South, and by the failed 1938 Integralist putsch, which prompted the stationing of troops among the German communities as part of the nationality policy. An important commercial deal was signed between Brazil and the United States at the beginning of 1939, and the entente between the two countries was strengthened in September 1940 with the granting of a US$ 20 million loan from the Export-Import Bank of the USA to build the Volta Redonda steelworks in Brazil. Military agreements soon followed, which made Brazilian bases available in the event of an attack on the USA by a non-American power. By 1941 Brazil's foreign policy hinged on its relations with the USA, and Brazil finally declared war on Germany and Italy on 21 August 1942, in response to torpedo attacks on Brazilian shipping off the north-eastern coast. The opening credits of *For all* are preceded by a series of sketches depicting Brazilian ships being sunk by German submarines.

2.   The author interviewed Buza Ferraz via electronic mail on 11 September 2000.

3.   In the *chanchada O homem do sputnik* (*Sputnik Man*, Carlos Manga, 1959), for example, Oscarito's character, Anastácio Fortuna, is lured to the then capital city from his ramshackle home in the interior in an effort to make money from the discovery of what he believes to be a sputnik satellite in his backyard. On hearing of his find the Americans, Russians and French send spies to Rio to try to get their hands on the 'sputnik' (which turns out to be nothing more than a weather vane that has fallen off a church roof). Anastácio and his wife are spellbound by the sophistication of Rio, its high-class inhabitants and foreign visitors. Like Sandoval, Oscarito's character is an ingenuous and bumbling fool alongside the slick, polished foreigners.

4.   In *Esse milhão é meu* Felismino makes a fool of himself with the show-girl Arlete by falling for her deception, and visually by way of his fumbling advances, which provide a comic foil to her poise and almost choreographed seduction routine. His father-in-law is clearly another feminized, anti-macho male, whose freedom is curtailed by his domineering wife, and who claims to be tired when he thinks

she is trying to wake him during the night for carnal activity. He wants to hear all about his son-in-law's nocturnal antics, as his only source of sexual pleasure is vicarious. In the *chanchada* men are ritually humiliated and portrayed as guileless fools, blinded by desire to trickery and lies.

5.   The term *malandragem* refers to the lifestyle of idleness, petty crime, drinking, gambling and womanizing which was favoured by the mythical *malandro* or mixed-race spiv or hustler, who was something of an anti-hero in the poorer quarters of Rio de Janeiro in the first decades of the twentieth century, and who came to be venerated in the lyrics of samba. The concept of *jeitinho* has been described by Lívia Neves de H. Barbosa as 'a fast, efficient, and last-minute way of accomplishing a goal by breaking a universalistic rule and using instead one's informal social or personal resources.' Lívia Neves de H. Barbosa, 'The Brazilian *Jeitinho*: An Exercise in National Identity', in David J. Hess and Roberto A. Da Matta (eds), *The Brazilian Puzzle: Culture on the Borderlands of the Western World* (New York, Columbia University Press, 1995), p 36.

6.   Rick Altman, *The American Film Musical* (Bloomington and Indianapolis, Indiana University Press, 1987), p 51.

7.   The term *forró*, which is applied to a variety of dance-oriented, accordion-driven north-eastern styles of music, originally meant a party or a place to play dance music. Although some speculate that it is derived from the English 'for all', others trace its origins back to the word *forrobodó*, a term meaning revelry or party that may have been in use as early as the first half of the eighteenth century. Chris McGowan and Ricardo Pessanha, *The Brazilian Sound: Samba, Bossa Nova and the Popular Music of Brazil* (Philadelphia, Temple University Press, 1998), p 142.

8.   Altman: *The American Film Musical*, p 238.

9.   Over two dozen 'south-of-the-border' musicals were produced in Hollywood in the 1940s, as well as countless individual 'Latin' numbers in other musicals. As the only part of the world within reach not torn apart by the war, Latin America came to represent a utopian vision of life. The USA identified its southern neighbours with rhythm, life and a certain looseness of morals. MGM was late to jump on this bandwagon, and only did so in 1945 with *Yolanda and the Thief* (Vincente Minnelli), a musical fantasy with Mexican settings. Perhaps the best-known examples are 20th Century Fox's 'Good Neighbour' musicals, such as *Down Argentine Way* (Irving Cummings, 1940), *Weekend in Havana* (Walter Lang, 1941) and *That Night in Rio* (Irving Cummings,1941), all of which starred Carmen Miranda.

10.   Allen L. Woll, *The Hollywood Musical Goes to War* (Chicago, Nelson-Hall, 1983), p 157.

11.   Altman: *The American Film Musical*, p 51.

12.   In the *chanchada Matar ou correr* Oscarito plays the sheriff, a yellow-bellied buffoon who is terrified of the villains, frequently bursts into tears, and is even afraid of riding a horse. He forms a blatant iro-

nic contrast with the heroic Gary Cooper of *High Noon*. The diminutive black star of countless *chanchadas*, Grande Otelo, plays an
equally timid cowboy. The casting of an Afro-Brazilian in this role
adds a further dimension to the undermining of the Hollywood
model and the values that underpin it, since the Western is a cinematic genre which traditionally upholds the ideals of both machis-
mo and Wasp supremacy, and one in which black actors are cons-
picuous by their absence. *High Noon* was a new-style Western, critically acclaimed and subject to various allegorical interpretations.
Read initially as a liberal critique of McCarthy's witch-hunts of the
50s (the script was written by the blacklist victim, Carl Foreman,
and proved to be his last for a Hollywood movie), it was subsequently seen by some critics as an allegory of US foreign policy and
the Korean War. By parodying the film, the director of this *chanchada*, Carlos Manga, brings these intellectual interpretations
abruptly down to earth, and seems to be making his views of
Hollywood's didactic and lofty pretensions plain.

13.   Christopher Porterfield, 'Dissonant Duet: A Review of *New York,
      New York*', *Time*, 27 June 1977.

14.   Penelope Gilliatt, 'Review of *New York, New York*', *New Yorker*, 4 July
      1977.

15.   David Robinson, 'Review of *New York, New York*', *The Times*, 16
      September 1977.

16.   Jane Feuer, *The Hollywood Musical*, 2nd edn (Basingstoke and
      London, Macmillan, 1993), p 128.

17.   In interview, Buza Ferraz explained that the first part of this scene,
      in which the two women choose this song on the jukebox and then
      go up on stage to mime to it, was edited out of the final version of
      For all.

18.   Feuer: *The Hollywood Musical*, pp 127-8.

19.   Feuer: *The Hollywood Musical*, p 126; p 130.

20.   Feuer: *The Hollywood Musical*, p 73.

21.   Altman: *The American Film Musical*, p 61.

22.   Rob Wilson, 'Bloody Mary Meets Lois-Ann Yamanaka: Imagining
      Hawaiian Locality from *South Pacific* to Bamboo Ridge', *Public
      Culture* (Journal of the Society for Transnational Cultural Studies)
      18 (1995), pp 135-6.

23.   Richard Lippe, '*New York, New York* and the Hollywood Musical',
      Movie 31/32 (1986), p 95.

24.   Marion Jordan, 'American Cinema in the 70s: *Yanks*', *Movie* 27/28,
      Winter 1980, p 104.

15

ImagiNation

José Carlos Avellar

1

Let's imagine something that could be compared to both an oyster and the wind. A shell, motionless, closed and yet also open on all sides, something that has neither shape nor a body, something that is pure movement. We can interpret the title of Walter Lima Jr.'s film, *A ostra e o vento* (*The Oyster and the Wind*, 1996) as a reference not only to the characters, to the sense of understanding between Marcela and Saulo (she is the oyster and he is the wind), or to the conflict between José and Marcela (he is the oyster and she is the wind), but also as an image that suggests to the audience a way of watching the film (or, in a wider sense, a way of watching all films). We can see the title as the first hint as to how the film is constructed, and as a reference to the idea that underpins the story and the way it is narrated.

The relationship between the audience and the film as it is being projected is open yet closed, fluid yet static. The film (which, contained within the screen as if inside a shell, escapes like a breath of air) is both the oyster and the wind. The audience (who sit in the cinema theatre as if inside a shell and let their imaginations wander freely) are the wind and the oyster. If we continue with this analogy we could perhaps define the audio-visual industry's output as just the wind and nothing more, which implies that the audience is just the oyster. In relatively recent times in the history of the cinema (when various national cinemas existed) the relationship between the audience and the film was not simply based on what occurred during its screening. The audience continued to watch the film even after the screen had gone blank. In the last few years (when a single model of cinema has emerged) the relationship between the film and the audience has tended to wear thin as soon as they set eyes on each other. It tends to be a case of love at first sight, without a second glance.

2

At the end of the silent era we imagined that the cinema allowed us to see more, and more clearly. (As Dziga Vertov said in his film *Kino-Eye*, 1924, the cinema represented 'the possibility of making the invisible visible, or illuminating the darkness, of seeing without boundaries or distances.') But then Mário Peixoto showed us that, in reality, the cinema makes us see less, and less clearly, and that its strength lies precisely in this incomplete way of seeing. As the title of the film suggests, in *Limite* (*Limit*, 1931) what we see in every shot and in the way of establishing a connection between them, is something in the image that limits our vision. The narrative hides more than it reveals. What we see is only there to establish a tension with what is off screen. In this case cinema conceals, hides and cuts. It all begins with a cut, as if the order to stop filming ('cut!') had started the action, and the cry of 'lights, camera, action!' had brought it to an end.

At that time we imagined that fictional films were very important (the market for such films was even greater than it is today) but then Humberto Mauro said that Brazil was the ideal country for the documentary, 'because the raw materials are everywhere.' The important things were studios and the star system, in the eyes of the industry, whereas Mauro said that in a documentary 'the lead role is not played by any actor, but by the camera.' He also said that 'cinema is a waterfall, dynamic, beautiful and never-ending,' that 'people should not film nature when they want to, but at the time that nature chooses,' and that on seeing 'a water-fall I don't go right up to it but, instead, I hide behind a banana tree, waiting for the right moment.' *Ganga bruta* (*Rough Diamond*, Humberto Mauro, 1933) combines elements of the fictional film (with the camera sometimes in the lead role, moving as if it saw the world through the eyes of a drunken man) with those of the documentary (with the camera sometimes observing quietly and for long periods of time the landscapes and people before it). As its title suggests, this film presents itself as raw material, a rough diamond in need of polishing, dulled by the audience's gaze.

As Walter Lima Jr. stated, it is significant

> that within Brazilian Cinema there are two films that are such
> clear archetypes of Brazil's eternal quest, namely *Limite* and
> *Ganga bruta*. They represent something that you have to pol-
> ish and something that determines its own space, suggesting
> at the same time that something more exists beyond its con-
> fines. This is strange, but in some ways it creates a parameter.[1]

In the dialogue between these two silent films, one made shortly
after the other, a 'way of speaking' is created that is similar to the
cry of the sailor who, high up in the crow's nest, shouts 'Land!'

3

Once upon a time, when sitting in front of the Lumière brothers'
cinematograph, the audience closed their eyes, turned their faces
away, made as if to run, in order to get out of the path of the train
at La Ciotat station, that was threatening to jump through the
screen into the cinema theatre. But today it does not matter what
kind of nightmare threatens to jump out of the television into our
homes. We keep our eyes wide open, but do not focus our attention on anything at all. We try to defend ourselves against what we
see without turning away from it. At home, but also outside the
home, in any other place, we behave in some ways like the character of Ninhinha in *A terceira margem do rio* (*The Third Bank of the
River*, 1994), by Nelson Pereira dos Santos. To comply with her
grandmother's wishes, this little girl puts her hand inside the set
and brings into the living room the sweets being advertized on the
television. At home, but in a no man's land, where reality does not
exist, in front of an image that from time to time puts its hand into
reality to grab hold of something, in front of a television, the viewer can repeat to himself what the Portuguese character Pedro says
to the Brazilian Paco, who has recently arrived in Lisbon in *Terra
estrangeira* (*Foreign Land*, 1995), by Walter Salles and Daniela
Thomas: 'This is not a place to find anyone. It is the ideal place to
lose someone or to lose yourself.'

It is no coincidence that television has been a constant presence in Brazilian films, not only as an object in the corner of the
set but as a character the same as any other. Television is the villain who kills Paco's mother in *Terra estrangeira* when it broadcasts
Fernando Collor's new economic policy, the magician who gives

sweets to Ninhinha in *A terceira margem do rio*, the policeman who closes in on Japa and Branquinha, the two shantytown kids holed up in an American's house in Rio in Murilo Salles' *Como nascem os anjos* (*How Angels Are Born*, 1996) the policeman who invades the personal drama of Dalva and Vítor in *Um céu de estrelas* (*A Starry Sky*, 1997) by Tata Amaral, the corrupt policeman who rigs the elections in Lúcia Murat's *Doces poderes* (*Sweet Powers*, 1996), and the surrogate lover who moves in with Dora, bought with the money that she earned by selling the young boy Josué in Walter Salles' *Central do Brasil* (*Central Station*, 1998).

4

Let's imagine an idea not yet articulated such as a speech when it exists in written form only. This is like the opening images, shaky and almost entirely white, of *Vidas secas* (*Barren Lives*, 1963), by Nelson Pereira dos Santos: long shots, almost empty, white on white, the camera in the hands of the photographer as he walks along, unstable, as if it too were a migrant driven off the land by the drought, alongside Fabiano, Sinhá Vitória, their two sons, and the dog Baleia. The sun burns everything there is to see and is more blinding than revealing. The image is almost always unsteady and reveals more about itself than it does about its subject. Even when fixed on a tripod the camera moves off centre, 'de-frames' and cuts in order to compose an image of unstable equilibrium like those that are produced with a hand-held camera. When Fabiano encounters the soldier lost in the scrubland, for example, we see on screen the shoulder and the left arm of the cowhand as he clutches a knife. And that is all. At this point Fabiano is just a man made up of a part of his arm, his hand, a knife and half an eye. We cannot see his face. Or rather we see a face that is part eye and part knife, just the blade. The images appear on the screen like thoughts spoken aloud, like the visual equivalent of speech. They are the visual equivalent of the most accentuated pronunciation of a word and the half-swallowed sound of another word in the middle of a sentence. They are like the gesture that accompanies speech and completes the meaning of what is only half said. They are like punctuation that is sometimes irregular, like pauses that indicate a search for the right term. In short, the intense whiteness and the shakiness of the image can be interpreted as corresponding to every kind of imperfection that comes to light when the spoken word is compared to the written word.

25. Alva (Sonja Saurin), Ninhinha (Barbara Brandt) and Liojorge (Ilya São Paulo) in *A terceira margem do rio*.

Furthermore, let us imagine speech that is not even organized like a language, an essential phenomenon, rudimentary, the expression of a pure state, completely unarticulated. This brings to mind *Deus e o diabo na terra do sol* (*Black God, White Devil,* 1964), by Glauber Rocha. Cinema in Latin America was searching for a new way of looking at things, inspired by Italian neo-realism, when Glauber's film exploded onto the screen. The camera accompanies the cowhand Manuel towards the sea, it circles around Corisco and Rosa's kiss, it descends, in a whip lash, from the white sky towards Sebastião on the top of Monte Santo, it breaks up into a rapid succession of lightning flashes while Antônio das Mortes shoots at the holy men, it zigzags from Dadá's face to that of the blind man Júlio, it fixes its gaze on the bandit's clothes, it stumbles in the dry, thorny vegetation of the scrubland, it stridently cries out that stronger are the powers of the people, and it shuts itself away in a tense and uneasy silence. This kind of cinema is all about the way in which the camera interferes with the scene in front of it and not the scene in itself. The scene is just a sketch for the creation of a dramatic space that takes shape in the minds of the audience. It is, in fact, the camera that acts in the scene, always scribbling over the image (a type of illiterate writing that looks like the graffiti that covers the walls of Brazilian cities today). These invisible elements make us feel or understand that a film is not the image that is shown on the screen, and that it is not what the audience sees during the screening, or at least it is not only that.

A film is also and predominantly made up of images that we invent inspired by what we have seen. From the moment that the film is projected, dragged along by a camera that refuses to observe the scene from a tranquil, comfortable position, the audience is urged not to behave like spectators. They must participate in the creative process, there and then, while the film on the screen messes up everything that language has neatly ordered. It is neither an unknown, foreign language nor a case of misused language. It is as if no language existed yet, as if everything is still waiting to be created, as if a new way of feeling and thinking about the world was being invented at that very moment, as if words were in the air that had never been uttered before. To put it another way, let's think about language as a type of cinema generated by the bringing together of two very different planes, sometimes apparently in conflict but in truth complementary, namely the spoken and the written word. The former is natural and open like a documentary, whereas the latter is disciplined and constructed like a fictional film.

Let's think of 1960s cinema as equivalent to the spoken word, not because it attempted to interpret visually the way that Brazilians speak, and not because it tried to rely on the written word in order to give structure to its narrative. In the 1960s, cinema was more *spoken* than *written*. It expressed itself by using the direct and only partially articulated elements of spoken language, by using the equivalent, so to speak, of the word before the word existed. It recalled a time when in order to express something that still had not been given a name, there was only an interjection, a cry, a groan, a mute gesture, a way of speaking that owed more to feeling than to reason.

(Let's remember what we were imagining back in 1960. Reality was experienced as if it were a film. The whole of life itself 'in its collection of actions is a natural and living cinema: and in this respect it is linguistically the equivalent of spoken language.' If memory and dreams are like 'primordial schemes', cinema is the 'written moment of this natural and complete language, that is the action of men in reality.' Cinema is like *the written language of reality*, or so Pasolini imagined.[2] At the same time *Cinema Novo* imagined itself as spoken language, both *natural and complete, action in reality,* almost as if on the screen film did not exist at all but rather reality itself, the performance putting itself forward as a *re-presentation/reinvention* of reality, as the first language. It is the very first language, a thought just as it occurs, in the wilderness, on the frontier, at the precise moment between the unconscious/conscious absence/presence and the possibility of gaining form and expression. We should remember what Fernando Birri was imagining in relation to *Vidas secas* and *Deus e o diabo na terra do sol* at that time:

> *Vidas secas* is the film that a whole generation of Latin American directors, to which I belong, would like to have made years ago... It is the highest point reached until now by Latin American cinema (new and old). And in this respect, it is a classic film. And precisely for this reason, now old and overtaken by historical circumstance, this kind of cinema is rarely made any more. *Deus e o diabo na terra do sol* appears to be a very powerful, ambiguous, exalted, contaminated, shocking film, and more lyrical than epic. With this ground-breaking film that, as Neruda wanted to achieve with his poetry, drags along with it pure and impure material, Glauber Rocha, by now not a director but an author, made a timeless and tremendously contemporary work ... So this is not a case of opposition, but rather of historical continuity.) [3]

5

Let's imagine that prior to the 1960s Brazilian filmmakers had been trying to write before they could talk, as if a language could first appear in its written form, with the spoken word developing later. Or as if they had been trying to write down what Hollywood cinema was saying. *Vidas secas* and *Deus e o diabo na terra do sol* appeared at a time when Brazilians were making films that were an illustration of an idea thought up before the accompanying image, which was devised in its written form and frequently by other people, outside Brazil. In Brazil films were made as if they were merely a means of bringing together different kinds of shots (close-ups, long shots, *plongées*, *contre-plongées*, panning shots, tracking shots, tilts, and so on). The image captured by a hand-held camera (which reproduces all of these techniques and in doing so alters them all) and improvization during filming were, from the outset, the most distinguishing features of Brazilian films from the 1960s. In truth, this type of filming, that revealed the nervous presence of the camera more than the scene in itself, was a creative intervention to render Brazil's cinematic discourse more complex. Glauber Rocha's *Terra em transe* (*Land in Anguish*, 1967) is a case in point. The scene is improvized not because it had not been properly thought through when the script was drawn up, but because it was continually being thought through during filming. The image trembled not as a result of any failing or lack of skill on the part of the photographer, but because at that time reality was dealt with in that way, a nervous, trembling discourse. The script was seen as a challenge to the filming, filming as a challenge to the montage and the film as a whole as a challenge to the audience. Cinema saw itself as a mode of expression that was complete, finished, on the screen, and yet incomplete, part of a process that does not come to an end when the film is screened. It saw itself as provoking images, providing a rough cut, an unedited version for the audience to refine and put in order in their imagination.

6

Let's imagine that a synthesis of the creative process of Brazilian Cinema can be found in the final part of *Memórias do cárcere* (*Memories of Prison*, 1984) by Nelson Pereira dos Santos. Novelist Graciliano Ramos, sitting on the earthen floor of the prison dorm, with his back against the wooden posts that support the roof, writes with the stub of a pencil on a sheet of crumpled paper. The other prisoners sit beside him to help him create the work. Mário Pinto brings him an old exercise book. Cubano gets him some pencils. Gaúcho brings him a wad of fresh paper. Suddenly Graciliano is surrounded by people who want to appear in the book. The writer receives from the other prisoners paper, pencils and stories to include in it. One says that he is in prison because he is poor, since only poor people go to prison. Another tells how his wife had been to prison more times than him. Yet another had been put in jail because of his involvement in strikes. The book that Graciliano writes is as much about the other prisoners who speak to him as it is about himself. All the prisoners contribute to the book. They defend it, as if it belonged to all of them. Gaúcho, who had stolen paper from the prison store, ends up in solitary confinement as soon as the theft is discovered, but he does not confess what he did with the paper. He is in the book, so it is his to defend. The guards enter the dorm to confiscate Graciliano's writing and they search the writer's belongings, but they find nothing. The prisoners have taken the sheets of paper and hidden them under their shirts and down their trousers, because they are all in the book. They defend it with their very bodies.

Let's imagine that an equally powerful image of synthesis of the Brazilian filmic creative process can be found in *Cabra marcado para morrer* (*Twenty Years After*, 1984) by Eduardo Coutinho, a documentary that began twenty years earlier as a work of fiction based on the assassination of the peasant leader João Pedro Teixeira. Filming had been interrupted by the military coup of 1964: the army invaded Engenho Galiléia, a co-operative farm in Pernambuco where the film was being made. A camera and negatives were seized, those who did not manage to escape were arrested and an official announcement declared the seizure of 'a vast quantity of subversive material in the arsenal at Galiléia'. This included 'films designed to incite peasant revolt and floodlights for late-night film shows, since training was intensive and lasted all day long.' Nearly twenty years later, Coutinho returned to finish the film, which would no longer be fictional but a documentary on what happened to those who took part in filming after 1964. In the film Coutinho, director and character in the story, talks to José Mariano, Severino, José Daniel, João Virgínio and João José, the actors from the interrupted film, and he also talks to Elizabeth Teixeira, widow of João Pedro who plays herself in the film. We could say that the film is pure dialogue. One man relates how he hid the camera and cans of film and how he helped others escape. Another reads from the introduction to *Kaputt*, a book left behind during the escape and which he kept as a souvenir of those involved in the film. The film reminds him of the story of Curzio Malaparte, who hid his texts during the war. Another man explains how he was arrested and mistreated in prison and how he had to go into hiding and assume a false identity. And at these moments when the interviewees enthusiastically recall their work on the film and how they suffered later, it is like a re-enactment of the scene from *Memórias do cárcere* in which Gaúcho goes into solitary confinement for stealing paper so that Graciliano can continue to write his book.

In the dialogue between these two films made almost at the same time it is readily apparent how Brazilian films have been made since the 1960s. Everything began more or less in the same way, with José Daniel protecting the camera, Mário Pinto arriving with an old exercise book, João Virgínio heading off for solitary confinement, Cubano bringing a pencil, the filmmaker himself, with his camera in his hand, on the prison floor, listening to tales from the prisoners around him. Graciliano, the protagonist of *Memórias do cárcere*, and Eduardo Coutinho, the director of *Cabra marcado para morrer*, are at one and the same time protagonist, artist and audience. At the precise moment when these films appear on screen the audience encounters someone behaving exactly like them, that is, concentrating on what ordinary people are saying. At the exact moment of screening they are invited to behave at the same time as spectator, protagonist and creator of the film, to imagine themselves in prison or in Galiléia, and on finding their own space, to freely invent their own cinema.

7

Let's imagine that making films is rather like dictating a letter to Dora of *Central do Brasil*. There is little chance that the letter will be posted and arrive at its destination. To continue the metaphor, as far as Brazilian Cinema is concerned, the chances are slim of Dora even taking the unlikely decision to post the letter and finding a post office and postman interested in distributing national mail. Letters, like films, come from abroad, written in another language and with a foreign stamp. Let's imagine that the cinema is not the best way to see films. Let's ask, just as Ricardo Dias did, shortly after the release of his documentary *Fé* (*Faith*, 1999), 'To what extent has cinema moved away from the public and not the other way round?'[4] The same thing that happened to Dias' film, in November 1999, soon happened to *Milagre em Juazeiro* (*Miracle in Juazeiro*, Wolney Oliveira, 1999) and shortly after to *O dia da caça* (*The Day of the Prey*, Alberto Graça, 1999). These films found numerous and sympathetic audiences beyond the commercial film circuits. The difficult task nowadays, according to Dias, 'is to take cinema to the public, and not to try to attract the public to the cinema.' For today's cinema theatres

> the work of attracting customers to shopping centres is more important than acting as cinema theatres per se. ...How many people, even if they are interested and have the financial means to do so, have never been to the cinema? How many people know how to go to the cinema?[5]

Carlos Diegues, in this volume, recalls that 'in spite of its population of 160 million, only about 70 million cinema tickets are sold in Brazil each year, to about 10 million consumers. This means that only 6 per cent of the Brazilian population goes to the cinema. There are some 1400 cinema theatres in Brazil.' Since the mid-1980s, 'the public is no longer going to the cinema as a consequence of the worsening economic recession and its resulting, growing and perverse concentration of income, which excludes the vast majority of Brazilians from today's consumer society.'

8

In the tale recounted in *Terra estrangeira*, a Brazilian girl Alex, who has emigrated to Portugal, sells her passport (a Brazilian passport, according to the buyer, is worthless), and she says she pities the Portuguese (because after the great effort of crossing the ocean they ended up discovering Brazil). When Alex acts and speaks in this way she is not only behaving correctly within the context of the story being narrated, but she is also, and primarily, expressing through drama a feeling that was common among young people of the Brazilian middle class at the beginning of the 1990s. The tale on screen relives in other dimensions what both the audience and characters of the film experienced in reality, namely the sense of belonging to a country that is no good, of having neither roots nor identity, of living in your own land as if it were a foreign land, of surviving (and here I borrow from two particular images in the film) like a ship stranded on a sand bank and like a car making a break for the border.

9

Let's imagine an image that is interested not exactly in revealing what it sees but rather its way of seeing. And let's even imagine that *Central do Brasil* looks at the story that it recounts, that of a retired teacher who earns a living by writing letters for people who do not know how to read, in a way that allows us to observe her as if she were a metaphor for the renaissance of Brazilian Cinema in the mid-1990s, after the paralysis caused by the corruption of the Collor government between 1990 and 1993. The story of Dora and Josué was not dreamed up with such a metaphor in mind, but (at least after understanding the essential message of the film) it can be read in this way, as a revival of the art of seeing. Once again Brazilians could tell stories in a language which belonged to all of them. They could rediscover their country and feel part of a specific space and time. The film includes scenes of landscapes and characters that left their mark on the cinema of the 1960s – the North-East, the *sertão* (backlands), those fleeing drought, pilgrims, ordinary workers from the poor suburbs of the big cities, and so on. It retraces the journey of migration of the characters of *Barren Lives*, but in the opposite direction. It follows in the footsteps of a woman who gradually, on transforming into words what she is told, experiences a process of 'resensitization'. The expression used by Walter Salles defines Dora's experience and as an extension of this, the experience of Brazilian Cinema in the last few years. The film and the audience, or rather cinema in its widest sense, has undergone a process of 'resensitization'. This process is to an extent the reunion of the father (the old *Cinema Novo*?) and the nation. It is a way of understanding Brazil, a country represented by such various figures as José, the protective and authoritarian father of *A ostra e o vento*, Osias, the impotent authoritarian who assumes paternity of the children who are not his in *Eu, tu, eles* (*Me You Them*, Andrucha Waddington, 2000), the absent father of Branquinha and Japa in *Como nascem os anjos* and the absent father of *Central do Brasil*.

The reunion of the father/fatherland is played out with all the ambiguity and tragedy that the story of Dora and Josué confer on the image of the father. He is at the same time the figure that Josué admires even though he does not know him, that Moisés scorns for having destroyed himself with drink and that Isaías hopes will come back home, to the family and to his carpentry. He is the rude and insensitive drunk, as Dora cannot forget, who left his family and who one day tried it on with his own daughter whom he did not recognize in the street. But he is also the affectionate train driver, as Dora eventually recalls, who one day let his little daughter drive the train that he operated. This reunion is also a rediscovery of a way of observing whose purpose is to invent the country through cinema – or vice-versa, for the invention of one implies the invention of the other. The creation of an image capable of capturing the essence of the country implies creating both cinema and then the country in its own image: imagiNation.

NOTES

1. Carlos Alberto de Mattos, 'Reiventar a luz, com alguma originali-
    dade' (an interview with Walter Lima Jr.), *Cinemais* 1,
    September/October 1996, pp 17-18.
2. See Pier Paolo Pasolini, 'Le scenario comme structure tendant a
    être une autre structure' and 'La langue écrite de la realité', in
    L'expérience hérétique – langue et cinéma (Paris, Payot, 1976).
3. Fernando Birri, 'Apuntes sobre la *guerra de guerrillas* del nuevo
    cine latinoamericano', *Ulysses* (Rome, 1968).
4. Ricardo Dias in a letter to the website www.zetafilmes.com.br,
    November 1999.
5. Dias: www.zetafilms.com.br.

Part seven
Epilogue

16

Then and now: cinema as history in the light of new media and new technologies

Laura Mulvey

Speaking as an afficionado of Brazilian Cinema, but by no means an expert, I am going to try to begin this chapter by considering some contextual issues that, I hope, relate to the discussion of the Brazilian Cinema's 'renaissance' but will contribute another, more general, perspective. I am particularly interested in ways in which the essays in this volume address questions of history: the history of Brazil since *Cinema Novo* and the history of Brazilian Cinema itself. These discussions, in turn, raise questions about 'political' time and 'cinematic' time which inter-relate in this story.

I have also been influenced, in my reflections here, by broad parallels between the Brazilian and the British film experience of the 1960s and 70s. The 60s saw the high point of *Cinema Novo*. But the British version of a radical cinema (influenced by, and part of, the conjuncture between cinema and left politics taking place contemporaneously in many different parts of the world) came later, then stretching, particularly in its feminist form, into the 70s. I would like to locate the radical aspirations of both cinemas within wider questions of political, cultural and economic changes that have taken place since that period. It goes almost without saying that it is difficult to compare *Cinema Novo*, an outstanding contributor to world cinema, with the rather minor, low-profile, experimental cinemas of my own experience in my country. However, their different tribulations raise common issues that are of conceptual interest due to a similar pattern in their specific histories.

The similar pattern may be found in the close relations between left politics and the cinema in the 1960s and a sense of loss, disorientation and disillusion that followed, concentrated above all in the 80s. A gap, a caesura, in aesthetic and political continuity developed that gives a distinct edge to the way that new cinema movements of the 1990s conceived of themselves; whether, that is, they did or did not try to relate to the lost, but still vivid, moment before the caesura. From this pattern, questions of conceptual interest arise. These are more general, relating outwards to the political climate within which the cinematic climate changed and are to do with the experience of temporality, the problem of epoch as something sensed but difficult to theorize. These are issues that, perhaps, can only be posed by the present within the political legacy of loss, discontinuity and a desire to find a way towards their interpretation. Unlike the British version of the story, the cinema of the Brazilian 'renaissance' directly raises the relation between a 'then' and a 'now' and confronts what meanings these cinema histories might have for the present. To re-iterate: it is the perception of a gap, of a loss of continuity, that is significant here. That is: how do we understand, now, the experiences of radical aspiration, and then loss, that characterize the history of the avant-gardes from the 60s/70s into the 80s/90s? And how can the contemporary revival of Brazilian Cinema contribute to more general speculation about cinema and history?

First of all, the radical cinemas of the 1960s, not only in Britain and Brazil but elsewhere, belong to a moment of political utopianism. As Ismail Xavier, in this volume, has emphasized, the cinema came to function as a significant symptom and symbol of a utopian teleology. Not only did this cinema articulate the desire for a better world but it also seemed to offer a means of achieving it:

> Aesthetic rupture and social criticism went along together, alienating people who expected naturalism and a didactic cinema. The best of *Cinema Novo* introduced textual references (not only related to parody), and a degree of opacity in those very images that conveyed its political engagement. ... Cinephilia, very strong then, meant utopian impulses, a belief in a better future for art and society. And the filmmaker saw him/herself as someone who had received a popular mandate that, in the Brazilian case, was conceived as coming from the very core of the nation.

As we all know, for the modernist tradition, the cinema was the art form and mass medium specific to the twentieth century that could provide the formal frame within which key issues of radical aesthetics could find expression. (As a precursor to the present topic, it has often been noticed how frequently the radical aesthetics of the 1960s look back to, and cite, the formative moments of the cinema-modernism conjuncture of the 20s. This is strikingly the case both in Brazil and Europe.) By the second half of the twentieth century, the cinema could mediate between modernity's proliferation of imagery, the prevalence of the society of the spectacle, and modernism's commitment to refract representation through a political and aesthetic scrutiny, to deny images transparency and authenticity. And, of course, out of this grew the cinema of self-reference and self-consciousness that marked all the radical cinemas of the period.

As Xavier has pointed out, cinephilia, a love of cinema as such, animates these connections. Belief in the cinema merges with belief in radical political change. So, a commitment to social transformation, essential for the political left, and a commitment to the cinema's place in enabling that transformation, precious to the radical avant-garde, work together in 1960s' radicalism. In a circular movement, the cinema had to be freed from its industrial and conventional trappings in order to become itself and to fulfil both its political and aesthetic destiny. One is tempted to speculate that the cinema's particular ability to visualize transformative processes, to see change in the making, chimed with this teleological aspiration. Annette Michelson notes the convergence between the cinema, political radicalism and modernism:

> The excitement, the exhilaration of artists and intellectuals not directly involved with [the cinema] was enormous. Indeed, a certain euphoria enveloped early film making and theory. For there was, ultimately, a very real sense in which the revolutionary aspirations of the modernist movement in literature and the arts, on the one hand, and of Marxist or Utopian tradition, on the other, could converge in the hopes and promises, yet undefined, of the new medium.[1]

These links between cinema's transformative potential and political aspiration are deeply marked by a teleological view of history and aesthetics, associated not only with Marxism itself but with all socialist and progressive movements. So, logically speaking, the crisis of modernism's characteristic leftwing understanding of time as moving into a future then also leads to a crisis in its conception of 'History'. Also reflecting on this problem of historical break, Susan Buck-Morss has re-located the collapse of communism from the specific histories of the socialist countries into the wider context of a crisis of the left more generally. She says:

> 'History' has failed us. No new chronology will erase that fact. History's betrayal is so profound that it cannot be forgiven by tacking on a 'post' era to it (post-modernism, post-Marxism). There is a real sense of tragedy in shattering the dreams of modernity – of social utopia, historical progress and material plenty for all. [2]

These are issues to do with change and continuity and to do with the question: how to find a way to stay in touch with a 'then' separated from 'now' by a familiar litany of phrases: the decline of the industrialized working-class (post-Fordism), globalization, neo-liberalism, the collapse of communism or, as we simply say in Britain, 'Thatcherism'. In Brazil, of course, the loss of continuity has been exacerbated by twenty years of dictatorship. Perry Anderson addresses the problem of 'gap' in his editorial for a new-look *New Left Review*, re-designed for the millennium, giving an illuminating analysis of the difference between the period of the review's founding (late 1950s and early 60s) and the moment in which he was writing. 'Four decades later, the environment in which *NLR* took shape has all but completely passed away.' He emphasizes the 'virtually uncontested consolidation, and universal diffusion, of neoliberalism' combined with the need for 'a lucid registration of historic defeat' of labour and the left in general. On a cultural front, perhaps the 'post-modern' rejection of history during the 1980s marked and expressed the break between the 'then' and the 'now'. This was a rejection, in the first instance, of the left ideological concept of 'History' but could be extended to the diachronic, the linear, the sequential on either an aesthetic or political level.[3]

It is impossible to detach the radical cinema's history from these accumulated crises. But the cinema itself went through a period of profound change during the 60s-90s decades alongside, coincident with, these other, political and economic, convulsions. In 1995, the cinema celebrated its centenary. For once, this temporal marker had a symbolic importance, drawing attention to the fact that, over the previous thirty years, its status and its nature had changed. The cinema, the emblem of twentieth century moderni- ty, had actually aged. By the time of its hundredth birthday, its century old, mechanical, technology had been overtaken by new, electronic and digital, technologies which gave a high profile to its ageing process. Despite the fact that people still go to the cinema in large numbers, and doubtless will continue to do so, most of them are likely to be introduced to the cinema electronically, either on television, roughly speaking from the 1960s, or on video, roughly speaking from the 70s. And alongside cinema going, con- sumption is increasingly on video and DVD.

By the 1990s, the digital had affected the production of images as well as their diffusion. So, as the cinema faced its own internal crisis alongside, in step with, the other crises mentioned above, its history then began to acquire its own division between the 'then' of celluloid recording and projection and the 'now' of a complex relation to other technologies and proliferating media. If the cin- ema in the 60s offered a framework or metaphor for contemporary radical aspiration, it is logical, perhaps, to try to consider whether its hybrid descendent might offer a framework or metaphor within which the problem of historical loss and discontinuity might be thought or imagined. The cinema in its present configuration, combining its long celluloid memory with its new digital capacity, might offer a means for negotiating across the divide.

Susan Buck-Morss continues the paragraph half quoted above in such a way as to suggest that attempts to negotiate across the divide are, indeed, of political importance in the present con- juncture. How precisely this task might be undertaken is itself interesting. To look backward from outside 'historical teleology' might seem to be simply nostalgic to Marxists or, on the other hand, nostalgic for historical teleology to post-modernists. As Buck-Morss puts it:

> But to submit to melancholy at this point would be to confer
> on the past a wholeness that never did exist, confusing the
> loss of the dream with the loss of the dream's realization.
> The alternative of political cynicism is equally problematic,
> because in denying the possibilities for change it prevents
> them; anticipating defeat it brings defeat into being. Rather
> than taking a self-ironizing distance from history's failure, we

– the we who might have nothing more or less in common than sharing this time – would do well to bring the ruins up close and work our way through the rubble in order to rescue the utopian hopes that modernity engendered because we cannot afford to let them disappear. There is no reason to believe that those utopian hopes caused history to go wrong, and every reason, based on the abuses of power that propelled history forward, to believe the opposite.[4]

Perry Anderson also suggests that one way of addressing the problems he discusses may lie in 're-weaving the threads of significance across the century'. There are two thought provoking metaphors here: 'working through the rubble of history' and 're-weaving the threads of significance', both of which point firmly towards an intellectual and political direction for now, but one which involves looking backwards at the forward looking cultures of modernity. This would inevitably involve moving beyond the ideological significance of 'History', with the connotations of failed progressivism evoked by Susan Buck-Morss, and also beyond the transitional moment of post-modern denial. Within this perspective, the new Brazilian Cinema is of particular interest.

Throughout the essays collected into this book, there is a recurring aesthetic and political issue: the way that the New Brazilian Cinema of the 1990s has re-visited the themes of *Cinema Novo*. As Lúcia Nagib says in her Introduction: '... it is now possible to assert that most of the new films maintain a strong historical link with Brazilian films of the past and that they share a number of features and tendencies.' Ismail Xavier, Ivana Bentes and Lúcia Nagib, again, in her chapter, look closely and critically at this historical link. They note the return, in 90s films, to the emblematic *Cinema Novo* subjects, particularly the *sertão* (the poverty striken North-East of Brazil) and the *favela* (the slums of Rio). In spite of their important collective emphasis on the difference between this 90s cinema and the *Cinema Novo*, and beyond their critical wariness about the return to these subjects, there is a sense that the cinematic renaissance marked, not a return to zero, but an *hommage* to the earlier cinema of social consciousness. From this perspective, the 're-working of national allegory' (Xavier's term), might represent a move towards an attempt to 'bring the ruins up close' and 'work through the rubble'. This would not constitute an a-historical, nostalgic, return to utopian hopes. But it could acknowledge the problems posed by historical caesura and recognize that culture, particularly in the privileged form of cinema, might be able to forge continuities of aspiration across traumatic political and economic change.

However, in these essays an accusation is explicitly levelled against the new cinema: iconographies and images that were, in the days of *Cinema Novo*, uncontaminated by sentiment and uncompromisingly in keeping with the real brutality of life, become a terrain in which contemporary dilemmas can be re-worked and reconciled. *Central do Brasil* (*Central Station*, Walter Salles, 1998) represents both sides of the coin. Ivana Bentes, in her chapter, in keeping with her tracing of Glauber Rocha's 'Aesthetics of Hunger' to a 90s 'cosmetics of hunger' makes the point:

> *Central do Brasil* offers the romantic *sertão*, the idealized return to the 'origins'. Its aesthetic realism, with citations of the *Cinema Novo*, offers a utopian wager like a fable. The *sertão* emerges as a projection of lost dignity and as the promised land of a reversed exodus from the seaside to the interior, a return of the failed and disinherited who were unable to survive in the big city. It is not a desired or politicized return, but an emotional return, led by circumstances. Thus the *sertão* becomes a land of social reconciliation and pacification...

It could, however, be argued that these citations of *Cinema Novo*, even if 'weak', are significant in their particular context. While post-modernity used citation to produce a sense of simultaneity and a flattening of the historical and the diachronic, these references back to the 1960s actually do the opposite. Out of an era in which 'history' suffered a defeat, its presence returns and is cautiously, perhaps tentatively, re-inscribed by a cinema that would like to use images 'sanctified' by the 60s to tell stories that have changed.

Perhaps my approach is affected by the lack of dialogue across the 'great divide' in Britain. The very interesting and flourishing new, 90s, artists' cinema in this country sees itself as a new departure, enabled by new technologies that have brought the moving image into the gallery and the art-world. There is no dialogue with the radical avant-garde of the 60s and the shift in context seems to dramatize the break. The British avant-garde of the 60s and 70s ranged across gallery and performance work, very much

within the ethos of modernist aesthetics, to feminist re-working of
narrative, to experimental documentary. The journal *Afterimage*
brought different strands of independent and experimental work
together.[5] And, in keeping with the radical, international, aspiration of the time, the cover of its first issue was taken from Glauber-
Rocha's *O dragão da maldade contra o santo guerreiro* (*Antonio das
Mortes*, 1969). Ultimately, although interesting work continued to
be done on a more individual basis through the 1980s, the movement fell in the face of two, quite disconnected events.

In 1979 Margaret Thatcher became Prime Minister, leading a
confident neo-liberal Conservative Government that very quickly
cut off the funding that had kept the British avant-garde alive. On
the other hand, in 1982 our fourth TV channel came on the air with
a positive brief to encourage experimental work. Channel Four
seemed, for a time at least, to open out new possibilities for radical
cinema to re-invent itself and reach a 'wider audience'. But the new
possibility offered by television was also emblematic of the decline
of 16mm format and its alternative exhibition spaces. It is perhaps
a combination of these factors that contributed so dramatically to
the British radical cinema's experience of caesura. The political
front, particularly feminism, went through a wave of depression and
disorientation that focused around the specific pleasure that our
first woman Prime Minister clearly took in dismantling the world's
oldest and most enduring trade-union movement. And, of course,
in common with intellectuals elsewhere, there was the first shock of
disorientation as the economic and political impact of 'globalization' seemed to be just too big to grasp.

I want to conclude by returning to the question of cinema in
the present climate of digital technology and its potential contribution to the difficulty of negotiating across the 'great divide'.
Practical, theoretical and allegorical aspects of the cinema join
together here. First of all, the birth of the cinema allowed the
world to be seen in all the detail of mechanical movement, with
consequent social and aesthetic implications, and offering a new
way of seeing. Now, also with a sense of novelty, the accumulated
cinematic record of the twentieth century offers, not so much a
new way of seeing the world in the present, but a telescope into the
past. Now anyone, with the simple touch of a digital button can
stop and think about the complexities of moving images with the
same space for reflection on time that has long been offered by the
still photograph. Rather than the voyeuristic tendency associated

with projected cinema, often discussed by feminists, a more 'pen-sive cinema', in Raymond Bellour's phrase, should emerge. Cinema can become a material allegory for the contemporary need to bring the 'rubble of history' up close and 're-weave the threads of significance'. But it can also provide a historically unprecedented 'time machine' with which to do so. The celluloid cinema may be there evidentially, a flawed but still indexical record of its moment, but also, and perhaps more crucially, it offers a more abstract, imaginative, means for reflecting on time itself. By a knight's move across into a different technological medium, it allows reflection on how time is inscribed into culture and politics and how it gets lost in the elusiveness of history. It is in this new context of thought about temporalities, their gaps and continuities, that the Brazilian 'renaissance' cinema's own reflection on its history seems relevant to problems posed by history today.

NOTES

1.   Annette Michelson, 'Film and the Radical Aspiration', in P. Adams Sitney (ed), *Film Culture Reader* (New York, Praeger, 1970), p 407.
2.   Susan Buck-Morss, *Dreamworld and Catastrophe. The Passing of Mass Utopia in East and West* (Cambridge, Mass., The MIT Press, 2000), p 68.
3.   Perry Anderson, editorial 'Renewals', *New Left Review*, January/February 2000, p 9.
4.   Buck-Morss: *Dreamworld and Catastrophe*, p 68.
5.   *Afterimage* 1, April 1970.

Index

A

1999], xxii, xxiii, 51, 58, 69, 99, 107, 117, 157-74
Proust, Marcel, 147
Pupo Filho, Gualter, 188

Q

Quadros, Jânio, 142
quatrilho, O [Fábio Barreto, 1995, nominated in 1996], 3, 8, 42
Queiroz, Eça de, xxiv, 42, 57, 193-202
Quem matou Pixote? [*Who Killed Pixote?*, José Joffily,1996], 52, 57
Quem roubou meu samba? [*Who Stole My Samba?*, José Carlos Burle,
    1958], 234
Quinn, Aidan, 221

R

Ramalho Jr., Francisco, 220
Ramos, Eurides, 233
Ramos, Fernão Pessoa, xiii, xxi, 65, 227
Ramos, Guiomar, 228
Ramos, Graciliano, 141, 166, 213, 252
rap do Pequeno Príncipe contra as Almas Sebosas, O [Paulo Caldas and
    Marcelo Luna, 2000], 103
Ratton, Carlos Alberto, 195
Ratton, Helvécio, xxiv, 42, 193-204
Raulino, Aloysio, 102
Recife de dentro para fora [*Recife from the Inside Out*, Kátia Mesel,
    1997], 102
Recife from the Inside Out – see *Recife de dentro para fora*
Reichenbach, Carlos, 59
Reis, Carlos, 194, 202
Reis, Major Tomás Luiz, 210-11, 222
Restier, Renato, 233
Rey, Geraldo del, 141, 155
Rezende, Sérgio, 42, 59, 122, 143-44, 158
Ribeiro, Darcy, 100
Ribeiro, José Tadeu, 195
Rigueira, Luciana, 226
Rio, João do, 159
Rio 40 Degrees – see *Rio 40 graus*
Rio Northern Zone – see *Rio Zona Norte*
Rio 40 graus [*Rio 40 Degrees*, Nelson Pereira dos Santos, 1955], 107,
    121, 132, 158-59, 162